Scotland Yard's
FIRST CASES

By the same author

The British Policewoman: Her Story
Marlborough Street: the Story of a London Court
Tales from Bow Street
Blue Murder: Policemen under Suspicion
Scotland Yard Casebook
Dead Image
Death In Perspective
Dead Born
Dead Centre

Scotland Yard's
FIRST
CASES

Joan Lock

ROBERT HALE • LONDON

ISBN 978-0-7090-9125-7

Robert Hale Limited
Clerkenwell House
Clerkenwell Green
London EC1R 0HT

www.halebooks.com

A catalogue record for this book is available
from the British Library

10 9 8 7 6 5 4 3 2 1

Typeset by Maggie Aldred
Printed in Great Britain by the MPG Books Group Ltd,
Bodmin and King's Lynn

Contents

Acknowledgements   6

Part One: In the beginning
1 The Edgware Road murder   9
2 New Police versus old   20
3 A plethora of suspects   31
4 The great and the Good   41

Part Two: Official!
5 First cases   55
6 Déjà vu   64
7 Murder! Murder!   78
8 Internal difficulties   90
9 'The electric constable   107
10 Strong mental excitement   116
11 Calling in the Yard   126
12 Government men   141
13 A nest of vipers   150
14 More murder   160
15 And more . . .   173
16 'Quite a Road murder'   186
17 Travelling men   197
18 Double trouble   212
19 Changes   228
20 The CID   240

Endnote   248
Source   249
Select bibliography   250
Index   252

Acknowledgements

I would like to thank Don Rumbelow for pointing me towards the newly discovered photograph of the Prince of Detectives, Jonathan Whicher, and Hampshire Country Council's Museums and Archives Service for promptly producing it for me; Keith Skinner and Alan Moss for information re police personnel; and PC Clark murder expert Lee Shelden for generously allowing me to use his sketch of Clark's beat and plan of the Dagenham area. Also, the ever-patient staff at the London Metropolitan Archives, the Metropolitan Police Historical Collection, the National Archives, the British Library and the British Library Newspapers, Colindale.

PART ONE
In the beginning

1

The Edgware Road murder

At ten past two on the afternoon of 28 December 1836, Constable Samuel Pegler, 104'S', was patrolling his beat down the east side of a snowy Edgware Road when he heard panic-stricken shouts of 'Police! Police!' coming from across the way near the Pine Apple tollgate.

As Constable Pegler was well aware, the Edgware Road was a divisional border: 'S' being on the east side and 'T' on the west. Divisional borders were not lightly crossed by constables of the New Police, but such was the urgency of the shout that Pegler rushed across to the beckoning workman, who took him to see a large sack he had dragged from behind an upturned flagstone. Inside the sack was the nude torso of a woman. The arms were still attached but there were no legs and no head.

At that moment two 'T' Division officers, a sergeant and a constable, hove into view, and between them they loaded the torso on to a wheelbarrow from the nearby building site and took it to Paddington Workhouse. Here it was examined by the parish surgeon, whose pronounced opinion was that the victim was middle-aged, of above middle height and had the mark of a wedding ring on one of the fingers of her toil-worn hands.

He found no indication of disease. Indeed, the woman appeared to have been remarkably healthy, and since there were no marks indicating she had recently been bled or blistered it would seem she had not been taken ill shortly before her death. The fact that the dissection of her body was so crude indicated that it had not been done for the purpose of an anatomical lecture. The surgeon estimated that she had been dead about twenty-four hours although, given the current severe weather, he conceded that it may have been longer.

Constable Pegler set about retrieving the cord and some rags found near the sack and some wood shavings – probably of mahogany – from inside the sack. He went on to search the half-completed villas on the building site but found no further clues.

He was of the opinion that the death had occurred at least three days earlier, based on the fact that at about 8 p.m. on Christmas Eve he had seen an old chaise-cart[1] covered with mud, as if it had travelled a considerable distance, drawn up near the spot where the sack had been found. At the time he had been suspicious that 'something was going on' – possibly theft of building materials. But although he had kept the cart in view for twenty minutes, he had seen no activity near it and before his suspicions could be confirmed it had been driven away.

Maybe, he suggested, the murderer had been depositing the remains. He also pointed out that there was no impacted snow *under* the sack, even though heavy snow had been falling since Christmas morning and had collected at either end of the flagstone tunnel. This indicated that the sack must have been left before the snow began to fall.

We know Constable Pegler's thoughts on the subject because he shared them with a *Times* reporter. Perhaps it was foolish and naive of him to give away so many clues at such an early stage, but in those days of such limited means of communication they could have helped a newspaper reader to recall some useful information.

There were no New Police detectives to investigate the crime. It had been difficult enough to get Londoners to accept uniformed members when they were established in 1829, so the employment of what the public saw as plain clothes 'police spies' was out of the question. Consequently, murders and other serious crimes were dealt with by the uniformed officers of the division on which they had occurred.

On this occasion the man in charge was Inspector George Feltham, a member of the Bow Street Horse Patrol, which had recently been handed over to the New Police. As for Pegler, he had joined in September 1830, had resigned in April 1834, then rejoined seven months later – a common pattern. Life in the New Police was hard but it could be harder outside.

Given that forensic science was then practically non-existent (no blood-grouping, DNA or fingerprinting) and Feltham's detection experience limited, he must have viewed the challenge with some trepidation; today an unidentified body still poses sometimes unsolvable problems, even if the head is still attached. The surgeon did his best to help find clues, coming up with the interesting but at this stage not terribly useful information that the victim had not been a virgin and had an 'unusual interior malformation' which would make it impossible for her to have a child.

Inspector Feltham questioned the man who had discovered the sack and then the three policemen. Clearly Pegler had given the matter some thought, indicating he had an enquiring mind, so, even though the body had not been found on his division, he was assigned to aid Inspector Feltham on this enquiry.

The news of the finding of the torso spread with alarming rapidity. Already, large crowds had gathered outside the workhouse and the building site. But spreading the news to those who needed to know it quickly – the rest of the force – was another matter. No telephone, telegraph, radio or email, and the Penny Post had not yet been introduced.

What the police did have was their route paper system, by which details of the latest unsolved crimes and suspects could be passed on to the surrounding divisions, who passed them on again – like the ripples of a stone thrown into a pond. The system was quite efficient in its way, but of course the big problem was keeping the information up to date.

Despite this news-spreading the investigation got nowhere until, ten days after the torso had been found, Inspector Feltham received a message from police in distant Stepney in London's East End. They had, they said, something which might interest him: a head.

A local lock-keeper on the Regent's Canal, which wound its way across north London, had found it difficult to close one of the sluice-gates. He realized that some object was wedged there and set about retrieving it with a 'hitcher', or boathook. The object proved to be the head of a woman, of about forty to fifty years of age; it had clearly been removed from the body with a saw. Her right eye had been 'knocked out' and her jawbone broken.

The ever resourceful Pegler, who was given the job of carrying this head back to 'T' Division in a basket, now suggested that the murderer must have carried the body parts in the old chaise-cart, dropping them off whenever he found a suitable spot. Feltham pointed out that the distance between the two spots was seven miles and that there must have been somewhere suitable nearer to the Edgware Road than Stepney. Undaunted, Pegler replied that maybe the head had been dropped into the Regent's Canal as the cart crossed under the Edgware Road at Maida Hill, and had there been caught up on a barge and dragged down to Stepney.

In consequence, several men spent several days dragging the canal in the hope of finding the legs as well, but with no luck. The head proved to have severe bruising over one eye, probably occurring during life, and a torn earlobe. However, even this discovery failed to answer the most pressing question: who was she? To help identify her, the head was preserved in spirits and put on display where members of the public, who could claim good reason to do so, were allowed to view it. Many did, most probably out of morbid curiosity.

Despite the reported 'unceasing exertions' of Inspector Feltham and Constable Pegler the case went cold again until, two months later, an ostler cutting willow canes on the side of a water-filled ditch in Camberwell spotted a large, half-submerged sack. Inside were a pair of legs – which turned out to fit the trunk.

The fact that Camberwell was a long way south of the Edgware

Road and on the other side of the River Thames rather knocked on the head Pegler's idea that the Regent's Canal had been the murderer's dumping ground. But at least he had had an idea, and its pursuit had helped the police appear unceasing in their endeavours to catch the perpetrators of the Edgware Road murder – very important when they were constantly ridiculed by the press and adversely compared to the Bow Street Runners, who were still operating and many of whom had the press in their pockets.

The placement of the body parts certainly defied any obvious reasoning, particularly at a time when the means of transport were so limited. Some modern profilers tell us that most murderers don't stray far from home, even though they now have cars to assist them. Yet here were these remains, distributed in a twenty-one-mile circle. Stepney was seven miles east of the Edgware Road, and Camberwell was further away and on the other side of the river. This, at a time when there were no cars or bicycles and no underground railway – indeed, the capital's first train, from London Bridge to Deptford, had only been introduced earlier that year. Even Mr Shillibeer's horse-drawn omnibuses had begun moving around London on limited routes just a few years earlier.

Maybe Pegler's chaise-cart had been used. Maybe more than one person was involved.

The Camberwell parcel did at least give police an opportunity to show more 'due diligence' – another term beloved of the press. The legs had been wrapped in a piece of sacking, on which remained five printed letters: 'erwell'. Clearly the whole word had read 'Camberwell'.

Transport was also a problem for the New Police. They had none of their own, were supposed to walk the first three miles on any enquiry, and had a hard time justifying to the Commissioners any bus or cab expenses. However, they found their way to Camberwell and, with the help of a 'P' Division inspector, traced the owner of the sack.

Three years earlier, he told them, he had sent potatoes to Covent

Garden in such sacks, so the enquiry switched to that venue which was, of course, knee deep in sacks. But no-one recognized this particular one. Another dead end and still no identification. It was now almost three months since that snowy day on the Edgware Road.

Then, suddenly, a man named William Gay who lived in Goodge Street, off Tottenham Court Road, began to wonder why he had not heard from his sister, Hannah Brown, for three months. She lived in Union Street near the Middlesex Hospital, a strong woman who 'owned a mangle' and so was able to earn her living by washing and mangling. Come to think of it, wasn't it just before Christmas he had last seen her? He went to view the head, which was still on display at the office of Mr Girdwood, the Paddington surgeon who had examined the various portions of the body.

By now the front of the face was fairly unrecognizable so Gay was uncertain, but he felt it had the *look* of Hannah and had a damaged ear-piercing just like hers. He did know she had been involved with a man over Camberwell way, and wasn't that where the legs were found? He had overheard his sister telling her best friend, his employer Mrs Blanchard, that she was going to marry this man. She had not told *him* because they were not on speaking terms at the time. Then again, he recalled, two days after Christmas the prospective bridegroom, a Mr James Greenacre, had turned up, and Gay had overheard him informing Mrs Blanchard that the wedding was off because he had found that Hannah had been deceiving him about property she claimed to own.

James Greenacre was 'traced up'. Feltham obtained an arrest warrant and, with PC Pegler, went to his address, where they found him in bed with a woman named Sarah Gale. At first Greenacre denied even knowing Hannah but he soon caved in and admitted that he had. He showed some bravado by telling the policemen they were lucky to have caught him as he and Sarah were leaving for America in the morning, and indicated the boxes, 'tightly corded', containing their luggage. From one of these Greenacre extracted his greatcoat to keep him warm on his cab journey to Paddington Police Station.

Around midday Greenacre was taken to appear before the magistrate at Marylebone Public Office,[2] travelling in a hackney cab with a mob trailing them all the way. While he was inside the crowd swelled to thousands.

Constable Pegler was the first witness. It seems he was nervous, possibly because of the number of local worthies cramming the courtroom, including the superintendent of 'T' Division, and the fact that Mr Rawlinson, the magistrate, kept interrupting him to clarify the facts. At one point he instructed, 'Now speak slowly and deliberately; what was it you found?'

Mr Rawlinson may have been trying to help the constable – the stipendiary magistrates had become a combination of police chief and examining magistrate – or he may have intended to undermine an officer of the Metropolitan Police, as some tended to do, sensing that their own powers were under threat.

Apparently the accused did not cut a prepossessing figure. He was around fifty years of age, of middle height and rather stout. He looked very weak, owing, *The Times* reported, to his determined attempt to strangle himself with a handkerchief while in the cells at Paddington Police Station. Only bleeding and other measures, it assured its readers, had rendered him fit for his appearance in the dock.

Those present were in for something of a shock when Mr Rawlinson enquired of Greenacre whether, before the case was adjourned for a week, he had anything to say. He certainly had. It all came spilling out as he explained just how Hannah's 'accidental' death had occurred.

They had been together in his lodgings when each began accusing the other of exaggerating their wealth. (Greenacre admitted that he had represented to her that he was a man of property, 'as people do'.) Hannah, who was rather drunk, had been reeling back and forward in a rocking chair when (Greenacre admitted) he grew angry and put his foot on the chair, sending her falling backwards with great violence. She hit her head and could not be roused. He realized she was dead and, thinking no-one would believe his story, proceeded in the manner already revealed.

It turned out that he was right: neither the inquest jury nor the trial jury believed his story. After all, there were signs of injury to the front as well as to the back of the head where the eye had been knocked out. Then there was the fact that those who knew her insisted that Hannah was a genteel 'well-conducted woman' who did not drink, and also that Greenacre was shown to be in possession of some sovereigns and other articles belonging to her. Also, Pegler had found a witness who stated that the sack had come from a mangle-maker's which Greenacre had visited *before* Hannah's purported death – which suggested premeditation. He was found guilty and sentenced to death.

Greenacre had insisted throughout that the woman Gale knew nothing, but Hannah's earrings were found in her pocket and there was a bloodstained handkerchief in her trunk. Then Pegler

James Greenacre, who murdered Hannah Brown. Charles Dickens once halted a portrait sitting because he thought the artist was making him look like Greenacre

produced a child's dress found in Sarah Gale's room. It was patched with nankeen, matching one of the scraps found alongside the sack containing the torso. Gale was convicted of being an accessory after the fact and sentenced to be transported for life.

In his final confession – he made three – Greenacre admitted he had struck Hannah with a rolling pin during their quarrel but insisted he had not meant to kill her. He turned out to have a murky past. His marriage to Hannah would have been his fourth to a woman of property, and since her death he had advertised for another prospective bride.

But he had his pride. He could not wait to put Pegler and Feltham right about the order in which he had disposed of Hannah's remains. He had, he claimed, first taken her head to Stepney on one of Mr Shillibeer's new omnibuses, and dropped it into the canal. On Christmas Day he had put the legs into the nearby Camberwell Marshes. On Boxing Day, he had taken the trunk to the Edgware Road. The first part of that journey had been by cart, when someone had given him a lift. When that proved too slow, he had completed it by cab.

Presuming he was telling the truth, this proved Pegler wrong about the trunk having been in the Edgware Road since Christmas morning, but right about Hannah having been dead more than twenty-four hours. He had also matched up the scraps of material found with the body to the child's dress, and his discovery of the mahogany shavings in the first sack had led to the tracking down of the mangle-maker. More to the point, he had shown some reasoning and initiative. This had gained him press approbation and the attention of Commissioner Richard Mayne.

Therefore, it is not surprising that when, only a week after Greenacre's execution, there was another murder hue and cry (this time on Pegler's own 'S' Division) he was instructed to assist Inspector Aggs with the enquiry.

William Aggs was obviously quite a bright man, having been taken on by the New Police as a sergeant in February 1830 and promoted to inspector in December of the same year. Such rapid promotion was probably aided by the generally low standard of many of the recruits and the enormous dismissal rate due to drunkenness and offences against Commissioner Rowan's strict discipline code.

The victim this time was a barmaid, Eliza Davis, who had been found dead with her throat cut just after opening time (6 a.m.) at the King's Arms public house just off the Hampstead Road. Blood was found on the street door handle, and on the bar counter were a bloodstained knife, a penny, and a half-consumed glass of ale. Mr Wadley, the publican, exclaimed that he knew who must have done it – an 'ill-looking fellow' who came in first thing every morning and asked for a knife with which to cut his bread.

What more could Aggs and Pegler want? This time they had a complete, identified body. They knew the time of death fairly accurately and had been handed an instant suspect. Soon they were off in pursuit of the 'ill-looking fellow' (then meaning ugly or evil-looking). Fortunately, Mr Wadley provided a fuller description. The suspect was a tall, thin man of about thirty, with light whiskers. He wore a blue coat, a Scotch plaid waistcoat, fustian trousers and a white apron.

For the rest of the month Constable Pegler and Inspector Aggs, together with a Constable Roderick, were constantly on the move. On foot and – risking lack of recompense – by omnibus, coach, and hackney cab, they went to and from the West End, Lambeth, the City, Greenwich, Islington, Pimlico, Camden Town, Neasden, the Marshalsea Prison, Mayfair and St Albans, following up all possible suspects and bringing many back to the King's Arms to be identified by Mr Wadley – which they never were.

The description changed: the pot-boy insisted the man wore a black coat, black silk neckerchief and moleskin trousers. His nationality altered as well: he was a foreigner named André. No, Zucelli. No, he was English. The net widened. Men were arrested in Hounslow, Beckenham, Cheltenham, Bath, Windsor, Hull . . .

The most obvious suspect was, of course, Mr Wadley himself. He had not even bothered to open his bedroom door when the pot-boy shouted news of the murder – merely told him to fetch the police and a surgeon. He had also taken his time to get dressed before appearing, even though he admitted having previously opened the door to Eliza Davis when handing her the keys. It is possible that Pegler, faced with a ready-made suspect, had stopped deducing or that Aggs was not listening to him.

Their expenses did indeed prove very difficult to prise from the Commissioners, themselves kept very short of funds by the government and some parishes who, encouraged by the likes of Bow Street's Chief Magistrate, Frederick Roe, were refusing to pay the police rate.

Inspector Aggs put in a bill for £10 13s 6½d for a month's travel and subsistence for himself, PC Pegler and witnesses. Commissioner Mayne demanded detailed explanations for the refreshment portion, which totalled £6 9s 10½d. An aggrieved Aggs begged to state that during the entire time he had not had a single meal at home with the exception of breakfast, 'and sometimes not that, neither did the PC' and that it had often been two o'clock in the morning before he got home to Hampstead and Pegler to St John's Wood. Policemen had to eat, whether away from home or not.

Mayne replied implacably that he could only authorize occasional dining away from home. Anything extra to that should only be incurred after first obtaining the permission of the Commissioners. Aggs was obliged to submit a breakdown of his costs, which were in excess of estimated eating-at-home costs. This reduced the sum by about half.

However, Commissioner Rowan was kinder and authorized payment of the difference between what Aggs had claimed and what was initially granted: 'Let this sum be paid to Inspector Aggs as a reward from the fund for good conduct,' he wrote in the margin of Inspector Aggs's expenses claim.

Meanwhile the case remained unsolved, but it was to re-emerge years later.

2

New Police versus old

It was a strange situation. The Metropolitan Police – or New Police – had been established in London in 1829, but there were still other police officers operating from the several public offices run by paid magistrates. Bow Street, of course, held most sway and its beat was countrywide.

Successively, Bow Street Runner Henry Goddard investigated a murder at Stamford in Lincolnshire, executed warrants in London and Dover and, with Bow Street gaoler Joseph Shackell, arrested a Chartist agitator at Bury in Lancashire. The man arrested on warrant in London died in custody from an overdose of opium but Chief Magistrate Frederick Roe patted the officers reassuringly, complimenting them on the care they had given the prisoner – despite the fact they had obviously not searched him properly. This treatment contrasted sharply with the manner in which he harangued any members of the Metropolitan Police unfortunate enough to bring cases before him.

In fact, Bow Street's gaoler and officer Joseph Shackell had joined these New Police when they were formed. He was quickly promoted to sergeant but resigned three years later to return to Bow Street. Pay was poor in the Metropolitan Police, while the magistrates' men were given a retaining fee and were able to charge for their services, as well as taking a proportion of any reward or money that was refunded to banks when they acted as go-betweens. The Runners also got about a lot more, in plain clothes, and were not oppressed by the rigid discipline of the new force or the obligation to wear uniform both on and off duty.

But change was coming. In February 1837, Shackell was sent down to Uxbridge to investigate the murder of John Brill, a 15-year-old boy who had identified two poachers on the land of his employer, a wealthy farmer. Poaching and cattle-stealing crimes were something of a Bow Street speciality, provincial requests for their assistance coming largely from wealthy landowners. So one can imagine Frederick Roe's ire when he learned that the Commissioners had sent down Sergeant Otway of the New Police to assist Shackell and the local constable – at the request of the owner of the wood in which the boy's body had been found and the renter of the game. Uxbridge was beyond the Metropolitan Police boundaries so Bow Street's countrywide permit was being usurped. Three men were detained but there was insufficient evidence to charge them.

Bow Street had lost their Foot Patrol when the New Police were established. In 1836 their Horse Patrol, which been founded in 1763 to rid London's approaches of highwaymen, was also handed over. This left only the Runners (the 'principal officers') and other officers whose work was the detection of crime.

The question of whether there should be any permanent plain clothes men in the New Police had been given a thorough airing in 1833 in the wake of the Sergeant Popay affair. PS Popay had obtained information about a forthcoming forbidden meeting in Coldbath Fields, Clerkenwell, by posing as a poor artist and infiltrating himself into the National Union of the Working Classes. The Commissioners had reacted to the news of this working-class defiance with a fine show of force and a riot had ensued, during which a PC Culley had been knifed to death. The inquest jury had become popular heroes after insisting on bringing in a verdict of justifiable homicide.

A subsequent Parliamentary Select Committee condemned the employment of 'police spies' as 'abhorrent to the feelings of

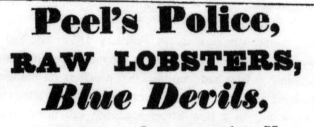

Poster showing resistance to the New Police

the people and alien to the spirit of the constitution'. Another committee discussed the organization of the New Police, comparing their performance to that of the old variety. Lambeth magistrate John Hardwick (a man much admired by Dickens) admitted that the Metropolitan Police were 'efficient in the preventative part of their duties' but claimed that they would 'ever be deficient' in the detective part thanks to their regulations and discipline. When asked what they could do about this, he advised that they should pick out their most intelligent men, put them in plain clothes, and train and employ them as a detective branch. Commissioner Mayne was already busy doing some discreet selection.

Another woman named Eliza was the victim of the next murder which the New Police were called upon to solve. Eliza Grimwood was a very beautiful prostitute, also known as 'the Countess', who lived close by Waterloo Bridge.

This time, the first constable called to the scene in the early morning of 26 May 1839 was 30-year-old Charles Burgess Goff of 'L' or Lambeth Division. As he arrived at the open door of 12 Wellington Terrace, the man who had taken him there suddenly departed and he found himself alone in a passageway with an open door at the far end. Beyond this, in a sordid, blood-spattered bedroom, he found the body of a half-dressed girl who looked as if she had fallen on her knees, then toppled over sideways.

Each era has its stereotypical means of murder. In the days of the open razor it was throat-cutting, and it seemed that was what had happened here. Despite his shock Goff noticed that there were two dents on the pillows of the double bed, indicating that two people had been lying there.

Standing gazing in horror at the body was a distressed young girl. Her name was Mary Fisher, she told him between sobs, and she was Eliza's servant.

Goff nodded towards the bed. 'She had somebody with her tonight?'

The girl explained that her mistress 'frequented the theatres' and had brought home a gentleman the previous evening. 'So Mr Hubbard slept upstairs.'

'Who is Mr Hubbard?'

'The master.'

'So where is he now?' Goff enquired.

'Gone to fetch the surgeon,' was the reply.

Goff passed this information on to the divisional superintendent and then to Inspector Field, the man put in charge of the case. Having shown some initiative, Goff was told to assist Field with his enquiries.

Charles Frederick Field, the son of a publican, had spent much of his youth trying to make his way as an actor in London's unlicensed theatres, but had been one of the first to apply to join when the Metropolitan or New Police were launched. Having a higher standard of education and intelligence than the average new recruit – many of whom were labourers or farm workers – he was taken on as a sergeant. Promoted to inspector the following year, he was sent south of the river to Lambeth, then home to numerous brothels and thieves' haunts.

Lambeth might be seedy and on the south side of the river but it was conveniently placed to allow its inhabitants easy access to the well-to-do, on whom they could prey or from whom they could seek custom. This was thanks to the splendid new Waterloo Bridge, which led almost directly into the glamorous theatre-land of the Strand and Aldwych.

Evidently, Eliza had put this gateway to good use. Wearing her pale brown dress and flower-trimmed blue silk bonnet, and with a feather boa draped saucily around her neck, she would regularly cross over to the theatres to pick up clients. According to her young servant the man she had brought home the night before was tall, well-dressed and of gentlemanly appearance. Mary was unable to describe him further because the night had been dark and she had not taken a candle to the door when she had gone to let them in.

Mr Cooke, the surgeon who examined her body, stated that Eliza had obviously committed suicide by cutting her own throat (almost decapitating herself in the process). An agitated Hubbard declared he could not think why his dear Eliza should have done away with herself – she seemed quite happy. She must have done it with the old razor he had given her to cut her corns.

Field, now thirty-four years old and an officer of some experience in this crime-ridden area, arrived after the doctor had left and disagreed with his diagnosis. He asked him to come back and take a closer look, pointing out that the woman also had a deep cut across the back of her neck and defensive wounds to her hands, which she could scarcely have made herself. Mr Cooke had to agree that this did look suspicious and decided that, after all, the 'remarkably handsome' Eliza must have been murdered. It was later revealed that she had also been stabbed once in her chest and twice in her stomach, through her stays, making this conclusion even more undeniable.

Unlike some of his predecessors Field resisted the impulse to rush off in pursuit of a shadowy suspect and instead concentrated his efforts nearer home. First, he made a thorough search of the rest of the house, starting with the bedroom of William Hubbard, a bricklayer and Eliza's live-in lover – and, from the tone of his subsequent written reports, the person he instantly suspected.

It had been Hubbard who had found the body early in the morning when he came down from his attic room, which he occupied alone when Eliza had company. He claimed he had been passing the back-parlour-cum-bedroom when he had seen Eliza's candlestick lying on the hall mat near the front door. (The 'candle factor' was an important clue at crime scenes then, its whereabouts indicating where in-house suspects had actually been as opposed to where they said they had been – although some in-house offenders got wise and planted a candlestick by the door to suggest the crime was committed by an outsider.)

On seeing the candlestick there and noticing Eliza's open door,

Hubbard claimed, he had presumed that her visitor had not stopped the night, so had gone into her room and to his horror found it awash with her blood.

He rushed up to the lodger's room but, finding that she had a man with her, withdrew and instead went to tell the servant, who promptly became hysterical. Getting no sense from her he returned to the lodger's room, where he knocked on the door and told the couple what had happened. All oddly formal behaviour, given the circumstances.

The main item missing from Eliza's room (apart from the chamber pot, which was later found in the kitchen) was the murder weapon. Field took Hubbard's room apart but found nothing except three or four 'bloodstains' on the under-sheet which did not appear to be fresh. Between the sheets were several membership cards, one of which had blood on both sides. Hubbard's corduroy trousers were also marked with several small 'bloodstains'. If they were blood there was no way of telling whether they were human or animal, and sometimes it was difficult to prove that they were even blood at all. Hubbard's razor was found, as was the broken one he had given to Eliza. Neither showed any traces of blood.

The day after the finding of the body, Inspector Field and a Sergeant Price did take off in pursuit of Eliza's gentleman visitor. PC Goff drew the short straw, being left in charge of the house with strict instructions to keep an eye on the mournful Hubbard, who kept starting up from his stupor to cry, 'Oh, my dear Eliza! Oh, my dear Eliza! Oh, God! Oh, God!'

One of the most striking things about these early investigations is the amount of dashing about the lead investigator was obliged to do. This was due partly to the limited number of officers allotted to a case but also to the lack of rapid means of communicating developments. These days, the lead officer stays put for much of the time and his team do the dashing about; only in detective fiction does he (or she) continue to do all his own grass-roots enquiries.

The New Police did have some advantages over those of today, however. If communication and transport was extremely limited for them, so it was for their quarry. When it came to the ever-tricky problem of identification there may have been no CCTV, photographs or photo-fits, but the public did tend to be naturally divided (by their speech, dress and manner) into gentlemen, ladies and others; nowadays even earls wear jeans. The 'others' often subdivided themselves by dressing according to their trade: farm workers wore smocks, and personal descriptions included comments like 'dresses like a servant' or 'looks like a sailor'. Then again, many of the poor had only the clothes they stood up in, so what they were wearing at the time of the crime would be what they were wearing while they were being sought, 'bloodstains' and all.

Another advantage was that London was so much smaller than it is now and the same horse-drawn cabs plied a limited area nightly and usually returned to the same stand. Those drivers who covered the Strand area tended to remember crossing Waterloo Bridge because they had to pay a much-resented twopenny toll.

Thus, quite quickly, Field 'traced out' the cabman who had brought Eliza home from the Strand Theatre. He claimed that Eliza's companion had 'very much the appearance of a gentleman'. The man was perhaps a little taller than his own five feet six inches; he was swarthy and wore very large whiskers but no 'moustachios'. The pair hadn't talked much, he recalled, but Eliza had told him he had a nice horse.

A musician on his way home from his evening stint at the Covent Garden Theatre recalled seeing such a gentleman entering 12 Wellington Terrace with a female at 12.15 a.m. and John Sharp, a newspaper reporter, remembered an 'unfortunate woman' (i.e. a prostitute) saying, 'He is here,' to her friend in the Strand Theatre. By this, he presumed she was referring to some man in the pit whom she recognized. Then he saw her go off to join the man. He later identified Eliza's body as that of the same woman. Doubtless her good looks made her especially noticeable and memorable.

Field was obliged to waste long days at the inquest sittings for which he had gathered these witnesses and also to do duty at the coronation ceremonies for the young Queen Victoria. In between he was never still, searching the 'dry arches' of the bridge, draining the cesspool at 12 Wellington Terrace and peering up its chimneys. He had the water pipes taken down and examined and the fields opposite combed. The houses of Hubbard's relatives received similar treatment but no suitable weapon was found.

By now it had been decided that the weapon would not, after all, be a razor but an extremely sharp-pointed knife. One of the medical men, *The Times* reported, was strongly of the opinion that it was 'one of those long, single-bladed Spanish knives with a spring to prevent it closing at the handle end of the blade'. Goff found a penknife under the floorboards but that, apparently, was not the weapon used.

The mystery of the man who had called PC Goff to the scene was solved when the lodger's visitor was located. He admitted that after Hubbard had burst in with the news and gone for a surgeon he had decided the police should also be informed, so had buttonholed the first officer he saw as he left.

Catherine Edwin, a fellow prostitute of Eliza's, turned up at the house claiming that a certain customer had become very obsessed with her friend. Eliza had called him 'her tormentor' or 'crack-whiskered Antonio' because he was Italian, although, Catherine told Goff, 'he spoke English just like you or me'.

She gave a very detailed description of the man. He was tall, with very full dark whiskers, green spectacles, dark green trousers, a frock coat, a primrose-coloured waistcoat, a broad-brimmed hat and a blue handkerchief,[1] and carried a cloak over his arm. It seemed one could hardly miss him, but Goff was suspicious of the woman's motives because while he had been distracted answering the door she had had the opportunity to speak to Hubbard.

Nonetheless, Field, Goff and Sergeant Price went to 'places of public resort of foreigners' such as hotels, gambling houses and the opera house, and made enquiries at the Passport Office, docks and wharves as to whether a swarthy foreigner had embarked there recently.

Hubbard was always kept very much in view as a suspect, particularly after they discovered that he had been violent not only towards his estranged wife but also to Eliza (who was his first cousin). It seems that he had been very jealous about her, especially with regard to one customer with whom she planned to go to the Epsom Races. He had even threatened to 'do them both in'. To cap it all, he had been seen around the Waterloo Road in the early morning before the discovery of Eliza's body.

Unfortunately, the water was being muddied by inquest witnesses who contradicted each other – and themselves. Some of them may have been telling lies so they could claim the reward money which was being offered or out of fear of the violent Hubbard. One, who had come forward with startling evidence of seeing a bloodied man at the door of 12 Wellington Terrace, had failed to pick Hubbard out of a line-up, had later accused someone else, and was found to be known locally as being a little wanting mentally.

As always, much time was wasted following up information from anonymous letters, but one writer gave his name – John Walter Cavendish – and stated that he had some vital information. He was the gentlemanly person who had come home with Eliza intending to stay the night, but he had been almost thrown out by a belligerent man who had come down from upstairs. Police were unable to trace the writer, but he promised that if his letter was printed in the newspapers he would come forward to give evidence.

Finally, worried that Hubbard was about to abscond, Field arrested him and took him before a Lambeth magistrate, who felt there was insufficient evidence to hold the suspect. Unless John Walter Cavendish came forward, he said, he would have to dismiss the case, but he did adjourn the hearing to give the man time to appear. Meanwhile, the crowd outside were howling that Hubbard was the murderer and should be sent to the gallows.

When the court reassembled Cavendish's name was again called, but when there was no response Hubbard was set free.

Although hard evidence was difficult to come by in those days before forensic aids, Field had shown himself capable of conducting an investigation. Goff had also demonstrated sufficient initiative to become what was being termed 'an active officer' – one of Mayne's selected men. He proved himself further by finding and arresting a prisoner who had been at large for some time after escaping from police custody when a mob of ruffians had attacked them at Barnet Fair.

3

A plethora of suspects

'Police! Police!'

The shouts came from the open door of 35 Princes Street, Soho, just after midnight on 3 June 1839. A passer-by fetched PC Timothy Gimlet, who saw smoke billowing out from the ground floor. His rattle summoned two more constables and, with the help of bystanders, they managed to put out the fire in the back room.

'There is a body in here,' one of the bystanders pointed out, causing PC Thomas Chilman to get down on his hands and knees to feel around in the lingering smoke. He soon located a pair of feet and legs, a great deal of blood and many feathers. Near the body was a heavy sash-window weight matted with hair; later, when PC Chilman presented this in court as a possible weapon, he had to admit that there was no way of telling whether the hair was animal or human. Inside a drawer was found a knife which looked as if it had recently been wiped of blood.

The victim, 55-year-old Robert Westwood, was a watchmaker and the inventor of 'the celebrated eight-day watch'. In those days merely owning a watch indicated that you were a person of some substance, and you could risk your very life by carrying it about. Mr Westwood had dozens of watches on his premises in Princes Street, many of them extremely valuable. Although the bedrooms were above the shop, fear of burglary caused him to sleep in the back room of the ground floor instead – but only after double-locking and chaining the street doors.

However, despite all his security precautions, the watchmaker had been battered about the head, his throat slashed and his clothing set on fire.

In this case there was to be no difficulty in finding suspects – quite the reverse. First, since there were no signs of forced entry, there were the other residents. The elderly Mrs Westwood (at least twenty years older than her husband) claimed that she first became aware something might be wrong when, at around 11.30 p.m., she heard scuffling downstairs. Initially she had decided it was merely her husband catching the cat before putting it out, but fifteen minutes later she heard someone go out, closing the front door behind them. Only after she began to smell smoke and heard the occasional groan from the floor below did she go upstairs to fetch their new young maid and Mr Gerard, their elderly and deaf lodger, telling them she was sure her husband had been murdered.

It wasn't until the arrival of Westwood's foreman, Charles Louis Serouche, that it was revealed that over eighty of the most valuable timepieces were missing, including several of the patent eight-day watches, some made of gold. Moreover, it was evident that the murderer knew which were the most valuable pieces and where they were kept. The foreman was suspect, of course, particularly since he had lived on the premises until a recent disagreement with his employer. Police were soon to discover that having disagreements with Mr Westwood was not unusual.

Messengers were sent dashing off with route papers listing and describing the stolen property, and at 8 p.m. on the evening following the murder the inquest was opened. All the jury members were close neighbours of Westwood, and eight of them lived in the same street. This, given the man's irascible reputation, must have qualified them all as possible suspects.

In charge of this case was 'C' Division's most senior officer, Superintendent Baker, aided by Inspectors Jervis and Beresford.

The elderly Mrs Westwood soon pointed an accusing finger at two previous lodgers, William and Caroline Stevenson who, after her husband had asked them to leave only ten days earlier, had threatened to 'do for' him. The cause of the bad feeling had been domestic disputes plus Westwood's objection to the number and variety of Mrs Stevenson's admirers, who called when her husband was away. She insisted they came to see her unmarried sister, who lived with them.

Serouche, the foreman, appears to have done some mischief-making here, telling Westwood that he had seen Mrs Stevenson getting out of a cab 'without a bonnet' after being out all night, and that he had seen some of her women friends entering a brothel.

Consequently, she and her husband had argued and Stevenson had threatened Westwood. Mrs Stevenson became so upset by all this that she ran off home to her mother – inadvertently taking the shop keys with her. It wasn't until her mother had come across them, she claimed, that she became aware she still had them.

The last person to have seen the victim alive was the new servant, Maria Pritty, who was responsible for the final locking up after she let in the lodger at 11 p.m. The presence of not only lodgers but live-in servants in so many households complicated many early police enquiries. Such people were likely suspects not only because they had access, opportunity and knowledge of the premises and occupants, but also through possible motives of poverty, jealousy and the irritations of close-quarters living. Even if completely innocent they could make unreliable witnesses, being nervous of jeopardizing their jobs and/or homes. It looked, moreover, as if Maria Pritty could have further reason to lie when it was revealed that she had been almost fully dressed when the police arrived and also had been seen talking to some men while the others were trying to put out the fire.

A neighbour came forward, claiming that he had seen two middle-aged, lower-class men dressed in dark frock coats emerging from 35 Princes Street just after midnight. One of those helpful passers-by who had assisted with putting out the fire was a man named George Robinson. He had been wearing a frock coat and, said the witness, answered to the description of one of these suspect men.

Robinson was called upon to explain just what he had been doing in Princes Street at that hour, how he supported himself, and how he had come by that wound on his cheek. Neither the coroner nor the jury were happy with his replies, in which he contradicted himself and other witnesses. The wound, he claimed, was a burn from when he helped put out the fire. But one of the surgeons, in court to give evidence about the body, said it looked more like a graze to him.

The coroner and his jury pondered long on whether Robinson should be taken into custody. They finally decided he should be handed over to Inspector Beresford, who would examine Robinson's lodgings, make further enquiries, then decide whether to detain the man

After doing all this Beresford let Robinson go, claiming he could find no evidence against him. True, Robinson was in possession of Mr Westwood's hat, but he had made no secret of the fact, claiming he had mistaken it for his own in the hurry when police pushed him out of the premises. (Hats, accidentally left on scene or exchanged for those found there, also tended to feature in crime enquiries. Respectable people were rarely seen bareheaded out of doors, therefore the hatless became more noticeable and suspect.)

The Times made it plain that it favoured Mrs Westwood as a suspect, or at least an accomplice. The newspaper pointed out that, not long before, she had appealed to Marlborough Street magistrates to restrain her husband's violence against her. And didn't it seem odd that she pleaded ignorance of some anonymous threatening letters Westwood had received when he had told so many other people about them?

But it was evident that Westwood was a man of 'extremely irritable temper' and 'rather peculiar habits' – particularly when dealing with dissatisfied customers. A sea captain had had the watch he complained about snatched from his hand, thrown to the floor and stamped upon, and a young man found himself facing a pistol and a threat to blow his brains out if he didn't leave at once. The ranks of possible suspects were growing, and on the penultimate day of the inquest they were joined by a member of the jury. He, too, had once been foreman at 35 Princes Street 'but had lately opposed Westwood in business' and (alleged an anonymous letter to *The Times*) had threatened Westwood's life.

The jury brought in a verdict of murder by a person or persons unknown and congratulated Superintendent Baker and the two inspectors 'for their zeal, promptness and efficiency and for their efforts (tho' unsuccessful) to discover the perpetrators'.

According to the press, Sergeant Charles Otway was already assisting and now Commissioner Mayne sent in his big gun, Inspector Nicholas Pearce, to 'manage' the case.

Pearce, a six-foot Cornishman who had been a member of the Bow Street Foot Patrol, was another officer who had popped in and out of the Metropolitan Police. He had joined the new force in February 1830 as a sergeant and served in the East End before being transferred to the more glamorous 'A' or Whitehall Division. He soon resigned, but four months later he was back. Pay in the New Police might be low, discipline strict and hours long, but the force did offer the opportunity for advancement, particularly to those in at the beginning. Eighteen months after rejoining he was promoted to inspector and was soon being sent out from Scotland Yard to deal with difficult cases.

As Westwood's business relations had clearly been stormy Pearce drew up a list of all those who had worked for him: engravers, finishers, gilders, makers of dials, escapements, motions and hands – sixteen in all. There was even a 'secret springer' to question.

He also sent Beresford to trace the stolen watches at jewellers' and pawnbrokers' and, following information received, to a watchmaker in Gravesend. Beresford wrote from Chatham that he had had no luck at Gravesend but would go on to Maidstone the following day and return to Chatham in the evening. If he had not received further instructions by post he would return to London the day after that. But no such luck.

Beresford was 'guided on' to Broadstairs, where a boat had been reported stolen – possibly by some suspects, said to have been seen in the area, so that they could escape across the Channel where there would be better opportunities to sell the stolen property. The following day Beresford took the first stage coach to Ramsgate and the next day went on to Broadstairs. By the time he arrived at Broadstairs the boat owner was in Boulogne, retrieving his vessel from the French police. So the inspector trekked over to Dover to catch a direct steamboat to the French port. He arrived late in the evening only to discover that the French police had escorted the boat thief to the Belgian border, where they had set him free having believed his story that he was only a Prussian desperately trying to get home.

Of course, today such a wild goose chase would be unnecessary. A few phone calls or emails would have sorted out the whole thing.

Enquiries unearthed yet another disgruntled ex-employee and, Pearce reported to the Commissioners, he was a very likely suspect. William Campion had been sacked by Westwood four years previously, was known to be of bad character and, as Pearce pointed out, had worked in Paris and Holland, so would know about foreign markets for stolen goods. What's more, the man was now destitute, had made it known that this was due to Westwood's refusal to 'give him a character' and had been heard to say that 'some day he'd be damned if he did not cut his b****** throat'.

A watchmaker told Campion that police were enquiring about him and advised him to go and see them. He replied that when he heard about the murder he had intended to go to see Mrs Westwood but that his clothes were in such a state he had been too ashamed. Pearce and Otway searched for him well into the night, fearing he was now forewarned, and wondered whether to issue a wanted poster. Five days later Pearce saw Campion and reported firmly that the man had 'not the slightest degree of suspicion attached to him' as he was now employed, leading a regular life and had an alibi. Another dead end.

The police had always been aware of a group of people who had an extremely strong motive for murdering Robert Westwood: the relatives and friends of a young man named William Reading, who had been hanged on the watchmaker's evidence.

Twice during his thirty years in business Westwood had been robbed in a manner which may have helped sour his nature. Soon after he had commenced trading three men had broken in, tied him to a bedpost and stolen a number of valuable pieces. The second robbery occurred in August 1822, while he and his wife were at church. He had lost forty-four gold sovereigns, watches and jewellery worth about £2,000, a very large sum then.

A witness claimed to have seen William Reading loitering near the shop with four others. When apprehended, Reading had six sovereigns on him, two of which, Westwood swore, bore his special mark. This, plus a letter found on the suspect which asked his brother to get rid of certain items, had been sufficient to hang him. Ironically, had all this happened at the time of Westwood's murder seventeen years later, he might not have suffered such a fate as by then the number of capital offences had been drastically reduced.

There was little hard evidence to suggest that these relatives and friends had committed the murder but, possibly in desperation, Pearce now thought they must have, 'due to the considerable degree of malice used in the mangling of the body of their victim'. If they were the perpetrators they had waited a long time for revenge. One of Reading's brothers was now a watchmaker himself, but Pearce admitted he was not able to find anything against the man despite the fact he was being 'constantly watched by constables'. The friends were also enquired into, with two reported as having been seen wearing new clothes after previously being very shabby.

However, the arrival of a letter from New York put all other theories and suspects on the back burner. It concerned a certain Nicholas William Carron. He was not a new suspect, having been suggested early on by another anonymous letter-writer.

Following up anonymous letters usually only resulted in a waste of police time but this one had looked much more promising than most. It claimed that Carron, a paper-hanger who lived at 32

Princes Street – only two doors from the Westwoods – knew the watchmaker's premises well, having recently decorated them, and that he had been hard up at the time of the murder. Furthermore, Carron had 'concealed himself' all day following the murder, then left London having shaved off his whiskers, adopted a disguise and taken on a false name. He had been strangely agitated just before his departure and said he was thinking of going abroad. The fact that Carron was a paper-hanger was significant, given the discovery of the sash weight and a strange apron with large pockets (a paper-hanger's apron, it turned out) which had been found at the scene.

Inspector Beresford had been given the job of looking into these early allegations. John Lloyd, an ex-lodger of Carron's (who may have been the anonymous letter-writer), told him that Carron was being threatened by creditors and had been asked to leave his house just before the murder took place.

Beresford shamefacedly admitted that when following up the anonymous letter and discovering that Carron had indeed fled, he had decided that this was due solely to the fact that Carron's creditors were threatening him. He had left behind his wife and four children, telling them he was going to Blackheath to find work and would come back or write in about a week. Two of the children were put into a workhouse, two sent to relatives and the wife had gone back to her mother.

Now there was this letter from New York claiming that Carron had arrived there and that his wife was en route to join him. He had taken an apartment and was busy furnishing it in preparation for her arrival. He was shortly to send for his children and recompense all parties concerned for the expenses incurred. All very curious. Mrs Carron was not found at her mother's. She had left about two months earlier, saying she was going to travel, in service, with a French lady and would write soon. So far, no letter.

A red-faced Beresford suggested he interview Carron's ex-housekeeper, a widow with three children who had been thrown out when she became pregnant by him. He traced her to a Lincolnshire workhouse. She recognized the apron and sash weight as items she had seen about Carron's place and described the man as a bad character who spent a good deal of time with a prostitute in the Waterloo Road. (Eliza Grimwood, one wonders?)

Pearce had already sent reward notices to New York, escape across the Atlantic being commonplace. Now he took a chance and wrote to an old acquaintance, William Cartwright, who was living there. Cartwright was an ex-Metropolitan policeman – one of the many who had been dismissed in the early days. Pearce asked Cartwright to make discreet enquiries about Carron. If successful, there would be a reward. He received no reply so wrote again, twice. Still no reply.

Carron did indeed have creditors, but Beresford now found the sums owed them were paltry and the tales of their threats false.

Eventually, Pearce wrote to Cartwright again, this time under cover of a letter from Cartwright's sister. She received a reply from Cartwright complaining that he had gone to such expense making fruitless enquiries about Carron that he had been surprised he had not received replies to *his* three letters. He would write again soon nonetheless. He never did, and further enquiries indicated that he and Carron were now in cahoots.

Inspector Pearce, who liked to get around, suggested that if a person of good judgement who knew all about the case were to proceed to New York . . .?

There is no evidence that Pearce got his trip to New York or received any information from a Donald McLeod whom he had also asked to make enquiries over there.

Echoes of the case continued for some years. In 1841, an English boy from a brig docked in Quebec was approached by a man 'very dull and down looking and very heavy about the eyes' (and broadly answering Carron's description) who questioned him about the Westwood murder. In 1849, a convict in Bermuda named Carron's lodger, John Lloyd, as the murderer. In the interval Lloyd had been transported, served his time, returned and dropped out of sight. But Beresford, now a superintendent, thought the informant only wanted to be brought home to England – a common ploy. Suspects and alleged sightings of the stolen property continued to surface as late as 1854, but the murder was never solved.

To find *any* suspects can be difficult. In this case, there was a plethora but, unfortunately, no forensic means to pinpoint anyone. Nonetheless, it was clear that the police had made great efforts to solve the crime.

By the middle of 1839 Bow Street's worst fears were made real. The Home Secretary, Lord John Russell, was busy seeing that the provinces were given something similar to the Metropolitan Police and had also introduced his two Police Bills for improving the police in and near the metropolis. His aims were to be achieved by enlarging the area covered by the Metropolitan Police, incorporating the Thames Police, confining the powers of the magistrates to purely judicial matters and disbanding their officers. The New Police had won.

Bow Street Runner Henry Goddard went on to become the chief constable of Northamptonshire and Bow Street gaoler Shackell rejoined the Metropolitan Police – as an inspector. In the days when there was neither a detective branch nor any proper police training, the Commissioners could not afford to reject experienced men.

Meanwhile, Inspector Pearce and Sergeant Otway continued in their roles as 'active officers'. In February 1840, they chased embezzlers to Calais. In March, they prevented a duel between Prince Louis Napoleon Bonaparte and Comte Leon, and in May 1840 they were called in on two more murders.

The first was another particularly brutal burglary and the murder of an old man, Mr Templeman, in Islington. The local police, who had been handed the murderer, Richard Gould, had failed to consolidate the evidence and he had been acquitted. Word was that Gould was about to leave for Australia. Perhaps they could re-arrest him, this time for the robbery. Otway set about 'tracing him out'.

While he was gone, Pearce was called in on a case so important that, on hearing of it, Richard Mayne himself hurried to the scene.

4

The great and the Good

The New Police owed a great deal to Lord John Russell, son of the Duke of Bedford and member of a great Whig house. The previous Home Secretaries, Lord Melbourne and Lord Duncannon, had given them little support when there were early calls for their abolition from the press and magistrates. Indeed, Duncannon had conspired with Roe against them.

By contrast, during his four-year period in the post Lord John Russell had consolidated their position, enlarged their area of jurisdiction and taken some of the pressure off them by enabling the rest of England and Wales to set up similar organizations.

No surprise, then, that when Lord John's uncle, Lord William Russell, was found murdered in his bed, Commissioner Mayne hurried to the scene. Indeed, the Queen herself was soon sending Lord John horrified messages on hearing the rumour that his uncle had committed suicide.

Lord William Russell was an elderly and rather pernickety widower who, after years as a politician, had found himself too delicate to continue with the rough and tumble of Parliament so had withdrawn into a life largely centred on his club and his interest in art. He helped his brother, the Duke of Bedford, choose sculptures with which to adorn Woburn Abbey.

The first clue that anything had disturbed Lord William's well-ordered existence at his small but elegant house just behind Park Lane in Mayfair was at 7.15 on the morning of 6 May 1840, when the housemaid found the writing room and dining room in chaos and a heap of valuable objects by the unlocked front door – all of which indicated an aborted burglary.

She alerted Courvoisier, the 28-year-old Swiss valet, whom, unusually, she found already dressed except for his coat. When he saw the mess he exclaimed, 'My God, someone has been robbing us!'

She replied, 'For God's sake, let's go and see where his lordship is!'

They found him in lying in his four-poster bed with his throat cut.

The first police to arrive on the scene were two 'C' Division constables, Baldwin and Rose, quickly followed by a sergeant. Next came Inspector Tedman; he was a 'D', not 'C', Division officer but his station house in Marylebone Lane was nearer than 'C' Division's Vine Street. Tedman had joined the New Police on its establishment in 1829, exceeding the required height of five feet seven inches by only half an inch. He had become a sergeant the following year and an inspector four years later.

He found the valet Courvoisier holding his head with his hands, moaning, 'I shall lose my place and my character!'

Hurrying in from Vine Street once again came Superintendent Baker and Inspector Beresford. Then came Mayne, surgeons, Mayne's golden boy Inspector Pearce, noblemen making enquiries, relatives, and the multitude who were to surround the premises from that moment on.

The inquest was opened at 6 p.m. that evening in a nearby pub, as was the custom. Today's juries, encouraged by ludicrous TV displays of rapid forensic magic, are fixated on instant DNA. These inquest jurors had obviously been influenced more by the criticism of the police failure in recent murder cases such as those of the two Elizas and Mr Westwood.

After Tedman had described his questioning of the servants on his arrival, one juryman enquired, 'Is it not your duty to make directly to the room in which a murder or suicide is committed?'

Tedman agreed that it was, but said that finding the servants downstairs he had made a little enquiry first.

'Was it not your duty to send for the surgeon?' the juror persisted.

Tedman protested that from the account he had received, he was convinced the victim was already dead; besides, it was only two minutes before he went upstairs.

Inspector Beresford said he thought the marks on the back area door had been made by some instrument – when the door was open.

'I suggested to Inspector Pearce that we should search for it,' Beresford said, getting in before Pearce, adding that he had found a bent poker with a pointed end which fitted into the damaged latch. (At the subsequent trial, Pearce claimed to have found the bent poker, along with a suitable hammer and screwdriver, in the pantry – the valet's domain.)

The problem for the police was that it appeared to be an inside job. Although they knew some valuables were missing, and despite the heap of valuables found by the front door, there was no evidence that the likely suspect, the valet, had left the premises since the murder. So where was the loot? (The only other live-in servants were the housemaid and the cook.)

The 28-year-old Swiss valet was a man of charm and good appearance and his attentiveness had endeared him to his previous employers, but this had been his first unsupervised post and Lord William had found him wanting. The day before the murder he had failed to pass on a message to the coachman that he should pick Lord William up from his club and had lied about it afterwards. He had told the housemaid that if he had half of 'Old Billy's money' he wouldn't remain in England for long.

Courvoisier claimed that he had undressed his master at around half past twelve, warmed his bed[1] and left him with a rush light and a candle by which to read his book, *The Memoirs of Sir Samuel Romilly* (who, ironically, was a legal reformer). But the housemaid, a previous valet and his family all insisted that Lord William never read in bed and never allowed a candle in his room for fear of fire. He would be seen upstairs by lamplight and left with a rush light, which by morning would be burned out. But this light was only a third burned down. Beresford experimented with a similar rush light and found it took an hour and a half to burn down by a third – which tied in to the surgeon's estimated time of death.

Various possible suspects were investigated: previous servants, the coachman and groom, who lived off the premises, and Carr, an out-of-work servant who had visited Courvoisier the previous evening. He was found, questioned by Beresford and released. Tedman, a sergeant and a PC were left to keep an eye on the property and the valet.

'At the close of the second day,' *The Times* declared, '. . . it appears that the police are without any clue that can lead to the discovery and apprehension of the murderer.'

This was the fifth unsolved murder in two years, it went on. It wasn't that the New Police weren't trying nor that they weren't good at preventing crime. It was just that the set-up was wrong. As detectives, the officers of the former police establishments (the Runners) had seldom failed: therefore, 'recourse must again be had to their services'.

The press watched the house constantly for any clues. 'A sweep was sent for to the house in the course of yesterday,' *The Times* reported excitedly, giving rise 'to the notion that the murderer was still concealed on the premises, and that the sweep was to be sent up the chimney for the purpose of ascertaining if he had hidden himself there'.

In fact, Pearce *was* supervising a more thorough search of the house, assisted by workmen and two officers who had a reputation for finding things: a Constable Collier and a meek-mannered, sharp-eyed sergeant, Frederick Shaw, who had been part of the team on the Westwood murder. The officers had noticed that Courvoisier became more agitated when they looked around his pantry, and it was Pearce who discovered, tucked behind the skirting board, a Waterloo medal, a £10 banknote and a gold net purse containing gold rings and coins. They winkled out more of Lord William's possessions from under the water pipes and various other places in and around the pantry. But there was no sign of bulkier missing items, such as silver spoons. Nonetheless, they had enough and arrested the valet.

On the day after his committal to the Old Bailey for trial, *The Times* published a long letter signed 'DETECTOR' which answered the newspaper's criticisms that the New Police lacked detective skills. True, the Runners had been too hastily disbanded, but what should happen now was that twenty-five or thirty officers should be selected and added to the best of the now unemployed Runners to form a detective force to operate in plain clothes. They should be paid at the inspector's rate plus the other emoluments that the Runners had enjoyed. (Many ex-Runners had failed to apply for the New Police because of the low pay and over-strict discipline. They chose to become private investigators at a guinea a day plus expenses.)

But it was emoluments (in the form of rewards) which were to bring the officers under savage attack at the trial. Defence counsel Charles Phillips attacked them because the stolen articles had not been found on the premises until the day of the issue of the £400 reward notice. Prosecuting counsel responded that any reward money would have to be divided by so many that the officers would be unlikely to forfeit a man's life for the sake of their paltry share.

Pearce was attacked for bringing only part of one door and door post into court – to demonstrate how it had been damaged from the inside when open – when in fact he had also experimented on another door. He was almost accused of planting bloodstained gloves and hankies in the valet's box and criticized for asking the valet if he could now look him in the face when he showed him a stolen object he had found.

'Merciful God!' Phillips exclaimed. 'Such treatment was worthy only of the Inquisition!'

(Something of an exaggeration, one might think, but more an act of desperation on the part of Phillips. Years later the defence counsel admitted that at this stage he knew the valet was guilty: after the sudden production of the missing bulky items, Courvoisier had confessed to him but insisted he still plead not guilty, despite the fact that this might throw suspicion on the housemaid. Phillips was so overwhelmed by the knowledge that he acted very unprofessionally by consulting the judge, Baron Parke, who, furious at being so embarrassed, told him he must continue.)

These bulky items had been handed in after the trial had begun by Charlotte Piolaine, the English wife of a Frenchman. The couple kept the Hotel Dieppe in Leicester Square, where Couvoisier had worked briefly as a waiter several years earlier. He had suddenly popped up again shortly before the date of the murder, asking if he could leave a parcel with them. She had not known his name (they had called him Jean) nor with whom he was presently employed, and since she was so busy had only heard a little about the murder. It wasn't until her cousin saw an item in a French newspaper that she had made any connection. The silver spoons and forks in the parcel bore Lord William's crest: a goat.

The trial proceedings were completed by the proprietor of a hotel where Courvoisier had worked and the servants and mistress (Lady Julia Lockwood) from his previous post, all of whom spoke of his good character, kind-heartedness, humanity and inoffensiveness of disposition.

But the jury were unmoved. They found him guilty and he was sentenced to death. In one of his three subsequent reported confessions (all slightly different) he claimed that the motive for the murder was that Lord William had caught him stealing and had sacked him, but he later refuted this, saying his master was only displeased with him. For some reason he endeavoured to make the police look foolish by describing how he had deceived them every step of the way, although he also took some of that back. Later there was speculation that the reason no bloodstained clothing had been found was that he had been naked at the time of the murder.

The candle question was never adequately answered. Why cook up a story about Lord William reading in bed? In *Two Studies in Crime* (Hutchinson, 1959) Yseult Bridges suggests that the valet had lit his way to the bedroom with a wax candle from the dining room, then took it back to his own room before realizing that a wax candle in a silver holder would look suspicious in a servant's room (they were only allowed tallow candles). It was too late to return it so he quickly dumped it in Lord William's bedroom with the book.

Meanwhile, Sergeant Otway continued his efforts with regard to the botched Gould case. After his acquittal on the charge of murdering the old man Templeman in Islington, the Commissioners had learned, Richard Gould had confessed to the deputy governor at the prison where he had been held. Otway traced Gould to a ship at Gravesend which was about to depart for Sydney, Australia, and told him that a reward of £200 was about to be offered for the name of the murderer. He suggested that if he gave up his accomplice he could earn a useful sum with which to begin his new life in the Colony, implying that since he had been acquitted of the crime he could not be tried again.

After hesitating Gould agreed and gave a statement and names on the promise of £100 and payment of his delayed passage. Otway hotfooted it back to London and returned with a warrant for the burglary of Mr Templeman's house, a crime with which Gould had not been previously charged.

Once in the dock Gould retracted his statement, saying he had been coerced by Otway, but further evidence was presented regarding his efforts to acquire two 'screws' (skeleton keys), a dark lantern[2] and a penny rush light just before the robbery, and this helped convict him (burglars often had to take along their own light sources). Then there was the fact that he had told acquaintances about this elderly man with money and that he was able to buy new shoes on the day after the murder, despite being penniless the day before.

The judge, again Baron Parke, pointed out that there could be little doubt that Gould was not only the murderer but was willing to accuse an innocent person of the crime for money. He couldn't condemn him to death – the sentence was transportation for life – but, he added chillingly, he was authorized to add to this a still heavier punishment, which was that he be sent to a penal colony, there to pass the remainder of his life in hopeless slavery, poverty and misery of the worst description. That must have cheered Gould up. So the police had got their man, although there was some disapproval of the deception by which they had brought this about.

For about a year and a half there was something of a lull in embarrassing cases, and in March 1842 Inspector Pearce was much praised when he solved an old murder case at Eskdaleside in North Yorkshire.

But the respite was not to last. The next London saga began south of the river in Wandsworth at 8.45 p.m. on Wednesday 6 April 1842, when a shopkeeper complained to PC William Gardner that he had been robbed. A coachman by the name of Daniel Good had bought a pair of breeches, and after he had gone a boy assistant claimed he had stolen another pair and slipped them under his greatcoat flaps.

PC Gardner found Good at his master's stables in Putney, which he began to search. The coachman, vigorously denying the charge, accompanied him until they reached the last stable block, when he became anxious and said, 'Let's go to Wandsworth and make it all right.'

But the constable went on searching, and while taking a closer look at what he at first thought was a plucked goose realized it was part of a human body. Good ran off, locking the constable, two shop boys, the estate factor and his own son inside. It took fifteen minutes for them to escape and for the hue and cry to be raised.

By four o'clock the following morning all the stations within the sixty-mile Metropolitan Police area had been informed by route paper – a quite impressive feat, although how some stations handled this information was to prove critical. Some notified the beat men immediately while Inspector Tedman at Marylebone Lane, who received the notice at 3 a.m., decided to leave it to be read out to the early shift at 6 a.m.; after all, Putney was quite a long way away. It was his bad luck that the victim, Jane Sparks, or Jones, or Good, had actually lived on his patch just off Manchester Square, and it was to her lodgings Good had first hurried. She had not been seen there for three days since she had gone off to beard Good about the new woman in his life. He left there quite conspicuously at 5.15 a.m. that morning, piling their bed, a box and a large bundle onto a cab.

However, an alert beat PC had noted the number of the cab waiting outside Jane Good's address. Thus 'D' Division police were able to trace Good's route to Whitcombe Street near Trafalgar Square. A further cab had taken him to Spitalfields and the home of his first 'wife', Old Molly Good, but a sergeant who went there had been so crass with his enquiries that Good had probably been warned off and was now nowhere to be found.

It was an embarrassing chapter of accidents which provoked an inquest on the route paper system: the Wandsworth superintendent should have got the paper out before 11.15 p.m.; it should have been more detailed; once received at a police station the news should have been acted upon with more urgency; and so on. Some officers, including little Tedman, were suspended from duty without pay.

The reaction was partly due to another anti-police field day in the press. The fact that Jane Good's address had not been extracted from Daniel Good's son until the morning following the murder was another stick with which to beat them. Of course, these things always look simpler when viewed from outside, and in retrospect. Pearce, who had been called in, was treated more kindly by them. They reminded people of his success in the Courvoisier and Eskdaleside cases, and by now this familiar figure may have made some friends among the penny-a-liners.

The chief mistake of the New Police was their undue openness with the press together with a certain naivety, claimed Serjeant Ballantine, writing forty years later in *Some Experiences of a Barrister's Life* (Bentley, 1882). He pointed out that the old Bow Street Runners had not informed criminals who it was they wanted to catch, with what their trap was baited and where it would be laid. Nor did they have to waste their time writing endless reports. Instead, Charles Dickens commented – as a reporter, he had experience in dealing with them – they never lost a public occasion 'of jobbing and trading in mystery and making the most of themselves'.

Pearce knew that Good did not have the funds for flight but suspected that Old Molly Good, who kept a fruit stall, might be aiding him. Watch was kept on her and on the Channel ports and the docks, in case he tried to escape to France or New York. Sightings of him flooded in, but it was an ex-Wandsworth policeman who finally spotted him working on a new railway line near Tonbridge in Kent.

Despite all the criticism it was less than seven weeks after the finding of the body that Daniel Good was executed at Newgate for the murder of Jane Good.

There had been another atrocious murder while Daniel Good was awaiting trial: that of PC Timothy Daly, who was shot dead while chasing a 'highwayman' while another policeman and a member of the public were injured. The killer was captured immediately but now there were questions as to why unarmed police were sent after robbers – the Bow Street Runners had always carried pistols.

The second of two attempts on the life of the Queen soon settled the matter. In June 1842, the Commissioner sent a special report to the Home Office, defending his men regarding the Good murder – while admitting faults in the route paper handling – and pointing out that since the police had been established twenty-two murders had been committed. Fourteen of the murderers had been convicted, and in seven other cases the guilty parties were thought to be known but had escaped, either by fleeing the country or through lack of sufficient legal evidence to convict them. He cited Gould for the Templeman murder and the murder of Constable Culley at the Coldbath Fields riot, in which 'there is no reason whatever to doubt that the party who was tried but acquitted did commit the act'.

He pointed out that when the Metropolitan Police were set up there had been no 'provision for the performance of detective duties' because officers of Bow Street and magistrates' officers and others were exclusively thus engaged. Since then, when necessary, special officers from each division had been selected, but this was no longer convenient as it took men from divisional duties. Therefore, he asked for an increase of two inspectors and eight sergeants to act solely as detectives.

By 20 June he had his permission (although for two fewer than he requested) and the new detective force was announced by memorandum of 15 August 1842.

The two inspectors were to be paid £200 a year (£84 more than uniformed officers) and the six sergeants £73 (£10 more). The higher rates were to induce 'those most competent to enter it and to continue to exert themselves zealously without looking to advancement to other police appointments'. In other words, they should not expect any promotion beyond inspector.

Unsurprisingly, the new detectives were to be led by the tall, blue-eyed Cornishman, Nicholas Pearce, whose previous experience as a Bow Street Patrol had stood him in good stead. The second inspector was neither the keen but unfortunate Tedman nor the hard-working, high-profile Field, of the Westwood murder, but Sussex-born ex-chemist John Haynes. He had joined the force ten years earlier and was an expert on horse-stealing offences. On one occasion he had successfully used his experience to deduce how long it would take thieves who had looted a wrecked Indiaman off Margate to reach London, estimating how long the laden horse and cart could travel each day and so at which inns they would be obliged to stop.

Among the sergeants was Epsom-born, 39-year-old Stephen Thornton, veteran of the Westwood and Good murders, a man feared by pickpockets and the swell mob who plagued the Epsom Races because he was even wilier than they were. Ex-butcher Frederick Shaw had also been employed on the Westwood and Russell murder enquiries, and Sergeant Gerrett had worked as Pearce's assistant on the Good murder chase.

The remaining two had been constables at the time of their selection and so were given two steps up. Charles Burgess Goff had been first on the scene after the Eliza Grimwood murder in Waterloo and proved efficient enough to be seconded to assist Field in the abortive chase. Ex-Camberwell labourer, Jonathan Whicher, had gained experience of criminal London while patrolling the stews of St Giles. He stood just over the required height, was marked with the smallpox and, as Charles Dickens later noted, had 'a reserved and thoughtful air'.

The new branch was given tiny offices at Scotland Yard, which could scarcely have been more centrally located – down a side street very close to the southern end of Trafalgar Square, the dead centre of London and the point from which all distances from the capital are measured.

The Detective Branch was launched at last.

PART TWO
Official!

5

First cases

In 1844 a battered old wooden bridge linked the artists' haven of Chelsea to industrial Battersea on the south side of the Thames. The bridge was battered because boats tended to collide with its several wide piers when they passed between them. Nonetheless, be it battered or no, those wanting to cross the bridge were obliged to pay a toll.

At 10.30 one moonlit late April evening Thomas Hall, the toll-keeper on the Surrey or south side, was standing at the door of his booth when he saw a fine-looking woman of about forty years of age half running across the bridge towards him. She wore a light figured dress, a white straw bonnet, a black shawl and a grey fur boa. As she ran she kept exclaiming, 'Oh, dear! Oh, dear!'

When she drew closer she cried out, 'See how I have been ill used on the bridge!'

Hall recognized her as Mrs Sarah M'Farlane, a respectable local widow who ran a day and Sunday school close by in Bridge Street. As she collapsed he noticed blood running down the front of her dress.

Two policemen on duty nearby responded to shouts of 'Police! Police!' by dashing towards the bridge and the crowd gathering around the fallen woman. By now it was clear her throat had been cut.

She was removed to a nearby tavern, and while awaiting the surgeon she seemed to be wanting to say something. PC Frederick

Langton stooped over her, told the publican to listen and asked, 'Who did this to you, Mrs M'Farlane?'

He couldn't quite hear her reply but the publican told him she had whispered, 'Dalmas.'

They both knew she had been seeing a Frenchman named Augustus Dalmas.

'Was it Dalmas?' the PC asked.

'Yes,' was the faint reply and again, 'Yes.'

Six minutes later she died.

When the surgeon arrived he found she had received a wound to the right side of her neck about three inches long and an inch deep. It had, he decided, been inflicted by a very sharp instrument. No, he was to insist to the coroner, she could *not* have inflicted it upon herself. It had been done, he presumed, by a person standing behind her, to her right.

The local police acted quite quickly. Sarah M'Farlane had died around 10.30 p.m., and just after midnight PC Langton arrived at Dalmas's lodgings at Brompton on the Chelsea side. When a lighted candle always used by Dalmas was found outside his room by another lodger, it was assumed that the suspect had returned there, then left again. The landlord insisted that the candle had not been there when he returned home at 9.30 p.m. and that it was usually kept in Dalmas's room. Several letters, addressed to the victim and containing abuse about her and threats of suicide, were found on Dalmas's table.

Indeed, it was soon speculated in the press that it was probably Dalmas whom the driver and passenger on a knacker's cart (carrying three dead horses) had seen leaning over the edge of the bridge as they crossed in the wake of Mrs M'Farlane. They had called out to him not to jump. Maybe he had. He was certainly nowhere to be found.

Following their mother's death the year before, Sarah M'Farlane had given a home to Dalmas's daughters, Augusta, Charlotte and Caroline, and during the last few months Dalmas, otherwise known as Chaplin, had been 'paying attentions to her'. Charlotte and Caroline had since gone into service in Knightsbridge, and that very evening Sarah M'Farlane had accompanied Augusta over to Chelsea to her new job in service and had left arm in arm with Dalmas.

Local police lost no time in visiting the daughters. Augusta had not seen her father since she had arrived in her new post. However, the eldest daughter, Charlotte, had seen him at about 11.15 that very night. She had been sitting downstairs in the servants' quarters when she heard him pass the window and cough, which was his signal. He had been agitated, she admitted later to the coroner, and when asked why at first claimed he had poisoned Sarah M'Farlane.

When Charlotte fell to her knees in horror at this he denied it, saying he had only attempted to, and grasped the girl's hand. Something in his hand had cut his daughter's fingers, at which she had screamed and he had run away. He had also, she admitted, been acting strangely when she had met him earlier that day, having pulled down her shawl and felt her neck, claiming he was looking at a mole. 'I have no mole there,' she pointed out. He had also stamped his foot and said, 'Oh, Charlotte, I am mad. I am mad.'

With the victim and prime suspect already named, this crime was not much of a puzzle for the Detective Branch but, *The Times* assured its readers, the Commissioners had specially employed Inspector Haynes 'of the detective police force', and it was hoped that the officer would succeed in apprehending the murderer. The following day they reported that Inspectors Haynes and Pearce and Sergeant Whicher were endeavouring to trace the 'supposed assassin'. Meanwhile they claimed that some persons who knew Dalmas were of the opinion that he would not have sufficient courage to perpetrate an act of self-destruction, while others believed that he thought too much of himself to do so.

Route papers and wanted notices were sent out describing Augustus Dalmas as a chemist of about fifty years of age, five feet six inches in height, with dark hair, bald in the front, and with small square-cut whiskers. He was thought to be wearing a black surtout coat,[1] a black velvet waistcoat with blue glass buttons, a black stock[2] and a rather broad-brimmed hat.

What quickly became known as 'the Battersea Murder' had been committed on Monday evening, and at 1 a.m. on the following Saturday Dalmas saved police any further exertions and the press more speculation by turning up at Marylebone Lane Police Station. He claimed he was being hounded to death and that the newspapers had it all wrong – he hadn't murdered anyone. He and Mrs M'Farlane had had some gin and cloves at the Stag public house, had exchanged some strong observations about family affairs, she claiming his children were rather ungrateful to her. He had not gone on to the bridge with her at all.

Word soon got out, and by the time Haynes and 'V' Division's superintendent and sergeant collected Dalmas in a cab at 10.45 a.m. a large crowd had gathered. By virtue of some swift diversionary tactics they managed to get him on board and away, not pausing until they reached Chelsea Police Station, where they acquired two constables who were placed on the cab roof as additional protection. Then came the dash for Battersea Bridge, which was immediately closed behind them to prevent the surging, angry crowd from catching up.

When they finally arrived at Wandsworth Police Court the story which had begun at the inquest was continued, but it was all too much for Charlotte, who immediately fainted in the witness box. When she came round she was carried out, shrieking.

Oddly, on the same day as reporting all this, *The Times* launched into a tirade against the police:

THE BATTERSEA MURDER AND THE VIGILANCE OF THE POLICE.

The defect in the present system of police, as a detective force, as exhibited in the present case, is only exceeded by the remarkable instance of the miscreant Good, and is it not a little singular that the scene of the murder in both cases is in the same vicinity and not far apart?

Once the mistakes of the Good case were thoroughly raked over, those of the Battersea Murder were gone into. Dalmas had turned up at daughter Charlotte's three-quarters of an hour after the murder. He should have been caught then. He had pawned his coat in Bloomsbury[3] the next day, so obviously was not hiding himself, and he was French, which should have meant he was easy to find. He had obviously subsisted on the three shillings given him for the coat and had only given himself up because that had run out. (Lack of ready funds was a much greater handicap than it would be today, when so many people have credit cards.)

> . . . the Forresters or any of the officers of the defunct
> establishments would have been ashamed if they allowed
> such a person to escape their vigilance or be at large for
> three days . . . These two cases, added to those of Eliza Davis,
> Mr Shepherd, Eliza Grimwood and Mr Westwood, for the
> cold-blooded murder of whom not a single individual has
> ever been brought to justice, prove incontestably the necessity
> of a change in the present system of police to render it a
> 'detective' force.

John and Daniel Forrester were two famous brothers attached as constables to the Marshal's Office at the Mansion House, just as the Runners had been attached to Bow Street, and were still operating despite the formation of the City of London Police and its Detective Branch. As Donald Rumbelow points out in *I Spy Blue* (Macmillan, 1971), the Forresters had a marked advantage in that they could not only pick and choose their cases, leaving the dross for the official detectives, but were also able to charge high fees. Their 'long overdue suppression' was not to occur until 1857.

It is pretty clear some old jealousies were at work here in these unsigned columns and with little justification, given the quite prompt police action in the Dalmas murder.

The case went on to trial, with Dalmas still insisting he was not guilty. Sarah's dying declaration was disallowed because, it was said, she was not fully aware that she was dying when she gave it, despite the policeman insisting that several people had said she was, in her presence. But everyone knew what she had said by now, anyway, the words having been reported from the hearings at the inquest and police court.

A parade of witnesses gave evidence to seeing Dalmas and the victim shortly before: at the Stag public house drinking their quartern of gin and cloves, at a beer shop with a pint of porter, en route and on the bridge, and calling on daughter Charlotte. He was identified, by those who did not know him, mostly by his frock coat and broad-brimmed hat (hats were often vital in identification). It was 'something of a Frenchman's hat', the beer shopkeeper stated, and was quizzed about when he had learned that Dalmas was French. One witness said she had overheard the victim telling the accused she could not stop out that night, and another that he had said loudly and angrily, 'And so you won't!'

The jury were to learn that Sarah M'Farlane was quite well off but Dalmas was in financial difficulties; that her family was against the liaison; that her 16-year-old son William had sharpened Dalmas's knife at his request a few days earlier: 'It had four blades, two pen blades, one larger, and a sort of file – I sharpened the large one and returned it to him on the twentieth of April.' A few days later it killed his mother.

Letters from him among her effects were obviously from a man besotted, while the three on his table, not sent, accused her of being a gin-drinking prostitute having an affair with a married man, while leading Dalmas himself into debauchery as she bled him dry with her play-going three times a week, suppers, gin-drinking, coaches, cabs and omnibuses.

The judge looked askance at some of the identification witnesses (the reward system tended to make identification evidence suspect) but advised the jury to consider the whole picture. It took them about two and a half hours to find Augustus Dalmas guilty, at which verdict apparently he appeared 'totally unconcerned'. Next day he was sentenced to death.

While Dalmas was awaiting trial Pearce was 'especially employed' in searching for the suspect in 'the Supposed Murder at Wimbledon'. As you will have noticed, most murders became known by their venue, and 'supposed murder' was not an unusual qualification in cases of sudden death.

The reason that this became a 'supposed murder' was that the woman concerned, Charlotte Hall, had been heard shouting 'Murder!' several times by the lodgers in the adjoining rooms after her husband, Charles Hall, had returned home roaring drunk. He had decamped before dawn and had not been seen since. However, Dr Bright, who had examined the corpse, could not give an opinion as to whether death was due to natural causes (apoplexy) or whether a pillow had been held over her face.

The fellow-lodgers had not interfered when she shouted because they knew the relationship to be a stormy one. Nonetheless, they admitted Charlotte had been very afraid of her husband when he was drunk and that he had several times said he would 'do for her' – indeed, would pull out her windpipe. She, in turn, tended to scratch his face during their quarrels.

Following the postmortem the good doctor was no clearer in his mind. Pulmonary apoplexy was the cause, which could be natural or the result of suffocation, he said, and added that deaths from violence usually exhibited external injuries and there were none in this case.

This satisfied Mr Carter, the coroner (who, like most coroners then, had no medical qualifications). There was no need to go on, he felt, since the doctor had sworn the deceased's death was attributable to natural causes. One juror pointed out that they could hardly dismiss the other evidence from their minds. Nonetheless, the verdict was still death from natural causes. Reported *The Times*: 'The verdict created great astonishment throughout Wimbledon. Notwithstanding the return, we believe the police will not relax their exertions in apprehending the accused.'

And Pearce did arrest Charles Hall, but at the Old Bailey he was immediately found not guilty after Dr Bright, who had now become very sure of his opinion, announced that death was from natural causes.

Next came the 'Alleged Poisoning' case in Stepney, in which a James Cockburn Bellany faced charges of poisoning his wife. Bellany claimed that he had been taking small doses of prussic acid for indigestion; having broken the neck of a phial, he noticed that the acid had begun to spill so he had poured it into a tumbler and gone to get a replacement – leaving the tumbler near his wife Rachel's bedside. While away he had been distracted and began writing a letter, only to be interrupted by her screams.

He found her with the glass in her hand; she had died soon afterwards. It did not look good that he had not mentioned the broken phial of prussic acid so no-one had realized what was wrong with Rachel. Nor had he tried any of the accepted means of attempting to save her, even though he had some medical knowledge.

Since the pair had only just arrived from the North, 'it was deemed advisable to send an active and intelligent officer down to the North to institute enquiries', reported *The Times*, 'and Inspector Haynes of the detective force was dispatched on that mission'.

He came back with the information that the relationship between Bellany and his very pretty young and pregnant wife had by all accounts been very affectionate. He brought a posse of witnesses back, some to swear to this and others to swear to other pertinent matters, such as the fact that Rachel had quite recently inherited a lime works and a colliery from her deceased mother, which her husband had taken over. Before they had left for their visit to London, he had insisted that they both signed wills benefiting each other, telling her and others that this was a thing people generally did when they went away from home.

There was very little control of poisons at that time, and nor was there much expertise on the subject. How much had she taken? How much of the deadly prussic acid would kill? These were the nub of the arguments between the medical men. Few exact conclusions were drawn, although the chief expert, Dr Letheby, Professor of Medical Jurisprudence at London University, seemed to be of the opinion that Bellany perhaps might have made more effort to save Rachel, particularly since at one time he had been a surgeon and an apothecary. (Astonishingly, he had only revealed how she had come by the prussic acid *after* its presence had been revealed by the postmortem. He claimed to have been too ashamed!)

The jury (all male, of course) found him not guilty.

6

Déjà vu

Not all of the first cases handled by the new branch were murders or suspected murders. Many were the typical early Victorian crimes of forgery, coining, child stripping,[1] retail theft – particularly of jewellery and bolts of cloth – and servant/master offences.

To have servants to attend your every practical need may seem enviable to us now but, as we have seen, there were drawbacks. Servant/master crimes were to continue to provide a staple part of the police workload and also of that of the new detectives.

In May 1843 came a crime which had odd echoes of the Russell murder, although the perpetrator appeared to have learned some lessons from Courvoisier's mistakes. Not only did he not allow the stolen goods to linger on the premises but he also engineered a clever diversion while they were being removed. As the body of Irish peer Lord Fitzgerald and Vesci languished upstairs in his Belgravia home, his servants were ushered into the drawing room by the 52-year-old steward, George Howse, to be measured for their mourning attire. Meanwhile, a chaise-cart drew up outside, two men descended the area steps, proceeded to the butler's pantry and carried off a chest of silver plate worth £300.

Lord Fitzgerald had not been murdered; he had died of natural causes. Unfortunately for Howse, his steward for thirty years, the measuring of the cook had not taken long enough. Back at work, she spotted the men carrying the loot along the passageway and up the area steps. One of them she recognized as a man previously seen in the company of Howse.

The steward was arrested, as was a carman[2] named Fuller, whom the cook identified as being the one she had recognized. However, Fuller produced an alibi and was found not guilty. Howse was convicted and sentenced to fifteen years' 'transportation beyond the seas'.

The case had been dealt with mostly by the local uniformed police, but four months later Pearce brought Thomas Jenkins, alias Brummy, 'a well known member of the swell mob', before the magistrates at Queen Square, charged with being the second of the men who had carried off the silver. By the description he had been given, Pearce claimed, he had always thought it was Jenkins and so had kept a lookout. To consolidate his case Pearce attempted to throw in some more robbery charges, but the magistrate found the evidence for them insubstantial.

The cook swore that Jenkins was the second man she had seen climbing the area steps. No, she insisted, Pearce had not accompanied her to the prison where Jenkins was on remand and pointed him out. What's more, she insisted, the other man *had* been the acquitted Fuller. The under-butler also recognized Jenkins, and the butler was almost sure Jenkins was the man he had seen with Howse inspecting the pantry, as was the housekeeper, although she thought his whiskers had previously been fuller and his countenance paler.

In any event their evidence was sufficient to convince the judge and jury. Jenkins was found guilty and transported for seven years.

The following year Pearce and Haynes dashed off in pursuit of 27-year-old footman Edward Youngman Cotton and housemaid Henrietta Sharpe. Cotton's master, Mr Driver, Surveyor to the Commissioner of Woods and Forests, had returned to his Westminster home after a weekend in the country to find that the footman had decamped and the pantry, in which Cotton slept, had been almost destroyed by fire. Also missing were coins and banknotes worth around £50.

Pearce and Haynes 'traced out' the pair by finding the cabman who at the crack of dawn had taken them and their belongings on a long journey to a pub in Bromley in Kent.

Cotton was charged with 'theft from a specified place' (as opposed to theft after breaking and entering) and Sharpe with receiving three 7-shilling pieces from him. He pleaded not guilty, saying the reason for his flight was that two or three spoons had gone missing from the pantry and he was afraid to go back as he could not afford to replace them. However, a motley array of stolen items were found in his possession, such as a wine glass, a decanter, a light shade, a butter dish and clothes with the name Driver on them. He had an excuse for all of them including, oddly, that the decanter was to hold a pint and a half of gin to take to Henrietta when she was not feeling well. The pantry fire must have been accidental, he insisted. He had left the glass off the lamp when he lit it and could not remember whether he had put out the lamp before leaving. 'I had had a little drop to drink.'

Henrietta was found not guilty, but Cotton was convicted and sentenced to transportation for ten years. And Pearce was not finished with him yet. The charred remains of pawnbrokers' tickets had been found in Cotton's breeches in the pantry. They had the name of Stephen Chandler, Cotton's friend, on them. This time the charge was the rather more serious 'stealing from master'. It appeared that Cotton and Chandler had been pawning small items belonging to the Drivers, such as a silver marrow spoon, a butter knife, a silver tablespoon, some skewers and two pairs of boots, one pair of which Chandler was wearing when arrested.

Chandler was transported for ten years, and Cotton had another ten years added to his original sentence.

The fledgling Detective Branch was also given the task of handling the new extradition cases. The relatively unrestricted movement of criminals between countries, particularly Great Britain and France and Great Britain and the USA, had become quite a nuisance to the authorities of all three countries, and in 1843 new extradition treaties were ratified. The most difficult negotiations proved to be those between Great Britain and the USA. We were concerned that they might use the treaty to recapture runaway slaves guilty only of breaching slave laws, and they were concerned that we might use the treaty against the Irish.

These seemingly quite mundane extradition cases were to provide some surprisingly strange and dramatic moments. Indeed, Pearce ran into trouble with the French treaty straight away when he tried to extradite a man 'deeply implicated', as *The Times* had it, in the Custom House Fraud. This had taken place back in June 1842. Five valuable watches had passed through the West India Docks, supposedly en route for India. Twelve months later it was learned that the watches had never arrived at their destinations, and three customs officers were suspected of stealing them. The Forrester brothers had been put on the case but, pointed out *The Times*, even they had abandoned the pursuit 'in despair'.

One of the Custom House Fraud suspects (for whom a large reward had been offered) happened to be sitting it out in Calais, so in April 1843, taking advantage of the new powers ratified back in February, Pearce went over to fetch him. But, *The Times* reported, things did not quite work out as expected:

> As soon as the inspector's mission was known the accused claimed the protection of the French authorities, and immediately upon this, the inspector, in a very unceremonious manner, was informed by the gendarmes if he attempted to execute his mission he would subject himself to great personal danger. The inspector accordingly found it to be the most prudent course to return to England.

The problem was that the particular charge (presumably receiving) made against the man appeared not to be among those specified in the treaty.

The next extradition from France was more straightforward, and for the clearly specified crime of murder. Young Richard Dadd was an exceptionally gifted artist known particularly for his Oriental scenes and, later, for the miniaturist detail of his fairy and supernatural paintings, such as *The Fairy Feller's Master-Stroke*. Admitted to the Royal Academy at the early age of twenty, he became a founding member of a group of artists known as The Clique, alongside the likes of William Powell Frith, the celebrated painter of panoramas illustrating Victorian life.

In July 1842, Dadd was chosen to accompany an expedition throughout Europe and the Middle East during which conditions became quite gruelling. While on a trip down the Nile he began to show signs of being delusional, and on his return to England in the spring of 1843 he was diagnosed as being of unsound mind. His family took him to recuperate in the Kent countryside but his paranoia increased. He became convinced that his father was the devil in disguise, and while they were walking together in a park killed him with a knife and then fled.

Dadd was not to be found at his lodgings near Oxford Street but there were rumours and supposed sightings of him in London. *The Times* managed to get hold of three consecutive route papers, which gave full descriptions of the desperate young man and instructed police to search hotels, boarding houses, railway stations and docks as he was thought to have obtained a passport with which to travel abroad.

The following day, that newspaper demonstrated that it was not above profiting from the tragedy when it published an advertisement from *The Pictorial Times* announcing that their next issue, price sixpence, contained four illustrations by 'the supposed parricide', plus a memoir of his career.

The route papers did not achieve their aim, or perhaps were too late, for the next that was heard of 'the supposed parricide' was that he had been arrested at Fontainebleau, having attempted to murder with a razor a fellow passenger in the diligence[3] in which they were travelling.

The French held on to their prisoner while he served out a sentence for this offence (in a local asylum) and then agreed to surrender him to the British. Inspector May of 'K' Division and Detective Sergeant Frederick Shaw, he of the butcher-boy appearance, were sent out to collect this dangerous prisoner. It was not to prove a jolly experience, as Inspector May's subsequent report demonstrates.

On reaching Paris on 1 July 1844 and presenting themselves to the British ambassador as instructed, they were passed on from him to his secretary, to the French Minister of the Interior and then the French Minister of Foreign Affairs – with a day between each interview. At last they were told that a formal application would have to be made 'which would occupy some time'.

Three weeks later, they were again passed around until they eventually were handed a letter telling them to go straight to the Prefect of Beauvais, 'fifty-six miles from Paris'. They arrived there at 5 a.m. and saw the Prefect at 10 a.m. and then again at 2 p.m. He sent them on to Clermont, twenty-six miles away, where they arrived at 10 p.m. to learn that they, their prisoner and a gendarme were to leave at 11 p.m. 'the same night' and to proceed to Boulogne 'by post'. This last clearly rankled. Boulogne was over a hundred miles away and by now they must have been exhausted.

They arrived at Boulogne at 7 p.m. the next day and had great difficulty in finding somewhere to stay. When at last they were settled, they sat up all night with their deranged prisoner before catching the 8 a.m. steamer across the Channel. Anyone who has tried to keep a delusional, potentially violent person pacified will appreciate what a strain this must have been – and they weren't finished escorting him until he was finally presented to the magistrates at Rochester who had issued the warrant.

Eventually, Dadd was committed to Bethlem (also known as Bedlam) Psychiatric Hospital in London, where he was encouraged to keep on painting, and then moved on to Broadmoor asylum for the criminally insane. In 1987 one of his previously lost paintings, *The Halt in the Desert*, based on his Middle East sketches, was discovered on the BBC TV *Antiques Road Show*. Valued at £100,000 it was later bought by the British Museum.

Next into the extradition fray was the horse-thief expert, Inspector Haynes. He was responding to the first extradition request from the United States. The alleged offender was one John Cornstock Clinton, accused of altering the endorsements on certain US Treasury notes, an offence that was specified in the new treaty. However, Clinton's lawyer, Mr Chambers, argued that the offence had taken place before the treaty was ratified, and that it could not be used retrospectively.

Despite the Home Secretary's wishes that the preliminary hearing should be held at the principal police office, Bow Street, the case had been brought up at the Guildhall in the City of London, where Alderman T. Wood was in the chair.

Mr Bush, the lawyer acting for the US bank bringing the request, asked that Clinton just be discharged so that the officer with the warrant (Haynes) could do his duty. This turned out to be easier said than done, as *The Times* related:

> As soon as the prisoner stepped down from the bar the inspector seized him. Mr Chambers protested against the arrest, and denied the right of the officer to call on anyone to assist him in executing it. Mr Parker (assistant defence) called out to take down the name of every person who obstructed the prisoner's free egress. Someone told the prisoner he might knock down anyone who attempted to arrest him on an illegal warrant. The prisoner tried to force his way, and a general scuffle took place at the room door. The prisoner then retreated into the dock and demanded to see the warrant. While he was reading it Mr Chambers applied to Mr Alderman Wood to commit Inspector Haines [sic], and all who had assisted him, for contempt of court for taking a man into

custody in his presence when he had just discharged him. Mr Alderman Wood thought he could not take notice of the matter, though it would have been more decorous to make the capture in the outer room.

The prisoner's legal friends said so much about the illegality of the Secretary of State's warrant, that the City Police were at first afraid to assist the inspector, who had only two officers with him. The prisoner was then dragged forcibly out of the justice room, and carried to a cab at the door. The crowd, as usual, took part against the police, and, but for the timely help of four or five of the City policemen, the prisoner would have been rescued. The prisoner resisted by biting and kicking, but he was overpowered and taken to Bow Street for further examination.

The final verdict in the Clinton case was reached three weeks later in the chambers of judge Mr Baron Platt. After several therefores, insomuches and heretofores (clearly aware that the eyes of the Home Office and fellow lawmen were fixed upon him) he gave of his opinion that the treaty was not retrospective and, despite pleas from the prosecution that the Court of Queen's Bench might later disagree, released the prisoner.

Nor were the French happy with the way the treaty arrangements were working out. Indeed, their ambassador complained about their utter inefficiency, giving as an example a case in which the Lord Mayor (in a City case) refused the extradition of a man accused of fraudulent bankruptcy because it was not a crime in English law – even though it had been specified in the treaty.

Clearly, there were wrinkles to be ironed out before the new treaties became as effective as had been hoped.

'The Hungry Forties' were a time of social unrest and the new Detective Branch was soon drawn into the problems of the age. These included attacks or threatened attacks on prominent people.

Attempts on the Queen's life, as shown here by the Illustrated London News, *helped to justify the establishment of Scotland Yard's detective branch*

As pointed out earlier, it was the second of the two attacks on the Queen in 1842 which had helped the pressure for the formation of the branch.

The first attack had been committed by John Francis who, according to Prince Albert, was 'a swarthy ill-looking rascal'. He had fired at the Queen on two occasions when she was out riding in her carriage in May 1842, was caught, convicted of high treason and sentenced to death. On the day of his reprieve, while the sentence was being commuted to transportation for life, John William Bean pointed a pistol at Her Majesty as she was en route for the Chapel Royal. This time the potential assassin escaped. His identity was unknown, but it had been noticed that he was hunchbacked and soon all of London's hunchbacked men were being rounded up for identity parades.

The New Police did eventually get their man – or boy. He was found to be 'not more than twelve or thirteen years old' and his pistol had been packed with paper and tobacco. He was given eighteen months, and the New Police got their Detective Branch.

Economic hardship all over Europe was also causing foreign leaders to come under threat and thrones to totter. In June 1844, the detectives had their attention drawn to a Pole, Count Ostrowski, who was loudly proclaiming his intention to kill the Russian Tsar at the first opportunity. They arrested him, but since the Tsar was not in Britain at the time the matter was dealt with at Bow Street by the simple expedient of getting two sureties to keep an eye on him.

At the same sitting the Bench heard evidence about a clearly mentally disturbed man who was constantly sending letters to, and in modern parlance stalking, Sir Robert Peel. Peel, the founder of the New Police, was also in many eyes the architect of the current problems through his support of the Corn Laws.

In October 1844, Pearce was tasked with tracing the writer of a letter threatening the wealthy philanthropist Angela Georgina Burdett Coutts and the family's bank. The writer declared that he had accidentally become involved with a gang of starving men who had desperation in their hearts and were determined to seize Burdett Coutts's property by whatever means they could. He was trying to stop them, but the only thing that would cause them to abort their plans was £100 worth of solid gold. A letter should be placed in *The Times* stating that 'CC informs DD that his request had been complied with'. The gold should then be taken in a parcel by a small boy to the Monument, where the writer would be waiting.

All this was done but, unbelievably, the man escaped (with the parcel) from the policemen who had been in hiding waiting for him. Fortunately, the parcel contained only half a crown, but the gang were enraged by this, claimed the next letter, and were now demanding £500 of gold plus £100 for a passage to America. This time the meeting place was Southwark Bridge Road, where Pearce and Haynes were waiting and arrested the writer.

He turned out to be 20-year-old James Carruthers, a man (the newspapers claimed) of a most respectable appearance and (his defence claimed) from a most respectable family. He had tried but failed to earn his living by writing for the public press, and was now in a state of the most abject poverty, destitution and distress. His father was in Montreal, and it was his anxiety to join him which had made him commit the crime. 'Respectability' and good connections counted for much in those days.

Oddly, the prosecuting counsel, Mr Bodkin, agreed with the jury, who found Carruthers guilty but recommended mercy. Bodkin pointed out his youth, the respectability of his family and the acute distress he was labouring under at the time. Irish peer Lord Ranelagh, with whom Carruthers had been in service, 'gave him a character' and he received a sentence of twelve months' imprisonment. No hard labour and no transportation.

Lord Ranelagh was soon to pop up again.

On 28 October 1844, Queen Victoria opened the Royal Exchange, accompanied en route by a large entourage which included a troop of Life Guards and Silver Stick-in-Waiting. The sun shone, and 'Her Majesty was dressed in white satin, and wore a silver tiara set with brilliants, and looked remarkably well', reported *The Times*. Prince Albert also looked extremely well 'and repeatedly bowed to the cheers of the crowd'. The route was lined by 2,600 police, and 'Mr Pierce [sic] and several of the detective force were also on the alert'. The only fly in the ointment, it seemed, was that notorious rake, Lord Ranelagh, the seventh viscount (who later introduced actress Lillie Langtry, the Prince of Wales's future mistress, into London society).

When told to get off the carriageway and on to the pavement by Inspector Barton of 'G' Division, who was clearing the route for the Queen's return, Ranelagh resisted. He was pushed – violently, he was to claim – and struck out at the inspector, calling him a peasant. It turned into a scuffle, and subsequently the aristocrat charged the inspector with assault. Not surprisingly the policeman's colleagues, including Inspector Joseph Shackell of 'G' Division, gave evidence that the inspector was not the aggressor. The magistrate wisely decided, 'Who knows what really happened?' and dismissed the case.

The following month Inspector Shackell took over from Pearce in the Detective Branch. While gaoler and officer at Bow Street he had carried out several investigations of his own, including 'the alleged attempt to disfigure Madame Vestris' – a celebrated theatrical figure – with what appeared to be a bomb (possibly a publicity stunt).

He rejoined the Metropolitan Police as an inspector after Bow Street was stripped of its police powers in 1839, and in 1842 applied for the new Detective Branch. Failing that, he kept busy and in the limelight.

In late August 1844, a constable from Long Melford in Suffolk turned up at his police station in Shoreditch saying he had traced footsteps of thieves from a draper's house to the local railway station, where he had spotted a large parcel bound for Shoreditch and had followed it there.

The next day, Shackell told the Worship Street magistrate how he had immediately gone home, changed into private clothes, gone to the railway station and waited beside the package for two hours. When the thief turned up to claim it, he followed him and his parcel to a coffee shop, where two others joined the man in examining 'a great quantity of velvets, broadcloths and other valuable articles'. Shackell arrested them and all three were duly sent back to Suffolk to be dealt with.

Clearly Pearce – the man he was now replacing – was a forceful and dynamic character, but there had been hints that in his eagerness he occasionally sailed close to the wind, perhaps being too keen to nail his man, as in the early extradition from France fiasco, or too eager to over-egg the pudding by adding charges or doing a bit of evidential embroidery.

In August 1843, he had arrested German Leopold Meyer, a 20-year-old 'traveller',[4] for stealing a diamond ring from a jeweller's, and 21-year-old Robert Berg, his interpreter, for receiving it. The suspects had separated following the deed, but Pearce caught them and in Berg's pocketbook[5] found 'a portion of the ring in which the diamond had been set'.

Meyer pleaded guilty, and the prosecuting jeweller said he

wanted to recommend him for mercy as he had reason to believe he had been duped by his interpreter companion. Oddly, he added that Meyer was the son of a Prussian officer who fought at Waterloo. Berg pleaded complete innocence but the jury found him guilty, whereupon he asked to be able to speak, as *The Times* reported:

> . . . he wished to express his opinion of Inspector Pearce in order to guard others against being treated by him as he had been. He then denounced the inspector as a perjurer, and everything that was bad. He (the prisoner) had had his liberty sworn away by him and his gang, and many more would, in all probability, stand at that bar, and have all their happiness and hopes blasted, by similar practices, but God would eventually punish him for his evil deeds, and speak in vindication of the innocent. He (the prisoner) was quite sure the press would do him justice, and let the world know that he was innocent and that Pearce alone, was the author of all his misfortunes.

The judge was unimpressed and sentenced Berg to transportation for seven years. Meyer (the actual thief) received six months' hard labour. The court transcript of the case does not mention Berg's comments on Pearce – merely stating that he gave a long defence – nor the reason why Meyer was treated so lightly. This was brushed off with the fact that he pleaded guilty, was recommended to mercy and received a good character. All a little odd. Maybe it was that respectability and those contacts again.

It is impossible at this distance to judge the rights and wrongs of these matters, but one thing was clear: the new branch did need a strong and confident leader. The Commissioners had tried to retain Pearce's services by asking the Home Office to raise his pay from £200 to £250, which would have brought it in line with that of a divisional superintendent. What they had feared was happening: both detective inspectors had applied for the vacancy of superintendent of 'F' Division, which encompassed the prestigious Bow Street and Covent Garden area.

Mayne pointed out that it would be an injustice to pass Pearce over. The Home Office replied that the detectives received rewards as well as their salaries. Pearce and Haynes duly totalled up what they had received in a year: £75. This did not, Mayne explained, recompense them for their travel expenses, some of which, for various reasons, they could not claim back.

An unsigned Home Office note on the pertinent file squashed this reasoning:

> The situation of Detective Inspector is in many respects preferable to that of a Superintendent. He has not so much active out-of-door service, not so much hard work to undergo: and the peculiar business in which he is employed would be much more interesting to a police officer than the routine business of Superintendents. Besides, he is one of two, instead of being one of a body of officers and there is more room for the exercise of skill, more opportunity of fame, in his calling and duties, than of those of a Superintendent so that upon the whole, the service is in many respects preferable. £250 with the Rewards seems much too great a salary – especially when it is remembered that the Superintendent never receives rewards: his business being entirely unconnected with thief-taking.

Impressively argued. The job *was* more freewheeling, and Pearce and the detectives *had* already become famous. The names and ranks of police witnesses were always given in press reports and theirs were appended with 'of the detective department' or something similar. This and their freedom of movement must have seemed enviable to men who had to wear their uniform at all times, whether on or off duty. It was a fait accompli. Pearce became superintendent of 'F' Division, which meant that the branch was without its leader as it went into 1845 – and that turned out to be a murderous year.

7

Murder! Murder!

At around 7 p.m. on a particularly cold and frosty February evening in 1845 Mr Hilton, a baker, was calling on a customer, Mrs Beckwell, in Hampstead, when he heard distant cries of 'Murder!' coming from a nearby field. The cries sounded female.

'I thought that some man was beating his wife,' he was to say later. 'I entered the field to the extent of twenty rods,[1] but then I heard no more cries.'

Hilton asked the Beckwells' maid if she heard the cries, but she said nothing and closed the door on him. However, he passed on the information to PC Baldock whom he met a few minutes later. Baldock walked across the field but saw nothing, then met up with his sergeant and they both searched the field. Behind some railings on the frozen ground in the far west corner they found the body of a plump man of about forty years of age, lying in a pool of blood.

In his pockets were a couple of keys, a tin snuff-box and a letter from 'Caroline' telling the recipient she was pregnant. It was obvious that the victim had been a bit of a swell. His brown wrapper was of fine cloth with velvet facings and his bodycoat had a velvet collar. His dark blue, single-breasted Valencia waistcoat was decorated with 'small red flowers and sprigs', the *Observer* informed its readers the following day. 'His boots are Wellingtons[2] and his linen, which is of the very finest texture, is marked with a capital D in indelible ink.' A black handkerchief, white boot hose, black kid gloves and a hat completed the picture.

PC Baldock stayed with the body while his sergeant went off for a stretcher. He was not alone for long. Whistling along the path came a slight and dandified young man with a nonchalant air. 'Hello, policeman,' he exclaimed. 'What have you here?'

On being told it was someone whose throat had been cut, the young man asked, 'Do you think he is dead?' and promptly went down on his knees to take the victim's pulse. He decided the man was in fact dead, that it was 'a nasty job' and 'a serious case for the constable'. Then he offered the PC some brandy, pressed him to take a shilling and elected to wait with him until the stretcher arrived. Meanwhile, he confided that the victim could just as easily have been him as he often used this path, going to and from town, carrying money, despite warnings from his parents.

The body was found on Friday, and by the time the inquest was opened on the following Monday the victim had been identified as James De la Rue, an unmarried 33-year-old piano teacher who lived just off Euston Square in St Pancras. But there was no clue as to his killer. The ground had been too hard to register signs of a struggle or footprints[3] but, PC Baldock revealed, there was blood on the top rail of the fence 'where his hands had been'.

'What makes you say "his" hands?' asked the coroner, Thomas Wakley.

It was a bloody print of someone's fingers, the PC replied, and he had not seen blood on the victim's hands. A good answer. Today it would be a clue which could solve the case via DNA, blood type and fingerprints.

Wakley asked De la Rue's brother, Daniel, if he had any idea who might have done the deed but cautioned him not to say the name out loud. Coroners' courts often acted wrongly in this respect, he felt: 'When evidence which attaches suspicion to any person is made known he sees it and is consequently put on his guard ...They read in the newspapers the very things they want to know and they act accordingly.'

Indeed, Wakley claimed, this was the reason the murderers

of Marrs, Mrs Williamson[4] and Eliza Grimwood had remained undiscovered, and as for Mr Westwood, it had been positively stated that the perpetrator was actually in the inquest room: 'Under such circumstances of course the police are deprived of the best means of detecting the offender. It is not giving the police fair play.'

A good point. The detailed reporting of crimes as they took place in three separate arenas – coroners' courts, magistrates' courts and then the trial, quite apart from constant unbridled press speculation – was a great disadvantage to all who sought justice.

Charles Dickens thought Thomas Wakley, the surgeon and MP for Finsbury, 'nobly patient and humane'. Wakley was to become known for his improvements in coroner's court procedures, his founding of *The Lancet*, through which he attacked medical malpractice, and his campaigns against food adulteration and infant mortality due to neglect and baby farming.

The victim's brother said he had not the slightest suspicion of anyone but knew that his brother always carried a watch with a gold guard, made by Grafton of Fleet Street.

'Don't state that,' said Wakley, 'You must not state anything that may lead to a suspicion of parties.'

After hearing the witnesses Wakley had the court cleared 'of all strangers not excepting reporters', said *The Times*, 'remarking that he wished *to* have some consultation with the officers of the detective force. The consultation lasted an hour and a half after which he adjourned the inquest *sine die*.' The reconvening, he announced, would depend 'upon the information obtained by the police and upon the success of the detective force'.

The following evening a man named William Watson told Turnham Green Police Sergeant Scotney that on the previous Saturday he had been to see his parents and while there had been asked in by their lodgers, Mr and Mrs Hocker, who appeared to have come into some money. Their son, Thomas Henry Hocker, had offered him some rum but declined to talk about the terrible murder up in Hampstead, as it was depressing, so he sang a song instead. His father, however, seemed worried that Thomas had been up to something because the wrist of his shirt was torn, but Thomas claimed he had done it romping with some girls. Since then, William Watson told Sergeant Scotney, he had learned that the victim was James De la Rue – who, he knew, was a friend of Thomas Hocker.

Sergeant Scotney hotfooted it to Hammersmith Police Station, where he was instructed to go to Scotland Yard and inform Inspector Shackell or Haynes of this development. They were now handling the case. Why couldn't he go and arrest Hocker himself, Scotney wanted to know. Where was the encouragement to get information if it then had to be handed over? He could find neither Haynes nor Shackell at the Yard so took his information to the nearby police station, where Inspector Partridge consulted his superintendent and then hailed a cab which took them to Thomas Hocker's address, where they arrested him.

Under pressure from his brother Thomas Hocker produced the watch, saying his friend De la Rue had given it to him on the Friday morning, to pawn. He had given him several such articles over the past few months, he claimed, and produced the pawn tickets.

Later that morning, Thomas Hocker appeared at Marylebone Police Court charged with the murder. Inspector Partridge requested a remand, whereupon Shackell asked to say a few words.

'Have you any evidence to offer?' asked the magistrate.

'Yes, sir. I have some very important evidence,' Shackell replied, obviously eager to reinsert the detective department into the case.

He could prove that the watch was indeed De la Rue's because it answered the description on a jeweller's receipt he had found on the victim's premises and, what was more, it was seen on the victim by his landlord's daughter at 2 p.m. on the Friday. Hocker had claimed he had been given it on the Friday morning – when he had last seen De la Rue. It was indeed damning evidence.

Haynes, Partridge and Shackell got to work. At Hocker's lodgings they found a bloodstained wristband and, at his parents' home, a shirt with the wristband missing, muddied and bloodstained stockings and a black ebony cane with a split end. Had he taken his cane when he went out on Friday, the father was asked. Yes, was the reply. And where had Thomas said he had got the money he came back with? Borrowed from a friend, Mrs Edwards, the father replied. 'I have got a sovereign of it, and if it is not true I will give it up.'

The following morning the inquest was resumed before a displeased coroner, angry that the accused was not present when evidence was to be heard which could militate against him. Apparently when the Commissioners had formed the Metropolitan Police they had not deemed the coroners' courts of sufficient importance to issue instructions about bringing prisoners before them. He raged on about the petty jealousies of magistrates and attitudes towards coroners' courts which he was no longer prepared to tolerate.

The trouble between Mr Wakley and the police continued in earnest the following Saturday, when Thomas Hocker was still not produced despite the coroner having been to see the Home Secretary, who had granted permission, and despite him writing a letter to the prison governor making this clear. (The prison governor had said he still needed the magistrate's permission to release the prisoner. This had been obtained, but the governor then insisted he needed it in writing.) Wakley was furious that the police had not kept him informed about the capture of Hocker. Had they done so the case could have gone straight to trial without going near the police courts. When he learned that the delay was partly due to Scotney being unable to find the two detectives, he displayed appropriate disgust. Coroners could commit to trial if the jury accused a particular person: there was precedence for this. Indeed there was, but clearly the police were caught in the power struggle between coroners and magistrates, who were probably still sulking about their loss of police powers.

Next time the coroner's hearing was graced by the presence of both suspects (the brother, James Hocker, was also under some suspicion) and all the witnesses who had attended the police court. Mrs Edwards denied having lent Hocker any money and told the coroner he had been paying court to Sarah Jane Philps, a young woman who lived with her. Miss Philps (who was duly shielded from the sight of Hocker) described how he had shown her the watch and a ring which was too big for him. It was his but he didn't wear it, he had said, because he did not like jewellery. She noticed that there was blood on his shirt front but he had explained it away by saying he had cut his nose while indulging in some horseplay. The coroner discharged the brother, then got his desired verdict from the jury of 'wilful murder' against Thomas Henry Hocker.

The police court hearing the next day proved something of an anti-climax, despite the magistrate Mr Rawlinson telling Miss Philps that she must tell the whole story as if she had never heard it before. The late arrival and early departure of Shackell and Haynes – delayed by a case at the Old Bailey – probably did not help. Perhaps through pique, Rawlinson adjourned the proceedings for a week.

Meanwhile, a PC James Euston was placed in Hocker's cell at court – a not uncommon ploy. Hocker complained to the PC about a barman who had failed to identify him as having been in his pub at the time of the murder despite being given a large tip at the time. He also described his visit to the scene, and his offering Baldock some brandy and giving him a shilling. Baldock was now put on the spot. This was the first anyone had heard about the man who had kept him company that night. He hadn't mentioned it, Baldock claimed, because it hadn't seemed important, and he hadn't realized the man was the accused because he had been muffled up against the cold when he saw him. Mr Rawlinson accused him of withholding facts because of the shilling and remarked that it was not up to him to judge what was important.

What the *Morning Chronicle* thought was important and had been dropping heavy hints about (gleaned from 'unimpeachable sources') was that the principal occupation in Hocker's dissolute life was the deluding of females and meeting the deceased in the field for, it was believed, 'the worst of purposes'. Hocker had received

£150 from De la Rue, said the paper, but had realized that his victim was not going to pay him any more. In other words, what had been going on was homosexual prostitution and blackmail.

The *Chronicle* also informed its readers that 'in the discovery of the leading facts . . . the greatest credit is due to Mr Shackell, the intelligent and enterprising officer of the detective police'. Also, doubtless, someone who had many press contacts from his days as the Bow Street gaoler and who possibly was their 'unimpeachable source'.

Hocker was at last sent to trial, committed 'by myself as well as by the coroner's warrant', said Rawlinson.

The trial took only one day. No women were allowed in the courtroom owing (the *Morning Chronicle* explained) 'to the peculiar circumstances of the case'. There was, however, a dense crowd of influential males listening as Thomas Henry Hocker was found guilty and sentenced to death.

Just before 11 p.m. on Monday 31 March 1845, PC John James Allen of the 'E' or Holborn Division was on duty on a corner in St Giles when a man dashed out of a nearby house and ran past him. Running men always give vigilant policemen pause but also call for instant decision-making. PC Allen had often seen this man hanging around the area eyeing the prostitutes and talking to thieves. If necessary, he could doubtless find him again. The rookeries were a rough area, 'thickly inhabited', as the *Morning Chronicle* put it, 'by persons of the poorest, lowest, most abandoned, profligate and squalid description'. PC Allen decided not to pursue.

Six minutes later, a Mrs Palmer, servant at the house in question, which rented out threepenny rooms to prostitutes, also came running up the street and breathlessly informed the PC that a woman in there had been 'stuck'. That turned out to be an understatement. The plump middle-aged woman lying on her side in one of the rooms had been stabbed sixteen times and still had a large, black-handled carving knife buried in the back of her neck.

'The woman made a slight movement when I drew the knife out,' he was to report later. But by the time he got back with a surgeon, Mary Ann Brothers, or Tape, was dead.

Over on 'D' Division the following morning Inspector Tedman received information that Mary Ann Brothers had cohabited with a man called Meadows who lived in South Molton Street, Mayfair. Not about to be found wanting this time, Tedman hurried there but found the man had left for his work as a blacksmith in nearby Davies Street. He soon established that not only had Meadows been missing from work the previous afternoon but he had stayed out until after eleven o'clock. What was more, he had bloodstains on his clothes, his right hand and his handkerchief, all due, he claimed, to a violent nose-bleed. Tedman arrested him for the murder, although he should have known by now that he couldn't win, particularly as it was April Fool's Day.

The servant, the PC and one of Mary's fellow prostitutes all swore that Meadows was not the wanted man. In fact the murderer had advertised himself and his intentions to a ludicrous degree, asking several prostitutes the whereabouts of Mary Ann Brothers, complaining she had given him 'a loathsome disease', issuing threats that he would 'serve her out'. He even asked one of them, Irish Biddy, to examine his person to see whether he was indeed infected; she had been unable to come to a definite diagnosis. What they did not know was the man's name.

The murder happened on Monday evening. On Wednesday the *Morning Chronicle* was already complaining that the police had no clue, and by the following day that it was Eliza Grimwood and Eliza Davis all over again. We know that the murders of prostitutes are particularly difficult to solve, given the number and anonymity of suspects, but this suspect had almost put out flags. Witnesses, including the cutler who had sold him the knife, were practically queuing up.

The murder had occurred on 'E' but Pearce's 'F' Division shared St Giles. Old habits die hard, and having learned from Irish Biddy that the suspect had told her he was being treated for 'the clap', Pearce enquired at the local hospitals and picked out 20-year-old Joseph Connor who lived nearby as the most likely suspect on the King's College list. Pearce assumed, as *The Times* put it, 'the character of a gentleman from King's College' and went to arrest him. Pearce had been unremitting in his efforts, the newspaper claimed, therefore the allegation at the inquest that had a reward been offered the prisoner would have been taken sooner was ill-natured and unjustified.

Oddly enough, one of his own PCs, William Latham, 45F, told the coroner (Mr Wakley again) that he had suspected the murderer was Connor when he heard the description, but on informing his inspector and Superintendent Pearce he been told that five hundred others in London also answered the description and was sent to another beat. Had he been allowed the opportunity to apprehend Connor, he claimed, he could have done so forty-eight hours earlier.

It turned out that Connor could not have caught the clap from Mary Ann Brothers, Mr Partridge, the Professor of Anatomy at King's College, informed the courts. She herself did not suffer from it. She was clean.

As four of Pearce's most important witnessed were 'of low character', of no fixed abode and likely to be tampered with, Pearce asked that he be allowed to pay them a shilling a day via the workhouse governor to keep them available. The authorities were nervous but acquiesced. One of the flakiest trial witnesses turned out to be PC James Allen, who had seen the running man: 'I have no doubt who the man that passed me by was, but I would not swear positively – I have no doubt the prisoner was the man, but I would not swear to it positively – I have a strong belief that he is the man . . . I am in the habit of seeing him frequently . . .'

Despite aspersions being cast that some of the identification evidence was oddly similar, Connor was found guilty and sentenced to death.

In June, 1845, *The Times* reported that M. Vidocq's Exhibition was taking place in Regent Street. Given that it was this thief-turned-Head-of-Sûreté who had made the acceptance of the New Police and introduction of detectives so difficult, one can imagine the branch was not thrilled by this news, particularly as *Punch* had just dubbed them 'the Defective Force'.

In 1828, the year before the New Police hit the streets, a translation of Eugene François Vidocq's memoirs was published in London. Worse, in 1829, two months before the book's launch, a melodrama, *VIDOCQ! The French Police Spy*, was staged at the Surrey Theatre. The Frenchman had used his inside knowledge of crime to catch his fellow criminals and the response of the British public to this news was that they were not going to allow French-style police spies here.

Portrait by Achille Devéria (1800-1857)

Eugene François Vidocq the French former criminal who became head of the Sûreté

On show, *The Times* now reported breathlessly, were 'to be seen the costumes of all the various grades of society in Paris amongst which swindlers, rogues, thieves and plunderers may be suspected to associate, which costumes are understood to be the actual ones worn by M. Vidocq in his professional capacity, and used by him in discovering and arresting the criminals obnoxious to justice'.

But the principal curiosity in the collection, it went on, was Vidocq himself. 'He is a remarkably well built man, of extraordinary muscular power and exceedingly active. He stands when perfectly erect, five feet ten inches in height but by some strange process connected with his physical formation he has the facility of contracting his height several inches and in this diminished state to walk about, jump, etc.' His countenance, went on *The Times*, exhibited unflinching determination of character, strong powers of perception 'and that bluffness which denotes animal courage'. This paragon was also extremely intelligent, communicative and good-humoured and, though now seventy-two years of age, possessed 'all the strength, vigour and buoyancy of a man twenty-five years his junior'.

A few months after eulogizing this super police spy, that same newspaper launched another attack on the Metropolitan Police for allowing uniformed officers to go out in plain clothes, indeed assume various disguises 'such as the dresses of cobblers, itinerant greengrocers and costermongers' so as to catch members of the public who were passing bad coin.

Sir Robert Peel had lulled the public by promising no spies, it went on. 'The detective force seemed somewhat at variance with this assurance, but its object was confessedly useful, and, if restrained within proper limits might be allowed to exist without danger to the liberty of the subject.' However, there was something repugnant to the English mind in the bare idea of espionage – it smacked too strongly of France and Austria. The two kings of Scotland Yard had transgressed the law and violated the constitution, *The Times* concluded, and perhaps should be dethroned.

Shortly afterwards the kings of Scotland Yard (Mayne and

Rowan) issued a Police Order stating that no men on division should be called plain clothes men and that 'no man should disguise himself without particular orders from the superintendent' – and even then a strong case should be made out.

However, the following year was going to give them much more to worry about than policemen getting themselves up as cobblers and costermongers.

8

Internal difficulties

Where was Constable Clark? His sergeant had marched him out to the start of his beat at the Four Wants crossroads in Dagenham the previous evening at 9 p.m. He was seen again during the earlier hours of his shift, but not since, and now, at six the following morning, when he was supposed to be signing off duty at Dagenham Police Station, there was no sign of him.

PC Clark had only been at Dagenham for six weeks, having transferred there from Stepney along with his colleague PC Isaac Hickton. Indeed, the Metropolitan Police had only been at Dagenham for six years. When they were founded sixteen years earlier their area extended only seven miles from Charing Cross and had not included Dagenham.

To emphasize that they were a civil, not a military, force the uniform of the New Police was deliberately unmilitary. Thus the top hat, which was tough enough to stand upon, and tail coat. For protection, they carried a rattle with which to summon assistance, a truncheon and, sometimes, a cutlass. But despite their non-provoking uniform and the fact that it was emphasized that their role was largely preventive, much of the population had made it clear that they did not want the New Police. Thus several of the early murders the force had to investigate were those of their own men.

Despite these dangers twenty-year-old George Clark, a Bedfordshire farm labourer, applied to join. Things were hard on the land. These were the Hungry Forties when a loaf of bread had become very expensive, mainly because of the Corn Laws. Many rural workers were emigrating and quite a number joined the police, where they could at least get a regular wage and accommodation. Clark's first posting after he joined on 2 June 1845 had been to Stepney in London's East End.

If London had not wanted the New Police, rural areas – not previously included – wanted them even less. And Dagenham was then truly rural. The centre of the village was quite quaint and olde worlde but some cottages on its outskirts were little more than thatched mud huts. The surrounding land was flat and very fertile, supporting cornfields and market gardens, and across the Thameside marshes there was fishing in the river. Access to London was good

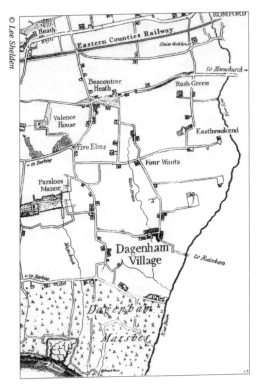

Map of Dagenham village, where murder victim PC Clark was stationed

91

via a main road on which a daily horse-bus operated. And for those who didn't want to take their produce to the capital by wagon there was the new railway line from Romford.

Soon, there were confrontations between the locals and the New Police. The locals thought the latter were over-officious, while the police wished to curb the theft of animals and produce, the poaching, the rick-burning and smuggling which went on in the area.

Clark had been at Stepney for just over a year when in May 1846 he and his colleague, PC Isaac Hickton, got the news that they were to be transferred to Dagenham. Also being drafted in was rookie PC Jonas Stevens, on his first posting.

The reason for this influx was a source of great embarrassment to the Commissioners. Clark and co. were to replace three other officers who had got into an argument in a local pub, then gone on a drunken rampage, cutlasses drawn. They had ended up in dock themselves, charged with assault and false imprisonment. Found guilty, they were fined and dismissed from the service.

There was little risk that George Clark would give any such trouble. He was reported to be extremely correct in his habits. An active Methodist, he soon became involved with Dagenham's Wesleyan chapel and was fond of handing out religious tracts to those he began to get to know on his beat. Many of these tracts attacked the demon drink.

He already knew PC Isaac Hickton, who had roomed with him at Stepney, and he was to live at Dagenham Police Station with the other new arrival, the rookie Jonas Stevens. The four other policemen already stationed there were all married men with families.

Now that the station had been brought up to strength again, Sergeant Parsons set about reorganizing the beats. Clark was given a night beat at Eastbrookend, which is north-east of Dagenham. It was very rural, with fields and marshes edged by deep ditches often filled with duckweed. Some roads were merely cart tracks and the beat was said to be very lonely in parts – a great contrast to the busy, lively Mile End Road.

Clark had been at Dagenham six weeks when, at 9 p.m. on Monday 29 June, he was marched out to the start of his beat at the Four Wants crossroads. He was armed with his rattle, a bull's-eye lantern, a truncheon and a cutlass. Cutlasses were only carried when confronting rioters or at night in unsafe areas.

He was seen at 10.30 p.m. by Luke White, who had a cottage in Oxlow Lane at the western end of his beat. Clark had been singing a hymn as he approached, White later recalled, and had said he had a tract for him although when he felt in his pockets he couldn't find it.

When Clark failed to report back to Dagenham Police Station at six the following morning Sergeant Parsons and his deputy, PC Kimpton, went round Clark's beat, each from opposite directions, but saw no sign of him. Sergeant Parsons confirmed that Clark had made his official meet with him at 1 a.m. at the Four Wants. He had not, however, turned up for his usual meeting with his colleague, PC Kimpton, shortly afterwards. Nor had he made his second official point with Parsons at 3 a.m.

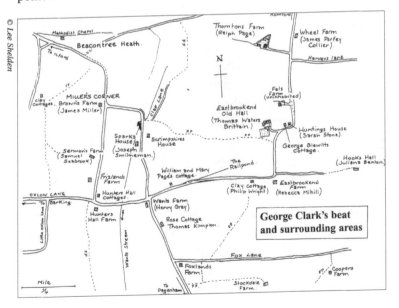

George Clark's beat and surrounding areas

93

PC Abia Butfoy had previously walked this beat so they got him out of bed to help with the search, but he had no luck either. A letter was sent to Clark's parents asking whether he had gone home or contacted them at all, and the matter was reported to Inspector Richardson at Ilford Police Station.

The rest of the day was spent searching ditches and ponds in case Clark had lost his way in the darkness and fallen in – which was not unlikely. During the previous eight years no fewer than five Met Police night-duty constables had drowned after falling into rivers, canals or docks. Sergeant Parsons' own policeman brother had fallen into a dry dock at Woolwich during a fog on the previous Christmas Day and later died of his injuries.

The policemen carried bulldog lanterns but these were of limited use on very dark nights in unlit areas. And, of course, the policeman was likely to be on his own when he fell in, weighed down with a heavy uniform, a rattle, a truncheon, a lantern and a cutlass, and very likely unable to swim.

The search for Constable Clark continued in sweltering heat. As he stood sweating by a farm gate, PC Kimpton told local farmer Ralph Page that all this searching was a waste of time. Clark's body was probably in a cornfield and wouldn't be found till harvest time. Page disagreed, saying that even a dog running into standing corn would leave a track. At that moment Sergeant Parsons appeared, declaring that they had searched all the cornfields and found nothing.

At 7.30 p.m. on the Friday, four days after Clark had gone missing, they were dragging yet another pond, this time in Ralph Page's farmyard, outside the range of Clark's beat, when Mrs Page came out and told them there was another pond they might like to look into – her two boys would show them where it was.

The boys led Kimpton and Butfoy through a potato field and on into a cornfield where they instantly noticed a strong and unpleasant smell. A few yards further on, they found a much-damaged police truncheon. One of the boys went on a little and saw something shining on a bank. It was Clark's bloodstained cutlass. As he turned round he saw the body of George Clark. The boys screamed so loudly that their mother heard them at the farmhouse.

Butfoy shouted, 'Here he lies!' drawing Sergeant Parsons and PCs Jonas Stevens and John Farnes to the spot. When Stevens got there he took one look, said, 'Oh, God,' and fainted on the spot. Small wonder.

PC Clark lay on his back, his legs crossed and his outstretched hand clutching a handful of corn. His face was very bruised and there was a large opening in the top of his skull, with his scalp laying alongside. There were deep cuts to the front and back of his neck and the ground around him was saturated with his blood and pieces of his bone.

When they had got over the initial shock Parsons said, 'See if his watch has gone.' As already noted, robberies and even murders were committed to acquire these valuable items. PC Farnes steeled himself to kneel down and search Clark's pockets. In them, he found Clark's silver watch, stopped at 3 a.m., and four half-crowns, four shillings and a halfpenny – quite a haul for any robber. In the greatcoat pocket he found Clark's rattle with a piece of paper wedged in it. His hat was missing. It was to be found nearby the following morning by farm labourer Joseph Palmer, undamaged and with Clark's handkerchief still neatly tucked inside. The surgeon concluded that a variety of weapons must have been used in this 'horrible and atrocious murder'.

At the inquest PC Abia Butfoy suggested that this could be a case of mistaken identity. *He* may have been the intended victim. Four months earlier on that same beat, he explained, he had had a run-in with beer-seller and marine store dealer William Walker, who had refused to open his bag for inspection. (Marine store dealers often dealt in smuggled or stolen goods.) Butfoy and Walker had come to blows. Eventually Walker did open the bag but then stalked off, exclaiming, 'I will be one with you for this.' In the dark, in the same area, Walker might have thought Clark was him, Butfoy now suggested.

The coroner agreed to release Clark's body for burial, confidently announcing that he was sure that in a few days the suspected parties would be in custody. How wrong he was. He was then approached by the boy's mother, begging to see the body of her only son. He told her he had no power to refuse but advised against it. She insisted and, *The Times* reported, 'the horrid spectacle had such an effect on her that she was led away insensible'.

But at least, with the mistaken identity idea, when the Scotland Yard detectives arrived – plus Superintendent Pearce – they had something to go on.

They soon found another mistaken identity theory going the rounds. Perhaps the victim was meant to be Sergeant Parsons. He had had a run-in with Amos Walker, brother of William, about some stolen hemlock and a quantity of brass and other metals. He had arrested Amos for theft but the magistrates had given him only a small fine and advised him to be more careful in future. Despite clearly not having supported the New Police the magistrates now declared themselves aghast at the murder and announced that every vigilance should be used to capture those responsible.

The detectives knew that a murder scene should be preserved, but by now it was well-trampled and becoming more so by the minute as the usual curious crowds began arriving. They were further hampered by the four-day delay between the murder and the finding of the body.

To start with they sought out anyone who had suffered injuries indicating they may have been in a fight. They toured the local hospitals, and on the urging of Pearce a newspaper appeal was published, although it was rendered rather ineffective when *The Times* gave the murder date as 13 June instead of the 30th. But a surgeon did come forward claiming to have treated a man who seemed to have received a blow to the neck. Since the man in question was well known to the police and had served several sentences in Ilford Gaol this seemed promising. But when they examined him they found only an old abscess just under his ear which had recently been drained.

Detective Sergeant Frederick Shaw, whom Dickens was to describe as 'a wiry little sergeant of meek demeanour and strong sense', was sent off to Woburn and Evesham, where Clark's fiancée lived, to see if he could find any love rival. Obviously his meek demeanour was a front, as with TV's Columbo, but on this occasion his guile was useless. He could find no jealous rival. There had been no arrest by the time the inquest was reconvened at the Cross Keys public house and the reason was, *The Times* thundered, that no reward had been offered. A notorious gang of smugglers operated in the area and any one of them would have informed on his mates for the money.

But the inquest did provide some startling new evidence from a surprise witness, farmer Ralph Page's wife Elizabeth. Before she had a chance to speak, Amos Walker leapt to his feet protesting that he and his brother were innocent of any murder. It was true they had quarrelled with Butfoy and Parsons, but they were innocent of any other allegations and wanted to stay in court in case the evidence maligned them further.

Mrs Page's story was worth waiting for. She told the jury that on the night they found Clark's body she had loaned the officers a coat to cover it, 'for decency's sake'. When they returned it around midnight they stayed to supper, and as they ate Kimpton told her that Sergeant Parsons had never even been on duty that night. He had been unwell and had asked him to take his horse and finish his duty for him.

Kimpton now denied having said any such thing and Jonas Stevens, who was also at the supper, insisted he had never heard Kimpton say it. Parsons denied having been absent that night and his men backed him up.

But other matters were preoccupying the coroner. Why was the lock on Clark's box broken? He kept his money and valuables in there. Clark had been quite careful with his money and there were rumours that some of the men were in debt to him. Stevens said Clark had lost the keys back in Stepney, and Hickton, who had roomed with Clark there, verified that he had broken open his own box.

Was Clark on good terms with his colleagues, the coroner wanted to know. Had they ever quarrelled with him about religion? Stevens insisted there was no bad feeling. Another surprise was that PC Hickton, who was on the adjacent beat, now claimed that Clark had failed to meet him as he usually did at 11 p.m. at Miller's farm. This placed his disappearance much earlier, and also put Parsons' claimed 1 a.m. meet with him in great doubt.

Another witness, Mrs Elizabeth Dodd, claimed to have actually seen Clark with his murderer. She'd been walking back from London where she'd been after a place (probably in domestic service) when at about eleven o'clock she had crossed Dagenham Fields. In a cornfield she had seen a tall man in a fustian coat who was asking a policeman the time. 'He then used improper language to him,' she said. 'I was very frightened as there was someone looking over the hedge.' When she got to Romford she met two girls who asked her whether she had heard some screams.

Finally, the coroner announced that further information had come to him and the police which was going to result in another adjournment, and also that it seemed likely Clark's body would have to be exhumed.

Reporting on the next inquest hearing on 23 July, *The Times* declared that 'the vast excitement created by this horrible occurrence has not in the least degree diminished'. By then, a reward notice had at last been issued.

The surgeon gave his evidence about the exhumed body. He had been asked, he said, to check whether the young constable had been shot, as had been rumoured, and whether his wounds could have been caused by his own cutlass. The answer to the first question was no, and to the second that it was possible that his cutlass had caused one of the main wounds but was not sharp enough to have caused the other two to the front and back of his neck. A medical colleague agreed and added the gruesome detail that the skull had not a particle of brain left in it.

Two more members of the Page family were called. Daughter Priscilla said she had heard Kimpton claiming he did Parsons' duty that night and that he had added that it wasn't the first time, either. Ralph Page, the man of the house, explained that he was not there on that night because he'd locked himself in his barn, guarding his corn. Others present at the supper sided with Kimpton – he had never said it. But on hearing this one juror exclaimed that he had heard one of these very witnesses say quite the opposite, several times.

At this juncture Parsons leapt to his feet, exclaiming that they were endeavouring to prove him the murderer. But help was at hand for him. His sister Julia gave evidence of how she had seen Parsons and Clark together that night, when she and Mrs Parsons had been coming back across the fields at about 9 p.m. after shopping in Romford. The sergeant had been on his horse and Clark had been walking beside him. They'd joked and exchanged pleasantries.

'The deceased,' she said, 'appeared to be in very good spirits.' Parsons' wife had been very tired and Clark had jokingly offered to put her on Parsons' horse. Her brother had come home at midnight to make out the report, then gone out again before 1 a.m. She hadn't seen him after that. Parsons also produced the landlord of the Cross Keys, who said he had served him a pint of porter while he was on duty at midnight, and a carter, who said he thought he had seen him on his horse around three or four in the morning. Curiously, the coroner accepted that Sergeant Parsons must have been on duty all night and adjourned the inquest for another month while further enquiries were made.

On 12 August three field labourers, Dennis Flinn, John Hennessey and Eileen Rankin, were brought before Ilford magistrates on suspicion of murdering PC Clark. When they were harvesting corn at a farm in Kent, Eileen Rankin had told two other labourers that she and Flinn had no need to be doing this sort of work as Flinn had been earning good money in London. But then he had assaulted a policeman and been obliged to flee. It had all resulted from a fight in a pub: a police sergeant had arrived to sort things out and been struck by a stone. Then Flinn and Hennessey had assaulted another policeman, who had been found dead in a field in the morning. It was all a bit garbled, and in fact the trio had been arrested merely to hold them while police investigated.

In court, Eileen Rankin denied ever telling this story – not surprising, given that a witness had heard Flinn threatening her if she didn't keep her mouth shut. But it was suspicious that two white gloves of the type worn by policemen had been found in her bag. She claimed she had been given them by a Margaret Driscoll to prevent her hands being injured by thistles while she was cutting corn.

Sergeant Edward Kendall, a new member of the Detective Branch, dashed off to Stratford, where Flinn said he had been working for a builder that night, to Mortlake, where Hennessey was supposed to have been, and to Loughton after Margaret Driscoll – and found that all their claims were true, the builder's foreman even producing time-books to back up Flinn's story. The trio were released.

Meanwhile PC Abia Butfoy took himself off to Scotland Yard where he spilled a quantity of beans. He admitted that neither he nor Parsons had been on duty that night, for the simple reason that they had got drunk together that day and were unfit for duty.

As a consequence of this revelation, all six of Dagenham's police officers – Parsons, Kimpton, Hickton, Farnes, Stevens and Butfoy – were suspended from duty.

Sergeant Kendall – another Cornishman and later described by Dickens as 'a light-haired, well-spoken, polite person' and 'a prodigious hand at pursuing private enquiries of a delicate nature' – was instructed not to let Parsons out of his sight.

Five days after Butfoy made his revelations, all six policemen appeared at the resumed inquest wearing 'private clothes'. The excitement in and around the courtroom and the local area was intense.

Butfoy was first on. He admitted to having lied previously and told how he had attended court on the morning in question, after which he and Parsons had got so drunk that the sergeant had excused him from his 3 p.m. to midnight duty. Then he added lethally, 'It looks strange that the sergeant does not account for his time from 9.30 to 11 p.m. that night and that Clark was not seen by a colleague who usually saw him at 11 p.m.'

The others, apart from Parsons, now admitted that they had also lied. They claimed that Parsons had told them that 'they were all in a mess and must stick to the tale' and had given them lists of the times they were to say they had seen him. Kimpton also admitted having taken over Parsons' duties at midnight but, oddly, claimed that Butfoy *had* been on duty. He had heard him report off duty by shouting, 'All right, Sergeant', as he passed the station at midnight. Parsons declared that they were all lying except him. He had been on duty that night and had not told them what to say afterwards.

Kendall was soon hot on another trail. It transpired that, despite being engaged to a girl back home, Clark had been seeing a woman named Susan Perry who was a domestic at Arbour Square Police Station. She had even been to Dagenham to see him. What's more, although she was separated from her husband, James, he was still very jealous concerning her. Even more suspicious, James Perry had been seen at Beacontree – which is no distance from Dagenham – on the night of the murder, leaving a public house with three other men.

Another new boy, Essex-born Detective Sergeant Edward Langley, was instructed to get into Perry's company. He did so on several occasions but failed to extract any helpful information, and no hard evidence could be found against the man. It appeared that he was jealous but only of another rival who had caused him and his wife to part.

Meanwhile, Joseph Palmer, the 36-year-old farm labourer who

had found Clark's missing hat in the cornfield, committed suicide by hanging himself from a rafter in his privy. His wife said his head was bad because of the heat and he was unhappy in his job, and that a few months earlier he had said to her that the devil had told him to kill himself. A verdict of temporary insanity was brought in by the inquest jury. The detectives then spent the next three days tracing a cabman who claimed to have picked up two tipsy gents covered in blood from near the East India Docks on the night in question. That also came to nothing.

Rumours were now rife that Parsons would emerge from the final inquest hearing charged with murder. The perceived motive was that Clark had disapproved of his drinking and neglect of duty and had threatened to report him. But Parsons was a slippery character and he turned up with a legal representative who objected to the prejudice that was being built up about his client. The coroner responded that he only had himself to blame.

Detectives produced another witness, George Dunning, one of the replacement constables who was living at the police station on the floor below Parsons. He recalled that one night he had heard Parsons and his sister quarrelling. She'd accused the sergeant of something. 'Do you mean this affair?' he had asked. 'Yes,' she had replied, 'and other things too.' Parsons had begun to cry but PC Dunning heard no more except the sergeant threatening to throw his sister downstairs if she did not hold her tongue.

The inquest jury returned a verdict of wilful murder by a person or persons unknown. Shortly afterwards Parsons' wife died of typhus. She'd recently given birth, and a local paper claimed that 'her husband's situation in this horrid affair played on her mind and accelerated her death'.

As always, the Yard was swamped with letters from people offering advice and claiming to have vital information. One, from a Bristol address, was signed by a Mr Bragg, who said he had some valuable information and wanted to know whether he could give it without bringing his name before the public at present. Would they write and tell him? They did better, they sent the ever-mobile Sergeant Kendall down post-haste to see him. But the Mr Bragg resident at the Bristol address denied all knowledge of the letter and promptly wrote another, not only to confirm this but also to illustrate that his handwriting was quite different.

Kendall was also sent to re-interview Elizabeth Dodd, who had claimed to have seen Clark in a field with his murderer. Now she denied having seen any such thing, saying she did not know the field in question and had not even been living in the area at the time – it had been a fortnight later that she had walked to London after a place.

'I find,' reported the detective wearily, 'that she is a person of bad character and is considered by many in Romford to be of unsound mind.'

Butfoy, Farnes and Stevens had admitted to lying at the inquest but, oddly, had not been properly sworn when first examined therefore perjury charges could not be laid against them and they were merely dismissed. The same was not true for Parsons, Hickton and Kimpton who were charged with conspiracy to pervert the course of justice, and Kimpton and Hickton also with perjury. Parsons and Hickton promptly fled.

Hickton was recaptured just before his trial was due to be held. Surprisingly, he was handed in by his own father and an old schoolfriend, Sergeant Harvey of the Derbyshire police. In fact he'd handed himself over to them so that they would be able to claim a reward for his capture which would help his poverty-stricken father. His and Kimpton's trial took place in July 1847, a year after the murder. They were found guilty of wilful and corrupt perjury and sentenced to be transported beyond the seas for a term of seven years. However, there was a backlog in the transportation arrangements so the first part of their sentence was to be served in the huge Millbank Penitentiary. Six months later, Kimpton was sent to one of the dreaded prison hulks at Woolwich. Such a move often proved a death sentence: disease was rife and mortality high in these decaying old ships which had been turned into temporary prisons.

Meanwhile, a soldier at Chatham confessed to Clark's murder. He was already in custody for desertion and now told Pearce that he and three other men had been poaching hares and rabbits when Clark had caught them. The detectives were not convinced; the soldier seemed to know so little about Dagenham. They suspected that he might be coming up with this tale to delay army punishment, which could be ferocious, especially as this was his fifth offence.

A senior police officer's laconic note in the margin of this file said, 'Game was not in season at this time nor likely to be shot in cornfields at night.' The man's relatives said he had not been right in the head since he'd had smallpox. Another dead end.

Parsons was still missing, doing what many fugitives did at the time, working on the new railway lines. He was eventually tracked down near Grimsby and brought back to await trial.

Meanwhile, a Mr Blairblock of Romford wrote to say that, shortly after the murder, a labourer had found a bloody smock frock, a jacket and trousers which had been thrown over a hedge on to a pile of night soil near Kimpton's cottage. Unable to get these clothes clean enough to make use of them, the labourer had buried them. He added cryptically, 'Ralph Page died on Monday under great suspicion of death by laudanum.'

Inevitably, it was the well-spoken, polite Sergeant Kendall who was sent down to have some conversation with Mr Blairblock. After extensive enquiries he found that the clothes had been buried in a gravel pit and would require a great deal of digging out, that the labourer did not remember exactly where to within three roods (about a quarter of an acre) and in any case the pits were very wet and the clothes were likely to have rotted away. So that line of enquiry was abandoned.

It was an exhausting time for the branch. Just getting from Westminster to Dagenham involved horse-bus to the railway station (6d), a train to Romford (1/9d second class) and then a fly from Romford to Dagenham (£3). Or they took a horse-bus all the way, which though cheaper took much longer and was much more tiring and uncomfortable. Such journeys made for long days and little home life.

Kendall was later to complain bitterly that, as usual, their expenses (including thirty-nine nights' lodgings) were proving hard to recoup. Pearce had asked him to take local policemen with him whenever he made an enquiry, in case they would let something slip. But he found he had to pay for all their refreshments. 'Most of the men,' he reported, 'had large families and consequently, no money to spend.' He also had to follow up every rumour 'and found in many instances after walking a great many miles and at great expense, that they emanated only from idle taproom talk'.

As for Ralph Page, the father of the two boys who led police to the body, and husband of Elizabeth who had reported Kimpton's revelation about Parsons not being on duty that night, his inquest jury could not reach a verdict as to cause of the death. Rumours suggested suicide. But he had taken laudanum after his rib was fractured in an election brawl and may have overdosed. Or, the doctor suggested, he might just have died of apoplexy as he had had two attacks before.

Parsons was eventually brought to trial in March 1848 but only on one charge, the Grand Jury[1] having decided that a charge of having suborned (in other words, encouraged others) to commit perjury did not stand up. And the judge halted his trial on a second charge, claiming that the sergeant had not been conspiring to defeat the ends of justice, merely to screen himself from neglect of duty charges – and he dismissed the case. So, astonishingly, Parsons got away with it. While Hickton and Kimpton, who had merely done his bidding, were to be sent to the other ends of the earth for a very long time, he went free.

Hickton did not stand up to prison life very well but, after many pleas from his father, in 1848 he was allowed to serve the rest of his sentence at Northampton Gaol. Kimpton remained on the hulk, where a cholera epidemic had broken out. Forty-four convicts succumbed; fourteen of them died but Kimpton survived and was released late in 1849. Meanwhile, in Whitechapel, Parsons was getting married again.

The inscription on one side of the monument in Dagenham churchyard opposite the still-standing Cross Keys public house reads:

This tribute of respect was erected by the inhabitants of this parish and his brother officers of the K Division of the Metropolitan Police.

And on the other:

Sacred to the memory of George Clark late a police constable of the K Division of Metropolitan Police who was inhumanly and barbarously murdered in a field at Eastbrook End in this parish whilst on duty on the night of the 29th June or the morning of the 30th June 1846 aged 20 years. His uniform good conduct gained him the respect of all who knew him and his melancholy end was universally deplored.

But these were not to be the last words on the subject.

9

'The electric constable'

The lack of a rapid means of communication was a great hindrance, not only when tracking down criminals but also when passing on force or inter-force information, something that was particularly important in a time of such social unrest. Police had only the postal service, messengers and the route paper system – until a wondrous new invention began to come to their aid: the electric telegraph.

During the 1830s Charles Wheatstone and William Fothergill Cook introduced the first working electric telegraph outside a laboratory, and in 1837 this was used to provide a link between Euston and Camden Town railway stations. In 1839 another link was introduced, this time between Paddington and West Drayton stations, and in 1843 this was extended to Slough. Though the distance covered was short, this 'electric constable'[1] was soon put to police use for keeping an eye on railway pickpockets, and on 1 January 1845 became the means of capturing a murderer, John Tawell.

Tawell had murdered his young mistress, Sarah Hart, by putting prussic acid in her beer. Her cries of agony had been heard by neighbours who saw him leaving her home and heading for Slough railway station. Noticeable by his Quaker dress, he was seen taking a train to Paddington.

A message was sent ahead, and on arrival Tawell was followed by a Great Western Railway constable in plain clothes. His 'shadowing' was not too wisely handled, as he left the suspect at his lodging house. The following morning 'D' Division's Inspector Wiggins accompanied the constable back there but, not surprisingly, Tawell had gone. Fortunately, they managed to track him down to the Jerusalem Coffee House, which he had visited the day before, and arrested him. He was taken back to Slough, charged with murder, convicted and hanged.

By 1849, about a third of the railway network had been connected by the electric telegraph, and its importance was judged so vital that during the lead-up to the huge Chartist meeting on Kennington Common in April 1848 a nervous government took over the system for a whole week, to prevent the sending of messages which might encourage the people countrywide to rise up.

Scotland Yard detectives were also to put the system to good use in their next big challenge in 1849.

One Friday afternoon in August 1849, a Mr Flynn informed PC Wright, an 'active officer'[2] of the 'M' or Southwark Division, that his cousin Patrick O'Connor, who was also a colleague in London Dock customs department, had not been at work that day. Nor was he to be found at his lodgings in the Mile End Road. Flynn had seen him the night before and knew he had been on his way to a supper engagement at 3 Minver Place in Bermondsey; he asked the PC to accompany him there to find out whether O'Connor had arrived.

The door of 3 Minver Place was answered by a handsome, well-dressed woman with a slight French accent. Yes, she told them, she had expected Mr O'Connor for dinner the previous evening but he had never arrived, which had surprised her since he was a man of such regular habits. Indeed, so surprised was she that she had gone to his lodgings to seek him out and had been even more surprised not to find him there. She had last seen him on Wednesday night, when he had left her house 'very tipsy'.

The 50-year-old O'Connor, a gauger of excisable liquor, had still not surfaced by Sunday and his relations, friends and colleagues were becoming increasingly concerned. (Their concern may not have been entirely altruistic given that O'Connor was quite wealthy, largely through money-lending, and possessed a great many French railway shares.) They went as far as distributing handbills offering a £10 reward for information, and two of them went to see the lady with the French accent, Maria Manning, who now appeared somewhat nervous but still puzzled by O'Connor's absence.

The relations and friends persisted, asking police to keep watch on the house. Flynn paid another visit with PC Wright to the now somewhat flurried and indisposed Mrs Manning, who murmured about 'poor O'Connor' who, she now recollected, could be somewhat erratic in his behaviour. She admitted that since he had gone missing she had twice visited his lodgings and had been allowed to stay alone in his room. But, she shrugged, that was nothing new.

Finally, Flynn broke open O'Connor's boxes to find them empty of cash and railway scrip. The following day police were to find 3 Minver Place in the same condition – empty. Three days later two PCs dug up the garden and gave the flat a more thorough search, during which PC Barnes (another active officer, and one of those who had helped capture Sergeant Parsons) noticed that some of the mortar between the kitchen flagstones looked damp. 'This arrested my attention,' he later reported. Underneath they found the naked body of a man, embedded face down in unslaked lime. On examination the corpse was found to have extensive fractures of the skull and a bullet wound in the head. Flynn quickly identified him as O'Connor by his very long jawbone and fine set of false teeth.

Details of the Swiss-born Mrs Manning's relationship with O'Connor were beginning to emerge. He had been her suitor when she was personal maid to Lady Blantyre but had been ousted by the younger Frederick Manning who, although only a railway guard, appeared to have better prospects. Manning had told her he expected a substantial inheritance from his mother and also had other ways of getting money. When he put these ways into practice he was sacked by the Great Western Railway, who objected to money going missing from their trains.

Discovery of O'Connor's remains

Manning became a publican in Taunton, but when a bullion raid took place on the GWR he was arrested as a suspect. Although he was released for lack of evidence, he and Maria ended up keeping a beer house in the Hackney Road. It was now that Maria, who had only wanted to escape from service into an easier life, discovered that O'Connor had become wealthy. They resumed contact. He became 'a family friend' and regular visitor to 3 Minver Place.

PC Barnes and his colleague, PC Burton, told the coroner the next day that they had the case well in hand, which seems a bit of an overstatement and may well have been an effort to stave off Yard involvement – a vain hope.

Inspector Frederick Field, who was about to replace Haynes in the department, was sent to France with Sergeant Whicher to search Parisian hotels and keep watch at railway stations. They were armed with Maria's description, which included the fact that she had a French accent and, more importantly, had a scar running from the right side of her chin towards her neck; scars are gold dust to pursuing police officers. The British consuls at Le Havre, Calais, Dieppe and Boulogne were alerted. An Atlantic crossings timetable had been found on the Mannings' mantelpiece and, since America continued to be a popular escape destination, it came as no surprise that two persons by the name of Manning had boarded the *Victoria*, an American packet ship.

Haynes had been promoted to superintendent of 'P' Division so remained in charge of the investigation on what was now his manor. He sent a telegraph to Detective Sergeants Langley and Thornton, who were busy searching ships in Portsmouth, telling them to stop and search the *Victoria*, which was about to pass Portland Bill. Easier said than done.

The ship failed to respond to signals instructing it to heave to so they appealed to the Royal Navy, who provided *Fire Queen*, a high-speed steam yacht, with which to give chase. Four and a half hours later the detectives boarded the passenger ship to find two sea-sick Mannings lying in their bunks: Mrs Rebecca Manning, who did not answer Maria's description, and her daughter.

In the end it was the meek-mannered, sharp-eyed Detective Sergeant Shaw who pulled the rabbit out of the hat in a good old-fashioned way by asking local cab drivers for information. He discovered that Mrs Manning had left home alone and in a great hurry on Monday 13 August, in a cab piled high with boxes and a carpet bag. This had taken her to London Bridge railway station, where she deposited the larger boxes with notices attached – 'Mrs Smith, passenger to Paris, to be left till called for' – and then went on to Euston station.

Among the heaps of clothes, personal possessions and bed linen inside the boxes were found a 'bloodstained' dress, labelled Maria de Roux (Maria's maiden name) and letters from O'Connor. At Euston, they were told that a woman answering Maria's description

111

with luggage marked 'Mrs Smith' had taken a train for Edinburgh on the previous Monday.

Now the electric telegraph really came into its own. Haynes used it to inform Superintendent Moxey, head of the Edinburgh police. The response was almost immediate. 'Mr Haynes had scarcely arrived at Scotland Yard on his return,' reported *The Times*, 'when a messenger from the Telegraph Office reached there, bearing intelligence that Maria Manning had been arrested.'

Another telegraph swiftly followed, giving details of property found on her, which included banknotes known to have been issued on O'Connor's cheques two days after his disappearance. She had been caught trying to sell some of the French railway stock.

Moxey and two Edinburgh city detectives escorted Mrs Manning on the seventeen-and-a-half-hour journey to London – travelling first class, which raised eyebrows at Scotland Yard. En route she confided to him that her husband was very violent towards her and it was terror of him which had made her take flight. Apparently Moxey was much affected, and after the first police court hearing asked to see her as she had expressed a strong desire to see him again before he left the capital.

But where was Frederick Manning? Before she took flight Maria had sent him out to sell their furniture. When he came back she was gone – *avec* the loot and almost everything else they still owned – so he too took flight.

Men answering his unlovely description (stout figure; florid complexion; full, bloated face; small, sandy whiskers; and a 'peculiar fall of the eyelids at the corners') were arrested from Dublin to John O'Groats. Whicher, back from France, was sent to Plymouth to search an Australian emigrant ship, and PC Lockyer and Sergeant Langley (who knew Manning, having worked on the GWR robbery) ended up in Jersey – where they caught him asleep in his lodgings.

He quickly fingered Maria as the murderer, claiming that he was afraid of her. She had asked O'Connor to go downstairs to wash his hands before dinner, he said, and at the foot of the stairs she had put one hand on his shoulder and shot him in the head with the other. When Haynes, who helped escort Manning back from Southampton, pointed out that there were other wounds to the head, he apparently made no reply but afterwards 'appeared low spirited'.

The Mannings stood trial each still blaming the other, but the Detective Branch had gathered some formidable evidence indicating that both had been well involved in what was a totally premeditated crime. A medical student, who had lodged with them up until 28 July but been asked to leave on the pretext that Maria's elderly mother was coming to live with them, described how Manning had confided to him that they had once got O'Connor into a state of intoxication by persuading him that port and brandy would help protect him against the cholera once again raging riverside. Once drunk, O'Connor had willed much of his wealth to Maria. More damningly, the student gave evidence that Frederick had pumped him as to what drugs would produce stupefaction but still allow a man to put his hand to paper to sign cheques; which was the most vulnerable part of the skull; whether an airgun made much of a noise when fired; and whether a murderer would go to heaven. Behind the ear was most likely to produce fatal results, the student told him. An airgun did not make much noise, but murderers could not enter heaven.

Tradesmen recalled that in late July Frederick had ordered a bushel of slaked lime 'for his garden'; on the day prior to the murder Maria had bought a strong shovel, and Frederick had recently purchased a crowbar or 'ripping chisel', thought to be the murder weapon. Later, he admitted that finding O'Connor was still alive and moaning after having been shot by Maria he had finished him off with the chisel. 'I'd never liked him well.'

They were both convicted and their execution, on 13 November, attracted the largest crowds ever to attend a public hanging – 30,000 to 50,000. Charles Dickens was there: in letters to *The Times* he condemned 'the wickedness and levity' of the crowd, and

MARIA MANNING.

G. F. MANNING.

*Frederick and Maria Manning, who murdered Joseph O'Connor
in 1849, as featured in* Mysteries of Police and Crime

in *Household Words* claimed he was haunted by the two figures. Apparently Maria's 'fine shape' was 'so elaborately corseted and artfully dressed, that it was quite unchanged in its trim appearance as it slowly swung from side to side'. (By contrast Frederick's 'limp, loose suit of clothes' looked 'as if the man had gone out of them'.) Maria's artful dress was made of black satin, which immediately went out of fashion.

Scotland Yard officials had other figures on their minds. They were still reeling not only from the first-class fares charged by Superintendent Moxey, but from his M&R (meals and refreshment rate) of £2 3s a day (for ten days) compared with the Metropolitan police superintendent's rate of £1 7s 6d.

When this was queried, Moxey responded by pointing out that, unlike the London superintendents, he was in charge of his entire force and these were the rates they granted him. Moxey also received £30 of the reward money (Haynes and Field, who had done much more work, received only £15) and claimed £15 for his electric telegraph messages, plus fivepence for a copy of *The Times* which, he said, he would not have needed for Maria's description had they sent him copies of the wanted notice, as they should have done.

Not a successful inter-force friendship-building exercise, then.

10

Strong mental excitement

Scotland Yard detectives mixed with all kinds of people in all sorts of places. They attended almost every notable event from Jenny Lind's final appearance to agricultural shows and royal occasions – indeed, any location which attracted 'the swell mob', who picked pockets and played confidence tricks on members of the public such as 'thimble-rigging' and 'gammoning a countryman'. Thimble-rigging was the old trick: under which thimble is the pea? Gammoning a countryman was deceiving some simple rural fellow out of money by, for instance, pretending to find him work.

The Epsom Races were a favourite haunt, and the detectives would wait at the railway station for the swell mob to appear and then pack them off home again. Those who slipped the net or had the sense to arrive by another form of transport might be caught, noted *The Illustrated London News*, by men like 'the wily Thornton' and popped into a portable prison which they dubbed 'Colonel Rowan's Cage' (Rowan being the other Commissioner).

The detectives were also allotted a curious assortment of other tasks, some on behalf of the government, such as the halting of General Flores' ships in London docks. General Juan José Flores was the deposed president of Ecuador. During the early 1830s he had fought to establish his country as an independent republic and been elected president, but he had hung on to power too long, as such men are wont to do. After being overthrown in a rebellion led by rival politicians he had left for Europe.

By the autumn of 1846, rumours abounded that Flores was building up an armed expedition to Ecuador with ships, men and armaments from Spain, Portugal and Great Britain. In response, more than fifty British businessmen (from Baring Brothers and Co. to N.M. Rothschild and Co.) who had interests in Ecuador and adjacent republics wrote to the Foreign Secretary, pointing out the dangers to their trade when 'the peace of these countries is threatened with invasion by a hostile expedition'.

The Times soon also informed its readers that 'several of the most active officers connected with the London Detective Police Force' were employed in ascertaining the accuracy of these rumours. The men from Scotland Yard shadowed Ecuadorian agents and discovered that 'equipments of the most warlike character were proved to have been the object of their visits'. Four suspect ships were seized as 'being unlawfully equipped, without the sanction of Her Majesty, for the purpose of commencing hostilities against a foreign power'. On board one were found 250 men who were to have been part of the invading army but 'seemed to have been recently in the most destitute condition'.

Another of the detectives' odder assignments was attending the meeting of the British Association for the Advancement of Science held in Oxford in June 1847. For the first time in the Association's erratic history, *The Times* announced, its meetings had been placed 'under the surveillance of the Metropolitan Police; those two intelligent officers of the detective police, Inspectors Haynes and Langley, having arrived yesterday'.

Scientific arrivals came from France, Germany, Prussia, Russia, Sweden, Norway and the United States. Those who came from the United Kingdom included the great chemist and physicist Dr Michael Faraday and astronomer Sir John Herschel. Also in attendance were the Prussian and US ambassadors, a sprinkling of aristocrats, Lucien Bonaparte (Napoleon's nephew) and Lord Baden-Powell. The detectives would be expected to protect the delegates from revolutionaries, the mentally disturbed and the swell mob, who seemed to be able infiltrate any gathering by adopting appropriate dress and mannerisms.

During the introductory general meeting, some of the latest discoveries were noted, such as the facts that air is affected by tidal movements and that electrical currents could be produced by muscular contractions (upon which Dr Faraday was to expound). The wonders of the electric telegraph were also celebrated in a touching story concerning the steamer *Hibernia*, which took news of our dearth of corn to Boston. This news was instantly transmitted by electric telegraph to New York where, the following day, the streets were filled with farmers' carts full of corn to be sent to England.

What Haynes (who had been a chemist, though probably pharmaceutical rather than research) and Langley made of all this there is no telling, but it does help illustrate the sheer variety of their work. Small wonder that when Charles Dickens met them in 1850 they gave the impression of being men 'habitually leading lives of strong mental excitement'.

It was his *Household Words* assistant, W. H. Wills, who first focused on the men who were to so fascinate the famous author. In Wills's article 'The Modern Science of Thief-Taking' he describes a case in which the uniformed constable called to a burglary suggested a domestic may have been responsible; however, a detective almost instantly divined that the thieves were members of the Dancing School gang – so defined by what we would now call their MO – who had gained entrance through the garret while the family were dining and the servants were occupied serving them. What's more, this oracle recovered most of the stolen jewellery before the fences had a chance to break it up and melt it down.

Wills also describes a detective sergeant catching a hotel thief by looking out for a man with a button missing from his shirt – his other shirt buttons matching up with one found at the scene. Another tale features the electrifying effect of the arrival of Sergeant Witchem of the detective police at a jolly gathering of members of the swell mob, who are attending an Oxford commemoration as uninvited guests. He packs them off home again by the next train.

The Scotland Yard detectives' first meeting with Charles Dickens took place over brandy ('not much') and cigars in his *Household Words* office just off the Strand 'one sultry evening at dusk' in the summer of 1850. Among the seven guests were two inspectors: Frederick Field and Robert Walker. Field 'one might have known, perhaps for what he is', wrote Dickens, but the schoolmasterly Scot Walker, 'never'. (Not surprising, since Walker was in fact not a detective but a member of the Executive Branch, which worked closely with the branch and sometimes helped them out.)

Three of the five sergeants present were branch originals: Thornton, Whicher and Shaw. The two others were newer men, Smith and Kendall. (Rather oddly, Dickens was to follow Wills's lead by slightly altering their names to Wield, Stalker, Dornton, Witchem, Straw, Mith and Fendall.)

The author met them just after the Mannings murder enquiry, for which, for once, they had been praised. The investigation had been, the *Morning Chronicle* pronounced, a marriage of new science and good detection. At the start of his piece 'A Detective Police Party',[1] Dickens made it plain that he had not been impressed by the 'Old Bow Street police', about whom there was a vast amount of humbug. Many were of very indifferent character, continually puffed up by incompetent magistrates anxious to conceal their own deficiencies; they consorted too much with thieves and were hand-in-glove with the penny-a-liners of that time.

But as for these new detectives, there was nothing 'lounging or slinking' in their manners. They had 'good eyes' with which they looked you full in the face when they spoke to you, unusual intelligence and an air of keen observation and quick perception. What struck him most forcibly was their camaraderie, each encouraging the other to tell their stories. These tales, Dickens says, demonstrate that despite press criticisms of the practice and official denials they frequently disguised themselves and revelled in the acting involved. (Field and Dickens had in common their early involvement with the London stage.) The tales also illustrate their advantage over divisional men in having the time and freedom to range around, following up specific crimes and criminals.

Field, who had handled the Eliza Grimwood murder back in 1838, was only a recent arrival in the Detective Branch. On its inception in 1842 he had applied but failed to become one of its two inspectors. In the interim he had been second in command at Deptford Royal Dockyard,[2] where police were tasked with curtailing the wholesale theft of goods and materials, preventing violence and coping with outbreaks of fire. Even in that capacity he had managed to gain appreciative press attention: 'Inspector Field performed wonders in his own person,' reported *The Times* after he had taken the dockyard's state-of-the-art fire engine to 'a Dreadful Fire' in Deptford High Street in 1841 and similarly to an 'Extensive Conflagration' in Deptford in 1844.

In 1847 Private George Hill of the 67th Foot Regiment stationed in Dublin confessed to the murder of Eliza Grimwood, and Field and Sergeant Goff went over to collect him. 'The magistrates of the Dublin Police consider there is a great deal of suspicion attached to the prisoner, but from the manner and behaviour of him,' Field reported back, 'I consider he is a designing, cunning artful fellow – very guarded in his observations.'

Indeed, Private Hill's own commanding officer deemed him 'a man of extreme bad character' and back in London Hill admitted that his confession, made when drunk, was only another of his attempts to get himself dismissed from the army, which he hated. He even had the gall to ask that the odium of being a supposed murderer be removed from him for the sake of his family, who were respectable. Notwithstanding the withdrawal of his confession, Field was obliged to produce the evidence to show that Hill could not have committed the murder. By then, confided *The Times*, Hubbard, the common-law husband and chief murder suspect, had been dead for two years.

In 1848 Field led a posse of three sergeants and thirty constables from the two dockyards to help police keep order at that last great Chartist meeting on Kennington Common over which the authorities were in such a panic, but which turned out peacefully.

Finally, in 1849, George Frederick Field arrived in the Detective Branch.

When reporting a case of annoyance of the Earl of Arundel and Surrey which Field was handling, *The Times* had described him as 'an old and experienced officer'. However, Dickens, in 'The Detective Police Party', saw him as 'a middle-aged man of a portly presence, with a large, moist, knowing eye, a husky voice and a habit of emphasizing his conversation by the aid of a corpulent forefinger, which is constantly in juxtaposition with his eyes or nose'.

Back at the meeting near the Strand, Field lauded Whicher as London's greatest authority on the swell mob, and after some prompting Whicher related his tale of 'the taking of Tally-ho

© *The Illustrated Times*

INSPECTOR FIELD, THE DETECTIVE OFFICER.

Charles Frederick Field, said to be the model for Inspector Bucket in Dickens's Bleak House

Thompson . . . a famous horse-stealer, couper and magsman'.[3] He had obviously taken enormous time, trouble and patience in the pursuit and employed much guile and intelligence before catching and arresting the man in Northampton.

Then Field described his pursuit of Fikey, a man who had been accused of forging debentures of the London and South Western Railway. The story illustrates that Field in his way was a consummate con man, and explains why the author found him so fascinating.

Field knew that Fikey had a factory on the Surrey side of the river where he bought second-hand carriages. But he had been unable to catch him there, so wrote a letter 'in an assumed name' stating he had a horse and shay (chaise) to dispose of – 'a reg'lar bargain' – and would drive it down next day to show him. Field and Shaw then hired 'a precious smart turn-out', but on arriving at the factory saw a number of 'strong fellows' at work and decided that to arrest Fikey on the premises would not be a good idea.

At first Fikey was unobtainable, but his brother eventually persuaded him to appear. Field told Dickens he could see that Fikey was taken with the 'precious smart turn-out' and the splendid horse which he saw him eyeing.

'Rising eight!' I says, rubbing his fore-legs. (Bless you, there ain't a man in the world who knows less of horses than I do, but I'd heard my friend at the Livery Stables say he was eight year old, so I says, as knowing as possible, 'Rising eight.')

Fikey was attracted by both the horse and the bargain price and was persuaded to give the turn-out a try. They drove past a pub so that one of the witnesses in there would get a sight of them through the window. But Fikey had shaved off his whiskers and the witness wasn't sure.

Fikey thought it was a clever little horse that trotted well and that the shay ran light. Field agreed, then pounced:

'And now, Mr Fikey, I may as well make it all right, without
wasting any more of your time. The fact is, I'm Inspector
Wield, and you're my prisoner.'

'You don't mean that?' he says.

'I do, indeed.'

'Then burn my body,' says Fikey, 'if this ain't *too* bad!'

Fikey was all for going back to his factory to get his coat but Field
sent for it 'and we drove him up to London, comfortable'.

There seems to have been no mention of the 'supposed murder'[4]
Field and Shaw had recently been helping investigate. The body
of servant Sarah Snelling had been found one Sunday morning on
the kitchen floor of her master's house in Clapham, with a roll of
kitchen carpet under her head. There were signs that a burglary
had taken place while her master, Mr Maddle, was out at church,
and he claimed to have lost some silver plate. But he could give no
description of it apart from three old teaspoons, which police later
found him using.

Police reports also made it clear that Maddle equivocated in his
evidence, gave signs of having a violent temper, was avaricious,
artful and untruthful. He informed them that he had only employed
Sarah because she was old and ugly and therefore he would not be
tempted, and as she was lowered into her grave he murmured, 'Ah,
poor girl, she is gone, she will tell no tales.'

Despite all this and their obvious deep suspicions they were
unable to arrest Maddle simply because no cause of death had been
established. There were no signs of violence on her body. Indeed,
the only untoward sign surgeons found was some inflammation of
the stomach lining. Its contents were duly tested for 'those poisons
frequently given, such as arsenic, prussic acid and oxalic acid' and
traces of the use of chloroform sought, but all with negative results.
The only conclusion the medical men could draw was that she could
have died from fright.

Field, Thornton and Smith visited Dickens's office on another evening, resulting in a piece entitled 'Three "Detective" Anecdotes', and the following year Field took the author around the sleazier dens of thieves and doss-houses in the East End, where apparently the inspector was treated like a sultan. They were, however, guarded by two uniformed constables. Their most dangerous moment, Dickens recalled, was when they met with some distinct sullenness in a kitchen 'crammed with thieves'. Throughout, he recorded, the burly Inspector Field was by turns bluffing, blustering, 'polite and soothing', 'sagacious, vigilant', but most of all he seemed to know everyone and every place and was 'at home wherever we go'. Bucket, in fact.[5]

The inspector absent from Dickens's first party may have been John Lund, a man of fifteen years' service but new to Scotland Yard. By then Inspector Haynes had been promoted to Superintendent of 'P' Division, and Inspector Shackell had retired in 1848 in rather mysterious circumstances.

Mayne had written to the Home Office, explaining that Shackell had become unfit for service because of ulcerated and diseased legs, for which the grounding had been laid by a kick he had received several years earlier. He asked that, although the inspector had been unable to attain the fifteen years' service required to entitle him to a superannuation allowance not exceeding half his present salary, his time as gaoler at Bow Street (five years) should be counted in, particularly as he had 'performed his duty with diligence and fidelity'.

Maybe so, but some embarrassment over Shackell's current appearance at Bristol Assizes as witness in a very complicated fraud case may also have made the process more urgent. It seemed that Shackell had been engaged in tracing gangs of bill-stealers and appeared to have become shadily embroiled in the process when negotiating the retrieval of stolen bills. In court he admitted having threatened one of the plaintiff's witnesses, telling him that if he got into the witness box he would be transported. Shackell claimed it was a joke. 'I was in liquor . . . but I was not drunk.' He had since apologized to the man.

Ramifications of this case emerged at bankruptcy court hearings two years later, one involving the grandson of Sir Walter Scott. In his summing up Mr Commissioner Goulburn was damning: 'The conduct of Shackell, the police inspector, throughout the affair, was that of a party to the system of fraud. It was a fortunate thing that the police force had got rid of him.'

He had escaped by the skin of his teeth, it seemed, although he had been granted his superannuation to the tune of £216 per annum. But Shackell was clearly a survivor. He popped up again in 1854 as the chief constable of Shrewsbury (Shropshire's county town) after the Borough Police Watch Committee decided that the force needed to be placed under the command of a thoroughly practical and experienced officer. The previous chief was demoted to make way for Shackell and the salary upped to £100.

11

Calling in the Yard

In the early hours of Saturday 28 September 1850, the Reverend George Edward Hollest, who lived in the parsonage in the hamlet of Frimley in Surrey, was awoken by the sound of footsteps and a light shining in his eyes. On each side of the bed there was a masked figure holding a pistol. Hollest, thinking they were his two sons playing jokes, told them not to be so silly at this hour (3 a.m.) and to go back to bed.

His wife Caroline realized it was no joke and screamed, whereupon the two masked intruders pointed the pistols at them, threatening to blow their brains out if they made another sound. Ignoring the threat Caroline leaped out of bed and reached for the bell rope to sound a warning, which caused one of the men to rush around the bed, seize her with such force that the rope broke, and hold the pistol to her head.

The 54-year-old Reverend Hollest was also a fighter. He too had jumped out of bed and was bending down, picking up the poker by the fireplace, when one of the assailants fired, hitting him in the stomach. The shock of the report caused the man holding Mrs Hollest to release his grip momentarily, and she rushed to the fireplace, seized a large handbell and rang it several times to wake the servants. As the men fled, the Reverend Hollest rushed into the next room, picked up a loaded gun and gave chase, firing off a shot at the fleeing figures as he did so. Only as he returned to his wife did he realize that he had been shot.

Even today a gunshot wound to the abdomen is liable to be life-threatening. In those days, before antibiotics and modern surgery, it was an almost inevitable death warrant. Sure enough, on the evening of the following day the Reverend Hollest died in agony. By then, Sergeant Edward Kendall of the Metropolitan Police Detective Branch had arrived on the scene.

Police forces which had no detectives, or were small or had few resources, had begun calling in the Yard to help them solve serious crimes. But Frimley was in the county of Surrey, which (apart from the areas which came within the boundaries of the Metropolitan Police) had no police force at all. Following the Municipal Corporations Act 1835, the towns of Guildford and Godalming in Surrey had each acquired their own police forces. Consequently, the surrounding rural areas which had not taken advantage of the County Police Act 1839, had become plagued by burglars and other criminals. Parsonages, often being the most substantial houses in a village and sometimes having church plate on the premises, became prime targets.

The fact that Surrey was within fairly easy reach of the London thieves added to rural anxieties. Everyone within thirty miles of London on the Surrey side was arming themselves, claimed one letter to *The Times*, while another correspondent described the county as having become a 'prairie of predatory excursion'.

When Kendall arrived in Frimley he examined the scullery window where the men had gained entrance to the parsonage, and found the mark of a naked foot in the doorway and a trace of blood. There were more naked footprints in the garden and under a tree, where there were marks on the ground 'such as would have been made by a corded jacket or trousers'; here he found a small piece of baize which turned out to be of the same material as the burglars' home-made masks.

However, the scene had already been gone over by Frimley's two parish constables and Inspector[1] Biddlecombe, chief of the tiny police force in the nearby small market town of Godalming. They had removed an umbrella and a stolen telescope from under the tree.

Meanwhile, Inspector Hollington, chief of police in the much larger town of Guildford, heard about the crime, decided who was probably responsible and went off in search of three likely suspects: Levi Harwood, James Jones and Hiram Smith. When he discovered that they had been absent from home on the night in question he arrested them. A fourth suspect was soon added to the group: Samuel Harwood, cousin of Levi.

So now four varieties of police were involved:

* Frimley's parish constables, who were merely householders taking their turn at the duty;
* Inspector Biddlecombe, of the Godalming police;
* Inspector Hollington, of the Guildford police; and
* Detective Sergeant Kendall of the Metropolitan Police.

None of them had ultimate authority but all were probably keen to demonstrate their superior methods. Not a recipe for success.

The seeds of possible dissension were quickly sown when *The Times* credited the Scotland Yard man with the decision to arrest the suspects. The fact that the coroner kept deferring to the Yard man can't have helped. But the officer whom Dickens had found 'a well-spoken, polite person who was a prodigious hand at pursuing private enquiries of a delicate nature' was also clearly aware of the potential problems. At the inquest, he stepped forward every now and then to prevent too much information being made public, but when the coroner asked him to relate the circumstances of the case he said, 'I beg your pardon, sir, but Inspector Biddlecombe was at Frimley before I arrived, and perhaps you would obtain a more correct history of the case by taking his evidence first.'

The coroner was clearly not pleased that Guildford's Inspector Hollington did not attend the resumed inquest. Perhaps he was sulking. It seemed that despite Kendall's efforts to be diplomatic, trouble was brewing. As *The Times* reported next day:

Nothing fresh whatever has transpired calculated to throw light on the perpetrators of the crime. The police are still actively engaged in their inquiries – Sergeant Kendall on the spot, Inspector Hollington at Guildford, and Inspector Biddlecombe between the two places. There is no doubt that each officer is using his best exertions, but from what transpired today there is too much reason to fear that a degree of jealousy mars their united operations.

But something fresh had in fact transpired: Hiram Smith had turned Queen's evidence or, in current parlance, become 'an approver'. The actual murderer was not allowed to escape justice in this fashion, but Smith insisted it was Levi Harwood, not him, who had fired the fatal shot.

The Times felt that a verbal report did not always convey the drama of the scene when an accomplice tries to shake the defence of his fellow criminals, as did Hiram Smith before the magistrates. So to help paint the picture it proceeded to supply vivid and slanderous descriptions of those involved. 'Hiram Smith who appears to have been the ringleader and plotter of the burglary is about the middle height, with narrow contracted shoulders, and a stooping figure. His face, which wears a sallow unhealthy hue, is extremely forbidding in expression, the features having that sharp prominent character which marks the rogue, while the doubtful and hesitating glance of the eye indicates a disposition at once cunning and irresolute.'

Levi Harwood, the man accused of firing the shot, was a ruffianly looking man with coarse and rugged features on a face betraying mastery of violent passions. He looked 'like one of those idle fellows, half ostlers, half anything else who were seen loitering about country inns waiting for any job that may turn up'. James Jones had flat and repulsive features and his whole physiognomy was expressive of a life of depravity and crime. He and Levi Harwood looked bold and determined fellows capable of carrying through any deed of violence they undertook.

The youngest, Samuel Harwood, was treated more kindly. He had great bodily strength, immense limbs and a slight cast in his eye, but good features and more frankness of manner than the rest.

According to approver Hiram Smith, on their walk from Guildford to Frimley the four men had armed themselves with two pistols loaded with stone marbles. They broke into the parsonage through the scullery window, and while three of them feasted on bread, beef, wine and spirits, the fourth, Sam Harwood, had kept watch outside, fortified by a decanter of wine and sheltered by an umbrella taken out to him when it began to rain. Then, reassured that their presence had not been noticed, all four men went up to the Hollests' bedroom, Samuel remaining by the bedroom door as he had no mask.

The other three simply denied all the charges, Levi Harwood claiming he had been in London and Jones that he had been out on the Downs watching the snares he had set for rabbits.

Witnesses identified Smith as having been in Frimley village a few days earlier on the pretext of selling crockery, presumably for the purpose of spying out the burglary prospects.

Caroline Hollest's view of the whole room had been obstructed by the bed curtains but she identified Levi Harwood's voice as that of the man who had held her and Smith's as that of the man who had fired the shot. Kendall gave evidence of finding a cut on Levi's foot which tied up with the blood found beside the footprint. The measurement of one of the footprints corresponded with Smith's right foot.

Many witnesses claimed to have seen the men on the road to Frimley that night, and a penny token found on one of them was identified by Mrs Hollest as having been among the bag of copper coins stolen from her house.

Samuel Harwood was found not guilty through lack of evidence, but was immediately re-arrested for a similar burglary elsewhere, for which he was convicted and transported for life.

James Jones and Levi Harwood were found guilty and hanged. Harwood, after much pressure at the last minute, confessed that he had indeed fired the shot which killed the Reverend Hollest.

The Frimley murder case had three major consequences.

The first was that Surrey got its County Constabulary. Indeed, the matter had been long mooted but the murder proved a tipping point. Within a month a Rural Police Committee had met in Reigate, Surrey, and the new force became operational in January 1851, while the Frimley murder suspects were awaiting trial.

Among the seventy men recruited by the new Surrey Constabulary was William Henry Biddlecombe, who became one of the first five superintendents as, shortly afterwards, did Guildford's chief, Charles Hollington. Oddly, one of Hollington's earliest acts in his new capacity was to write a furious letter to *The Times* in response to a magistrate's claim that the credit for breaking up the Frimley Gang went to Inspector Biddlecombe of the Godalming police. He (Hollington) had apprehended no fewer than six of them (six because he included two others who were transported for life for another local burglary) entirely on his own suspicions! The second consequence of the Frimley Murder was that when, in April 1851, the Reverend Joseph Smith of Walton in Cumberland became frightened by continuous knocking at his parsonage window at around midnight, he reached for the six-barrelled revolving pistol he had acquired following the Frimley Murder, opened the door and fired blindly into the night – killing a respected local landowner named William Armstrong. (Apparently Armstrong was drunk after a long market day and may have been trying to visit Ann Glendinning, a servant at the parsonage who had previously been in his service.)

The third major outcome of the Frimley murder, this time a joyful one, was that on 16 October 1852, at St Botolph's Church in the City of London, the victim's widow, 42-year-old Caroline Hollest, married the 'light-haired, well-spoken, polite', 37-year-old Detective Sergeant Edward Kendall.

Parsonages continued to be targeted. In fact, even while Kendall was at Frimley the new branch's Inspector Lund and Sergeants Whicher and Shaw were tracing the theft of a substantial amount of silver plate from the residence of a Roman Catholic priest at Bootle, near Liverpool, to a gold and silver refiner in the City of London. They telegraphed news of their find and details of the thieves thus gleaned to the Liverpool police, who replied with the report of the burglars' arrest within half an hour.

One reaction to this news reveals that fast telegraphic communication was by no means yet widespread. A writer to *The Times* enquired why, when the electric telegraph had aided the arrests of murderers Tawell and the Mannings, and now the rapid capture of the Liverpool plate thieves, the system had not yet been extended to the West Country, which had so many important ports and cities.

The Frimley Murder was not the first where the Yard had been called in since the withdrawal of the Bow Street Runners. In March 1842, just prior to the establishment of the Detective Branch, came a plea from the small town of Eskdaleside in Yorkshire for help in solving a murder which had occurred six months earlier. Inspector Nicholas Pearce was allotted the seemingly hopeless task of tracing a murderer after the trail had gone icy cold.

While her husband was out at Egton market, 61-year-old Elizabeth Robinson, a farmer's wife, had been found dead with her throat cut so ferociously that her head was almost severed from her body. Thirty-one sovereigns and some silver were missing. Panic ensued at the idea of such a crime having been committed during the day and the police from nearby Whitby rushed to arrest one suspect after another, then released them just as swiftly.

Firm suspicions eventually lighted on a local miller, William Hill, who was in the habit of delivering meal to Mrs Robinson on Tuesday mornings at around 10 a.m. and who was reputed to have quarrelled with the Robinsons about money. He swore she had been alive and well when he left her, but the surgeon said she had died before ten. Hill's statements to police seemed inconsistent and he was arrested, but there was insufficient evidence and he was discharged after a jury found there was no true bill.[2]

However, Hill was unable to shake off suspicion. The Marquis of Normanby, whose country seat was nearby and who had been Home Secretary from 1839 to 1841, went to see Commissioners Rowan and Mayne and they sent their most experienced man, Nicholas Pearce. He quickly decided that Hill was innocent and instead favoured the idea of someone from outside the district, on the grounds that there was evidence suggesting that someone had hidden in the cowshed and made a hole in the wall through which to spy on the house. Nearby had been found the remains of a loaf of bread 'made in a different manner from bread in that district'.

Also, back in turf-time (July) a woman servant had bumped into Thomas Redhead, a previous servant of the Robinsons, who had claimed to be in the area to see a friend – whom he failed to call upon. Redhead's mode of dress tallied with that of a stranger who had been seen around at the time of the murder. Redhead claimed to have arrived in Eskdaleside by the Stockton coach. Pearce traced his movements to Stockton-on-Tees, on to Hetton Colliery and Bishop Auckland, back south again to Darlington, and finally back to Bishop Auckland where he had died of smallpox three months earlier.

Nonetheless, Pearce persisted and discovered that Redhead had been working on the Shildon railway tunnel but had been absent for several days in July – when the servant had seen him – and again in September, at the time of the murder. He had arrived back in Shildon with sufficient money to pay off his debts, buy several things and invest in a grocery business. But his partner had tricked him out of his share, and from then on Redhead went downhill, speaking to no-one and subject to melancholy and fits of crying. It was reported that as he lay dying from smallpox he attempted to confess something but never managed to say what it was.

This conclusion, whether correct or not, greatly pleased the Whitby magistrates and gained the Metropolitan Police high praise at a time when they were much under attack for their tardiness in solving London murders.

By the early 1850s requests for assistance were coming regularly, but the Scotland Yard detectives were always hampered by their lack of local knowledge and co-operation, the time lag between the crime and their arrival on the scene, and the lack of forensic aid.

In December 1851, Sergeant Thornton was called in to assist on a throat-cutting murder enquiry in Bath, but he was disappointed when the pioneering forensic pathologist Alfred Swaine Taylor and an analytical chemist were unable to confirm that the copious blood

© The Illustrated Times

DRS. TAYLOR AND REES PERFORMING THEIR ANALYSIS.

Leading forensic toxicologist Professor Alfred Swaine
Taylor FCP (1806–80) (left) assisted by Dr Rees, a
lecturer in Materia Medica at Guys' Hospital

on the suspect's trousers was from a human being rather than, as the suspect claimed, from a bullock he had slaughtered.

While Kendall was involved with the Frimley murder investigation ex-butcher Sergeant Smith – whom Dickens described as smooth-faced with a fresh, bright complexion and a strange air of simplicity, and as being a dab hand at house-breakers – was dealing with a similar case (home invasion by a gang) at Frome in Somerset, a county also lacking a police force.

This was a more horrific crime. A 14-year-old girl, left alone in a farmhouse while her parents went to market, had been found brutally raped and murdered when they returned. As in the Hollest case, a group of three men had been seen acting suspiciously in the vicinity. One of them, William Bird, could not stop talking about the crime. He even began describing how it had been committed, including information which would have been known only to those involved (i.e. that after being assaulted she had been put in a barrel of whey).

Smith arrived on the scene at Frome five days later where he discovered, as in the De la Rue murder, a bloody handprint. As in that case, it was of little use.

One of the suspects, Sparrow, had a festering wound on his arm which could have been caused by a human bite, but odontology was not yet advanced enough to assist. (A few months earlier a London surgeon dentist had given an address to a dental college in Baltimore which 'dentistically considered' and compared the evidence in the Manning case with the recent US murder of Dr Parkman in Boston. However, in both cases this was about the tracing of false teeth which had resisted attempts to destroy the body.)

Smith arrested and charged the three Frome men but they were acquitted at trial.

Not long afterwards Somerset also got its county police, but by then there was no choice, thanks to the County and Borough Police Act 1856.

Adjacent Wiltshire already had a police force; indeed, it was one of the first eight counties in England and Wales to acquire one, having done so in 1839 largely because of the local magistrates. They had been impressed by the professionalism of the twenty-strong force of Metropolitan policemen sent down to answer their appeal to help quell rioting (due to Chartism and agricultural unrest in the town of Trowbridge), something which had been done without force or calling in the military.

In 1860, the Wiltshire magistrates again asked for help when they appealed to the Home Office to send down a detective to help them solve the murder of young Francis Saville Kent in the village of Road, set between the wool towns of Frome and Trowbridge. They had to ask twice, as at first it was pointed out that now that the County Police were established 'the assistance of London Officers is seldom resorted to'.

Following the second request Inspector Jonathan Whicher was sent down, so of course he was later than ever on the scene. Very late – fifteen days. It scarcely helped that the Wiltshire police's efforts to solve the murder had been ridiculed in both the local and the national press, and the demand had grown that the investigation be taken over by the best and most experienced detectives – the men from the Yard. The scene was set for non-cooperation. To add to the complications, the border with Somerset cut through the village: the murder scene was in Wiltshire while most of the village was in Somerset.

The story of the Murder at Road Hill House is an oft-told tale featured in various compilations by police historians, including myself, and has also been the subject of no fewer than four books. The most recent of these are the excellent *Cruelly Murdered* by Bernard Taylor (Souvenir Press 1979, revised 1989) and the best-selling *The Suspicions of Mr Whicher* by Kate Summerscale (Bloomsbury, 2008), which brought together much of the previous research and writings. Thus only an outline is necessary here.

On the morning of 29 June 1860, 3-year-old Francis Saville Kent was found dead, head down in the servants' privy at Road Hill

© Hampshire County Council Museums and Archives Service

Jonathan Whicher, the detective called in to
investigate the Road Murder in 1860

House. The cause of death was uncertain. Was it from suffocation? The stab wound to his chest? Or the cutting of his throat?

It quickly became obvious that it was an inside job by one of the twelve people who lived in the large house. These were the family: factory inspector Mr Samuel Kent (aged fifty-nine), his wife Mary (forty) and their children, Mary Ann (twenty-nine), Elizabeth (twenty-eight), Constance (sixteen) and William (fourteen) from Samuel's first marriage, and Mary Amelia (five), Francis (three) and Eveline (one) from his second. Then there were the live-in servants: nursemaid Elizabeth Gough (twenty-two), housemaid Sarah Cox (twenty-two) and cook Sarah Kerslake (twenty-three).

Extraordinarily, Wiltshire's Superintendent Foley, who knew Mr Kent socially, concentrated only on the servants. He quickly settled his suspicions on the young nursemaid Elizabeth Gough, not even searching or properly questioning members of the family lest they be disturbed or upset, and allowing Mr Kent to get away with various acts of non-cooperation.

Although the lone Yard man suffered several disadvantages, one thing in his favour was that he was likely to be neither influenced by local loyalties nor over-awed by important local personages.

*Road Hill House, where 3-year-old Francis
Saville Kent was murdered in 1860*

Whicher quickly came to suspect the daughter Constance, who had clearly been resentful of the attention given to the victim, the adored son of William Kent's second family. The fact that one of her nightdresses was missing helped consolidate this. He dashed about to Bath and Bristol where, from her schoolfriends, he gathered evidence of the girl's strong-mindedness, odd behaviour and jealousy of Francis; he then had the waters of the River Frome lowered in a (fruitless) search for the weapon.

When he explained his suspicions to the magistrates they insisted he arrest her, which he did. Then, during a week's remand, he endeavoured to find more evidence with the help of Sergeant Williamson, whom Mayne sent down on his request for assistance as he was 'awkwardly situated'; by this he meant the local police were not happy. He was right there. With their press briefings they were busy trying to discredit him and his theories about the murder, and they seemed to be succeeding. Their suspicions were still firmly fixed on the good-looking nursemaid Elizabeth Gough, and some were coming to include Mr Kent, now her supposed lover, the theory being that he had accidentally killed the boy while trying to quieten him as they made love.

When it came to the police court hearing, Constance was represented by a clever counsel, Mr Peter Edlin, brought down from Bristol, while the prosecution was unrepresented. It was true that Whicher's case was thin – and he knew it – but Edlin, who ran rings around the provincial court, made it sound mean and disgraceful, whipping the gallery into bursts of supportive applause. When Constance was released on bond the crowds outside cheered her and jeered Whicher as he left.

Worse was to come for Whicher, who on his return to London was to endure a vicious drubbing in the press which was to ruin his police career.

No doubt calling in the Yard was a useful move for chief constables or magistrates under pressure, but the resentment of the local police echoes down the years. Recently, when referring to a 160-year-old provincial murder enquiry in which a Yard man was partially involved, the force archivist exclaimed, 'Oh, yes, they used to come down thinking they knew *everything*!' and a senior detective in another rural force told me proudly, 'We *never* had to call in the Yard.'

12

Government men

Scotland Yard's offices were just off Whitehall, and this proximity to power led to the detectives being asked to make enquiries relating to offences which involved government departments, such as the ingenious fraud committed by ex-Admiralty clerk William J.R. Smith.

One of Smith's duties, before he was dismissed for misconduct in April 1847, had been to investigate financial claims sent in by ships' captains who had repatriated distressed or unemployed seamen from the British colonies. When Smith left he took with him some of the Admiralty registry books, which helped him set up his own repatriation scheme for fictitious sailors.

As the numbers of returning distressed seamen grew alarmingly, so eventually did Admiralty suspicions. Inspector Field and Sergeant Thornton were put on the case. They found that the *Mary Ann Jane* had not transported eight distressed seamen from Ceylon to Liverpool nor had the *Wanderer* brought ten British sailors from Canton to Liverpool, despite these claims being accompanied by signed declarations from the masters of the vessels and certificates from the secretaries to the governors of the colonies in question. In February 1850, when Smith sent his servant to collect the money on behalf of the skippers, the detectives were waiting.

They followed the servant to a pub where Smith was awaiting the handover. The fraudster was taken to Bow Street and then to the Old Bailey, where he pleaded guilty.

Another customer was the Metropolitan Commission of Sewers, which in August 1850 found that many of its Ordnance of the Metropolis maps, which were about to be engraved, had been destroyed by having a saturation of nitrate of silver poured over them. Field discovered that it was all down to office politics. A couple of employees in the District Sewers Office resented a new superintendent who had been brought in from outside.

Serious railway accidents were common in those early days of steam, and in one which occurred in June 1851 three people were killed on the short journey between Brighton and Lewes, in Sussex. These were the stoker and two passengers who had been thrown out of the open third-class carriage. The driver died later, following the amputation of both legs.

Who better to send to help investigate such an accident than one of those jacks-of-all-trades, a Scotland Yard detective? The 45-year-old Sergeant Edward Langley got this thankless task.

The accident (one of three in five weeks, claiming thirteen lives in all) turned out to have been caused by a sleeper on the line. Already under suspicion was ten-year-old James Edward Boakes, a boy obsessed by trains, who had been working in his family's potato garden overlooking the line and had raised the alarm after the accident. When Langley was taken to see James he asked him why he had at first admitted laying the sleeper on the line but now denied it. The boy was fretful and cried, but his father, who had stayed home from work to protect him, prevented any further questioning and, duly primed, the boy continued his denial at the inquest, backed up by his parents and a neighbour.

Langley believed the sleeper had been deliberately placed on the line, but there was no proving who had done so and he came in for some press criticism for pinpointing the young lad. Shades of Whicher at Road.

Back in Westminster, the branch's newest inspector, John Lund, witnessed a fire in the clock-tower of the almost completed new Houses of Parliament. Given the possibility that it might have been caused deliberately by such as the Chartists or the Fenians, Lund was sent in to investigate. It turned out to be an accident, but Lund having thus become the Yard's fire expert Mayne also sent him to observe the trial of Phillips's Patent Fire Annihilator in which a two-storey building, filled with timber and shavings saturated with turpentine and tar, was set on fire.

The Annihilator covered the blaze with a vapour, 'almost instantaneously extinguishing the flame', reported *The Times*, adding that 'within the hearing of our reporter' Lund had declared that had they had this machine at the Parliament fire (which took seven or eight engines and nearly an hour to control) 'it would have easily been got under'. The paper didn't mention whether Lund agreed with the inventor that such precautions should have been adopted for the forthcoming Great Exhibition to be held in the spectacular new Crystal Palace in Hyde Park, a venue considered so dangerous by the insurance companies that they would only insure it at very high premiums.

Of course, the 1851 Great Exhibition was the wonder of the decade. (The Crystal Palace *was* eventually destroyed by fire but not until 1936 at its new venue at Sydenham, in south London, where it was taken in 1864.) The vast glass and iron building was packed with industrial and scientific wonders, objets d'art and knick-knacks both British and foreign. *The Illustrated London News* declared that visitors found it 'a fairyland, a tour round the world'.

It also proved highly attractive to pickpockets and other thieves, many of whom were incoming foreigners and therefore not known to London's police. Fortunately, foreign policemen arrived along with the exhibits, and since Inspector Field took in a posse of detectives who were familiar with the London thieves those more liable to try their luck were, reported *The Times* disdainfully, 'clumsy performers from the country'.

Crimes involving the aristocracy also came the way of the Scotland Yard detectives. One of the oddest was that taken on by Sergeant Smith. It seemed that for years a man named Charles

Collins had been acquiring portraits and miniatures of lords, ladies, MPs and eminent military men by maintaining he wanted them to copy so as include them in such prestigious publications as *Portraits of Conservative Statesmen* and *The Female Aristocracy in the Reign of Queen Victoria.*

Having acquired the pictures (which were mostly daguerreotype photographs) Collins promptly pawned them, and when the tickets ran out many prominent persons found their images staring out from pawnbrokers' windows or, if sent on to the sale rooms, subject to the ignominy of rejection there. It was estimated that around a hundred likenesses had been so acquired, and Sergeant Smith soon found himself with over fifty pawn-tickets in various states of validity.

Unsurprisingly, although many complaints had been made to the Yard the eminent persons themselves were reluctant to come forward to aid prosecution and expose their vanity. At last Smith persuaded some to come forward: the Earl of Desart and Lord and Lady Paget. Smith took three charges to trial, but the victims failed to follow through as witnesses and Collins was found not guilty.

Most of the detectives' work was doled out to them in the form of 'dockets' which contained the bare facts of a crime or complaint. The docket would be 'marked out' to a particular officer and every action taken on the case would be noted in it. In *A Life's Reminiscences of Scotland Yard* (Leadenhall Press, 1893) ex-Sergeant Andrew Lansdowne names all his chapters 'Docket 1', 'Docket 2', and so on.

Almost as if designed to demonstrate that Scotland Yard detectives did not always wait for work to be brought to them was the case which resulted from a stroll across Trafalgar Square by Inspector Lund and Sergeant Whicher on Saturday 31 May 1851.

Loitering by the fountains they noticed a quite respectable-looking older man with a greatcoat over his arm. Whicher recognized him as returned convict John Tyler and decided he looked as if he was up to no good. They followed him to St James's Park, where he was soon joined by another respectable-looking older man whom they recognized as William Cauty, well known both in gambling circles and to the detectives.

After twenty minutes' chat the two men went to the London and Westminster Bank on the corner of St James's Square. Cauty entered. Tyler remained on the opposite corner until Cauty came out again and beckoned him over, and they both went in. Nothing untoward happened, and throughout June the detectives watched the pair go through this procedure three more times, always on a Saturday towards closing time at 4 p.m. and always with Tyler carrying a greatcoat over his arm, despite the increasingly warm weather.

Clearly, they were sussing the place out and awaiting some opportunity. The bank manager was informed and he admitted that on some occasions a cash box, containing from £20,000 to £30,000, was left exposed while the cashing up was taking place.

On the fourth occasion the arrival of a uniformed police sergeant to cash a cheque caused Tyler and Cauty to exit quickly, and it wasn't until the fifth visit that the deed was done. This time Tyler carried a black bag which appeared heavier when they came out than when they went in, although it contained only a few marked bank notes – it had been weighted down by a book.

The pair were stopped nearby and, realizing they had been caught red-handed, pleaded guilty at the Old Bailey, where Mr Justice Wightman told them that he felt obliged to sentence them to ten years' transportation even though he was aware that for men like themselves, who were over sixty, this was tantamount to transportation for life.

Although Lund and Whicher were praised for their detective skills, *The Times* soon published a critical letter under the heading 'DETECTION v PREVENTION', which asked what were the proper limits of the functions of the detective police. Would it not have been 'more English or rather more Christian' to have moved the box so that it was no longer a temptation? It also cited two or three other recent examples of questionable use of detective skills, including the placing a marked half-sovereign in a letter 'for the purpose of entrapping a thievish servant of the Post-office'.

As the 1850s got under way it became clear that the Scotland Yard detectives were no longer receiving all the attention. The City of London Detective Branch had been enlarged and become very active, particularly regarding financial crimes, and many larger cities such as Liverpool, Manchester and Sheffield had acquired their own detectives. Also, more of the Met's divisional plain clothes men had begun to appear in press reports and always by name, division and with the appellation 'detective'.

But these 'detectives' were still quite unofficial, as was made plain in a memo issued by Commissioner Mayne on 23 January 1854: 'Superintendents are reminded that there is no regulation in the service authorising the employment of police in plain clothes.'

When in plain clothes they were not preventing crime, as the sight of a uniformed constable would be and 'not under the control of public observation', he went on, 'and such a practice gives occasion to a charge of police being employed as spies and in other improper ways'. Still that fear. From now on, he insisted, superintendents must report why, how many and for what purpose such men had been employed.

In March 1852, the gentleman detective made what may have been his first appearance. 'Off runs the gentleman detective,' reported *The Times*, when describing the strenuous efforts made by an autograph expert bent on exposing as fakes some recently published letters supposed to be by Shelley. In contrast, the latest play at the Haymarket, *To Paris and Back for £5*, featured 'a burly detective'.

Even members of the public began to recognize the advantages of the title 'detective', which resulted in several charges of men falsely representing themselves as belonging to that elite group.

At the end of 1852 the 47-year-old Inspector Frederick Field, said to be the model for one of literature's favourite sleuths, Inspector Bucket in *Bleak House*, retired and opened a private enquiry office.

The personal publicity given him by Dickens must have helped him acquire customers despite Dickens going on record to say that Field was *not* the model for Bucket. He continued to make news – adverse news – in the Palmer poisoning case of 1856, when he was accused (possibly unjustly) of having withheld information (gained while investigating insurance claims regarding the victim) which could have saved a life.

In 1861 Field's police pension was stopped for six months because he insisted on giving the impression that he was still a police officer. His later years were troubled by particularly painful gout and he died in 1874 aged sixty-nine. I tracked down his grave in Brompton Road Cemetery in Chelsea. It was marked by a quite splendid plinth which carries an inscription very much in keeping with his talent for self-promotion when it states that he was a chief inspector – which was not true. There were no chief inspectors in the branch when he served.

Crimes connected with the ever-spreading railways continued to grow apace. Much of the pocket-picking and luggage theft was dealt with by the railway police, who now also had their own detectives, but there was a regular overspill into the lives of the Yard men, particularly with regard to railway share fraud, which was rife, and theft of goods in transit.

In 1851 Field had found himself deep in merino wool and *mousseline de laine* (a fine woollen material) which, after arriving from Paris via the London and South Western Railway, had been rerouted by a Nine Elms foreman to a draper and silk mercer in the Commercial Road. The foreman was nowhere to be found but Field caught and charged the draper and one other, who were found guilty of theft and receiving.

However, it was the interference with goods in transit in the other direction which was to become the sensation of the mid-1850s: the Great Bullion Robbery.

One evening in May 1855, three large boxes of gold bullion bound for France were placed in the guard's van of a London–Folkstone express. When the boxes were checked at Boulogne one of them was found to weigh less than it ought, while the other two were, oddly, slightly heavier than they were supposed to be. This was surprising given that the boxes had been bound with iron straps, sealed and weighed before being locked into Chubb's safes.

When the boxes were opened it was found that most of the gold had been removed and replaced by sacks of lead shot. Extensive

The men accused of the 1855 bullion robbery: Burgess (top left), Agar (top right) and Tester (bottom)

investigations turned up nothing. However, almost a year later one of those involved decided to come clean – for vengeful rather than altruistic reasons.

It transpired that the idea for the crime came from ex-railway employee William Pierce, who, with professional thief Ted Agar, sounded out current railway employees. From James Burgess, the guard who often accompanied the bullion train, they learned that they needed two sets of keys to open the boxes and that they should open them while he was the guard. Assistance from railway clerk George William Tester helped them get both the keys and the dates of the next delivery.

The deed was duly done, and no-one knew how until Agar, who by then was doing time for another crime, became an approver. He decided to tell all because money he had given to Pierce for the upkeep of his woman and child had soon been diverted to Pierce's own pockets.

The culprits were rounded up by Williamson, Thornton, Smith and Sergeant Richard Tanner, a young and eager new addition to the branch. Tester had escaped to Sweden and was pursued there by Tanner, only for him to find that he had returned home of his own accord.

Burgess appeared at his trial in his guard's uniform (possibly because that was what he was wearing when arrested). It was probably because he and Tester were convicted of theft from their master (the railway company) that they were transported for fourteen years while Pierce, the instigator, found guilty of a lesser charge, received only a two-year prison sentence.

13

A nest of vipers

In April 1853, after some months of surveillance, a Thames Division superintendent and Sergeant John Saunders (a rather shadowy figure in the Detective Branch) served a warrant on Mr William Hale and his son Robert. It claimed that at their Rotherhithe premises they had stored more than the legal amount of gunpowder allowed within three miles of the City of London and also that they had illegally manufactured the 1,600 war rockets found there.

William Hale protested that he was a legitimate rocket inventor who, to his misfortune, had failed to gain any orders from the British government. Despite this, and his having become bankrupt, he had managed to continue making and exporting them.

But it seems there was more to this Home Office and police interest than met the eye. They had not only noticed that some of his workmen were foreign refugees (Hungarian and German) but had discovered that two of them had been introduced to the Hales by Hungarian revolutionary Lajos Kossuth. These refugees and their fellow workmen, police claimed, were continuously warned not to talk about what they were doing.

Owing to the number of European revolutionaries taking refuge in Britain, the country was being referred to by some foreign powers as 'a nest of vipers' and 'the cesspit of Europe'. Two of the men whose presence most concerned these foreign powers were the Italian freedom fighter Giuseppe Mazzini and the aforesaid Lajos

Kossuth, who was actively encouraging his countrymen to rise against Austria to bring about an independent Hungary.

Hale denied the substance found on his premises was in fact gunpowder, so Saunders and other officers carried out experiments on it with a pistol in a Scotland Yard stable and declared the effect to be identical to gunpowder. A specimen of the largest rocket was produced in court and was reported to be about fourteen inches in length and two inches in diameter – which doesn't seem very large for a *war* rocket. Nonetheless, the magistrate clearly began to feel the technicalities of the case were beyond him and the case was carried over to the next Sessions.

It is impossible to overstate the attention and criticism the Rotherhithe War Rocket Factory prosecution attracted, particularly in Parliament – all much fanned by Mr Kossuth's stance of injured innocence.

What had happened to our treasured welcome for hunted refugees, commentators wanted to know. What on earth were our police doing watching them, persecuting them, *spying* on them? Others pointed out that Kossuth had made it plain to anyone who would listen that he meant to wage war and that he was stockpiling for that purpose in several countries. Was it not the Home Secretary's duty to see that no foreign refugees made warlike preparations against a friendly power? And, in any case, was Kossuth not supposed to obey our laws?

The Home Secretary, Lord Palmerston, refuted accusations that he had been bowing to pressure from foreign powers by resuscitating an old firework law. He had no desire to press hardly on Mr Hale but, he admitted, Austria 'felt aggrieved' at the goings on of refugees in this country. Encouraged by Palmerston's statement, William Hale wrote to him admitting guilt for inadvertently breaking the law and pleading for the proceedings to be abandoned, thus sparing him the expense and anxiety of a trial. The proceedings were abandoned, probably with relief all round.

The methods of another revolutionary, Frenchman Edward

Raynaud, were much lower key than those of Mr Kossuth. Raynaud wrote to the Prince de Joinville (who was the son of Louis Philippe, the late king of France, and lived in exile at Claremont in Surrey) offering to 'combine with him in an assassination attempt on Napoleon III the Emperor of France'. Or, if the Prince advanced him £20, he would carry it out by himself. A bargain assassination attempt, no less.

Sergeant Saunders traced poor, sickly Raynaud and arrested him. However, he was found not guilty of conspiring with others to murder Napoleon III. As the *Morning Chronicle* pointed out, there was no evidence that he possessed any 'infernal machines' with which to do the deed: he was merely out to extort money. The verdict may not have been to Raynaud's liking since he had told Sergeant Saunders that he was suffering from ill health and trusted he would get medical attention in prison.

Matters became more serious when, in 1856, Giuseppe Mazzini was joined in Britain by fellow revolutionary Felice Orsini, who had just escaped from an Italian prison. The French emperor was also *their* sworn target.

As Prince Louis Napoleon Bonaparte, he too had taken advantage of our tolerance of refugees. During the Prince's stay in Britain – from 1838 to 1840 and 1846 to 1848 – he had entered the police orbit several times. First, when his plans to duel with a man said to be Napoleon's natural son were thwarted by Pearce and Otway. Then, when he became a victim of a fraudster, and finally when he signed on as one of the special constables who accompanied the 1848 Chartist procession to Kennington Common.

Dubbed 'the depressed parrot' by some of his associates, he had since found reason to be cheerful by becoming the (rather authoritarian) emperor of France. Unfortunately, he failed to fulfil his promise to rid Italy of the despotic rule of Austria and the Papal states for which Napoleon I was partly to blame. In consequence, London's Italian revolutionaries not only plotted the French emperor's demise but began to make the requisite bombs and indeed in 1856 had already made one assassination attempt. They were about to try again – with terrible results.

One January evening in 1858 the heavy state coach, bearing the emperor and empress and flanked by a troop of lancers, arrived at the Paris Opera House. There was a heavy police presence. Inspector Herbert of the Sûreté was already on the alert after spotting Italian revolutionary, Giuseppe Pieri, in the crowd and arresting him. Now, just as the Emperor and Empress were about to alight there came a flurry of activity nearby followed by a deafening explosion, then another. A deafening silence fell over the scene before screams of terror and shrieks of pain began to rend the air. Two bombs had been thrown at the carriage. All around lay the dead and dying: lancers, policemen, members of the crowd and horses.

Inspector Herbert dashed forward to wrench open the door of the damaged coach just as a third bomb exploded beneath it, seriously wounding him. Two people had been killed outright, six more died within forty-eight hours and 156 were injured, some quite dreadfully. But, apart from a scratch to the emperor's nose and some inflammation to Eugenie's eye caused by flying glass, the coach's occupants were unharmed.

Three more revolutionaries, Antonio Gomez, Carlo di Rudio and Felice Orsini, himself wounded, were captured soon after.

Orsini was carrying a British passport in the name of Thomas Allsop. This led the trail back to London, where all the plotting and bomb-making had been carried out. The fiendish fragmenting grenades had been made to order by Mr Taylor of Birmingham and the filling provided by a French Communist refugee, Dr Simon Bernard. The whole was regarded as a grenade of 'unprecedented power'.

'France,' noted Baron Hubner, the Austrian ambassador, 'seemed as if drunk with anger and hatred of England.' This may have seemed a little unreasonable to Commissioner Mayne, who insisted that he had kept the Sûreté informed not only of the movements of Orsini and Pieri but also of their plans. (Later, the position was to be reversed when the Fenians began plotting and making their bombs in Paris, popping over to London to deposit them, then returning to the French capital via the night express and ferry.)

The emperor was an ally of Britain's and our government was soon pressured into action. They resuscitated an old Act of Parliament under which Bernard could be charged with being an accessory before the fact to the murder of two of those who died. French-speaking Sergeant Frederick Adolphus Williamson of the Detective Branch was sent to Dr Bernard's Bayswater lodgings to arrest him.

The jolly and popular Williamson was the son of one of the early police superintendents, and maybe for this reason had found his way into the branch only two years after joining in 1850. But he had shown determination. Being of Scottish, not foreign, stock he had to apply himself to off-duty study of languages while others were out enjoying themselves and earning a little extra money doing duty at theatres and music halls.

Williamson found that unlike the handsome, bearded Orsini, the 41-year-old Dr Bernard was not cast in the mould of romantic revolutionary. In fact he was rather short, with long, straggly black hair, sallow skin, a receding forehead, a large nose and a drooping moustache which failed to conceal his rabbit teeth. He was also rather deaf, which caused him to cup his ear to catch what Williamson said. He was, however, reputed to have a brave, simple and trusting nature and a genuine belief in the justness of his revolutionary causes. Moreover, the whole thing had been his idea.

Arriving at Bernard's lodgings, Williamson refused to let him go upstairs to change out of his dressing-gown but sent for his clothes and read out the warrant.

'If I have done wrong, I must suffer for it,' was Dr Bernard's ambiguous response.

Williamson, Smith and Saunders shuttled back and forth across the Channel, gathering evidence and taking with them the wife of Rudio and the girlfriend of Orsini, both men being now under sentence of death in France.

Bernard's trial began on a fine but distinctly chilly April morning. The floor of the Old Bailey courtroom was soon awash with French and Belgian witnesses – some blinded or on crutches – and the bench alive with persons of note, including the French ambassador and Sir Richard Mayne. Chartists and foreign refugees thronged the specially enlarged public gallery. French policemen, medical men, a gunsmith and a Parisian veterinary surgeon trooped in and out of the witness box.

Then came the British contingent, starting with Whicher, who reported having been unable to find Allsop for whom he had been searching for five weeks (he had fled England). He was followed by Sergeant Rogers, who was something of a revelation. It must have been his exploits that had allowed Mayne to warn the French police. Since the previous November, Rogers explained, he had been watching French and Italian refugees. (Doubtless police had been alerted by Bernard's loose tongue and his bomb test at Putney, about which the neighbours had complained.) A fluent French speaker, Rogers had attended political debates at Thomas Wyld's reading and debating rooms in Leicester Square where the refugees made their intentions all too clear.

'Rogers the spy', defence counsel Edward James insisted on calling him, claiming he was clearly in the pay of the French government who were trying to bring their spying, tyrannical ways to London. Much was also made of 'the ever-busy and ubiquitous Mr Saunders' and the trips to Paris of Williamson and Smith with their witness Eliza Rudio. In the event they did not get much out of her in court, for by now her husband had been reprieved while Orsini and Pieri had been guillotined.

Defence counsel James was also to make much of the oddity of a charge being brought for a crime committed in another country. The emperor, he told the all-British jury – Bernard had waived his right to a half-foreign jury, saying he trusted the British – was trying to destroy the very asylum of which he himself had taken advantage.

He implored them to show the French emperor that he could

not intimidate an English jury. He pleaded, 'Tell him that though six hundred thousand bayonets glittered before you, though the roar of the French cannon thundered in your ears, you will return a verdict which your own breasts and consciences will sanctify and approve . . .'

It was Waterloo all over again.

The jury, showing they were not intimidated by the notion of glittering French bayonets, found Dr Simon Bernard not guilty. This brought about, reported *The Times*, 'a loud shout of exultation' from the public gallery which was echoed by the crowds waiting outside.

The French government, having spent £30,000 on the prosecution, were furious but expediency soon healed the breach.

These days it tends to be an unexpected DNA hit or an airing on BBC TV's *Crimewatch* which resuscitates a cold crime, but in Victorian times they seemed to resurface all on their own, and not always because of soldiers wanting to escape military discipline or be sent home. Inspector Aggs followed up various later 'confessions' which surfaced regarding the murder of barmaid Eliza Davis back in 1837.

In 1842 he went over to the island of Jersey following up sightings of a suspect, and the case took on yet another lease of life in 1848 when a young man called in to tell Inspector Tedman that at the time of the murder he had been a servant in a house not far from the pub to which a frequent visitor had been the housekeeper's brother, a man named Holland.

The other servants had felt that Holland's clothes so resembled those described as worn by the suspect that, to prevent his capture, they held a collection which raised sufficient money for him to buy either a new hat or a pair of trousers. Holland, it seemed, had always been out and about early in the morning and was also an occasional customer at the King's Arms.

This information received some publicity which brought forth not only an offer of assistance from the now retired Aggs but a witness named Gee, who claimed to have seen a man run out of the pub at one o'clock on the fateful morning, pausing only to stoop over a gutter to wash the blood from his hands. Gee had told his master at the time and he had passed on the intelligence to Mr Rawlinson, the magistrate at Marylebone Lane Police Office, but he had 'treated the matter rather lightly'. Tedman went to see Aggs, who admitted that the running man evidence had been passed on to him but that he had paid little attention to it at the time – possibly because he had been dashing about hither and thither tracing so many other supposed suspects.

Tedman worked hard and spent his own money tracking Holland to Southampton but informed the Commissioners that he could not afford to pay Gee's fare down there to identify the man. They coughed up, but after all this time Gee proved uncertain whether Holland was the man he had seen that day and no further action was taken.

The murder of Constable Clark also came back into the news in a startling manner. In 1858 a Mrs Mary Smith began confiding in neighbours that she knew who had killed Constable Clark and her conscience was troubling her. She had lived with the guilty knowledge for over ten years and was now afraid of dying with it. What's more, she was being haunted by Clark's ghost. Nowadays, this might instantly mark her out as delusional, but of course such beliefs were quite common then.

Her story was this: she had once been married to William Page and their cottage had been the first habitation on Clark's beat. Earlier on the night in question she had told Clark that her husband was very violent towards her and asked if he would speak to him about it. He did so, warning Page that his behaviour could jeopardize his immortal soul. This had enraged him and he muttered dark threats about what he was going to do to Clark.

William Page and three mates – Ned Wood, George Chalk and George Blewett – had decided to steal corn that night from Eastbrookend Old Hall where two of them worked.

They had discussed the possibility of Clark catching them and decided that, should he do so, they would 'see him out'. He did catch them. Mrs Smith said she had been left outside the barn as lookout and when she saw Clark she shouted a warning to her husband inside. He came out and set about Clark with a heavy stick, calling to the others, who came out armed with pitchforks and other farm implements. They surrounded the hapless officer and she fled home. Even now the picture chills the blood.

Later that night, she had helped her husband burn his bloodstained smock and trousers. He told her they had killed the constable and carried him a quarter of a mile to the field where he was found. There, George Chalk had beaten Clark's head with the heel of his boot, possibly accounting for the absence of brain in the skull that the surgeon had reported. She also implicated Ralph Page, saying he had been waiting in his barn to receive the stolen corn – not to guard his own.

The story seemed convincing to the newly promoted Detective Inspector Whicher. Unfortunately, of those she had named, William Page had since died in an accident (his horse had bolted when frightened by a train, causing Page to be thrown under the wheels of his cart and be crushed), Ned Wood had hanged himself some time earlier and George Chalk was gone from Dagenham to, it was said, Australia. Only George Blewett was still around and he, naturally, vigorously denied the accusation.

Nevertheless, Whicher arrested him. At police court Blewett (who, incidentally was father to seventeen children) apparently cut an impressive figure physically and his impassive manner contrasted markedly with that of Mrs Smith, who was clearly a simple soul and inclined to wander when telling her tale. Blewett's counsel made mincemeat of her and, again, the police were without legal representation. Nonetheless, the magistrates sent Blewett before a Grand Jury for them to judge if there was a case to answer. They thought not and he was released.

So who killed Constable Clark? A rumour, passed down via

local police folklore, claimed that Parsons did, because Clark (who seemed to be popular with the ladies) had been having an affair with his wife. Smugglers having their style cramped by the keen young officer or being caught in the act by him were other favourite theories. The press always suspected that the locals knew much more than they were telling.

The mystery remains. I favour Mrs Smith's story.

Ironically, the Corn Laws, which had kept the price of bread so high and were partially responsible for the dire state of the farm workers, were being repealed as Clark lay dead clutching a handful of corn. Even more ironically, one of the persons who had most robustly opposed the repeal but in the end pushed it through was the man who founded the New Police, Sir Robert Peel.

14

More murder

Mrs Emsley was not answering her door. One of her tenants, Walter Emm, a shoemaker who occasionally collected some of the rents from her extensive properties, kept knocking but the wealthy seventy-year-old widow failed to respond.

He tried again on the following day and the next, with no more luck, so he informed Mr Rose, her solicitor, who told the local police.

They found the house in Grove Road, Bethnal Green, apparently undisturbed, but in the second-floor room it was a different story. Her body lay in a sea of congealed blood surrounded by rolls and fragments of wallpaper. The injuries she had suffered due to repeated blows to her head were so severe that pieces of bone had been driven right into her brain.

The lively 28-year-old Sergeant Richard Tanner and Sergeant William Thomas, an ex-grocer from Bagshot, were sent from Scotland Yard to investigate. They quickly learned that Mrs Emsley's nephew, Edward Jackson, a soldier stationed at Portsmouth, was known as a bad lot who frequently wrote home enquiring whether the old girl was dead yet as he expected to inherit something. However, the reply to a telegraph message sent to the Portsmouth police established that Jackson had not been absent from his barracks, and so began another enquiry with a seemingly limitless number of suspects but little hard evidence.

Detective officers were expected to submit regular detailed

reports. These, of course, were all handwritten, as was all the correspondence at the time, and not with a ball-point or fountain pen but with one which, every few words, had to be dipped into an ink bottle or well. (A form of self-filling pen had been invented but was plagued by ink spills so was not very popular.)

'There is nothing stolen which can be traced beyond a £10 cheque which has been stopped,' Inspector Thornton reported. No weapon had been left at the scene and no person was seen near the house on what they believed was the fateful evening. Some of Mrs Emsley's tenants were 'of the most depraved and lowest class', Thornton went on. 'She was in the habit of personally collecting the greater portion of her rents on a Monday and in consequence of her frequent litigation with her tenants, her very plain way of dressing and living, she became well-known at the East End of London.'

Her solicitor had warned her she would be murdered if she continued to go about alone among such bad and dangerous characters. Moreover, as Thornton – who was now in charge of the enquiry – pointed out, she had let many of her poor relatives know that she intended to leave her money to build almshouses. Suspects galore.

The wallpaper around the body was explained by the fact that she had bought a job lot at auction. Maybe someone had called upon her that fateful evening on the pretence of buying some. But then again, she was very careful who she let in: usually only those known to her, such as the shoemaker Walter Emm and an Irishman who did plastering and papering for her, ex-police sergeant James Mullins, who had been dismissed from the force following a conviction for larceny. But officers shadowing both men came up with nothing.

The body had been found on 17 August 1860. By 8 September, *The Times* was reporting that the police were 'ready to abandon the investigation as hopeless' but next day they made two arrests – the result of some very curious circumstances.

Ex-policeman Mullins had suddenly called on Sergeant Tanner at his home in Stepney. Since Tanner had interviewed him as a suspect, Mullins said, he had been using his police experience to study the case and had developed suspicions about the shoemaker, Emm, whom he began to follow. As a consequence he had seen Emm come out of his cottage at five in the morning, walk to a nearby ruin and bring out a large parcel. He took it into his home, only to re-emerge ten minutes later with a smaller parcel which he put in an adjacent shed. 'If this goes all right I'll take care of you,' Mullins assured Tanner, by which he meant he would give him a share of the reward, which had now risen from £100 to £300.

The parcel, which the detectives were unable to find until Mullins guided them to it, contained some spoons of the common type used by Mrs Emsley and the missing cheque. Emm was arrested but so was Mullins. The shoemaker, who had an alibi and no apparent knowledge of the parcel, was released, but Mullins was charged and sent for trial.

The press, who had been complaining about lack of progress, were not satisfied. The police had done it again, complained *The Illustrated Times*: they had arrested someone before they had sufficient evidence. The whole system was lamentably defective, particularly in the means of preserving inanimate objects. Why couldn't Mrs Emsley's wounds have been perpetuated by the simple means of a bag of plaster and why couldn't the crime scene have been photographed? Then there was the usual accusation of arrests not being made until good rewards were offered. 'This is the very root of evil! We actually employ, at the public charge, a body of low, cunning men called "detectives" and we hold out inducements of small fortunes to them *not to do their work.*'

The detectives worked hard to consolidate their case, even cutting out a section of Mrs Emsley's landing floorboard to take into court to show the partial imprint of a nailed boot to compare with a boot Mullins had been seen to throw away.

The surgeon in the case, Dr Gill, turned out to also be a keen amateur forensic scientist. He had examined the tape Tanner had found on Mullins's mantelpiece, he explained at the trial, and it was similar to that which had tied the parcel. Not only that, the ends corresponded exactly and there were the same number of strands in both pieces. No, he conceded, he was not engaged in the manufacture of tape but he *was* used to examining various fabrics under the microscope – for his own gratification. He pointed out that Inspector Thornton had been a draper and had found the same number when he counted them first.

Dr Gill also put Mullins's boot under his microscope and found three hairs, which 'in his opinion' were human and the colour of which corresponded with those of Mrs Emsley (no-one could say more than that he agreed) and he had found traces of blood on a silver pencil Mullins had sold following the murder. No, he had to admit, although the microscope was an infallible aid in proving the presence of blood there was, as yet, no test to prove it was human.

A host of witnesses swore to having seen Mullins in the vicinity of Grove Road on the night in question and in various other suspect locations and attitudes. But identification evidence was notoriously unreliable, the judge told the jury, and he dismissed most of the forensic evidence. His judgement may have been affected by the fact that he was currently embarrassed by accusations of biased summing up and the overturning of the verdict following a trial which had been complicated by the (admitted) mistake of expert witness Dr Alfred Swaine Taylor.

It came down to whether they believed Emm or Mullins, he told the jury. Why would Emm have secreted this parcel at dawn and why would he not have burned the incriminating cheque?

The jury had made the right decision, he told Mullins after they found him guilty, but he criticized the police for the weight of evidence they had brought, 'which only tended to embarrass the jury in coming to a decision'.

It seemed they were damned if they did and damned if they didn't, but truth to tell they *had* over-egged the pudding somewhat in this case.

163

Another murder, on 10 June 1861, had a feeling of the familiar about it, occurring as it did in a parsonage in Surrey. Of course, that county now had its own police force but, again, there were added complications. Tranquil Kingswood was only thirty yards over the border from the Met's 'P' Division and one of its officers, PC King, lived in the village and thus was first on the scene

This time the victim was not a parson but Mrs Martha Halliday, wife of the parish clerk, who had been acting as caretaker while the vicar was away. She was discovered lying dead in a bedroom, tied hand and foot, a sock stuffed in her mouth and held in place by a scarf, causing her to die of suffocation.

PC King informed both his own Metropolitan Police inspector and Superintendent Coward of the Surrey Constabulary, who when the Met inspector arrived assured him that the place had been searched and nothing was missing.

Mayne sent a detective down anyway and Inspector Whicher oversaw the enquiry.

Fortunately, the vigilance of another member of the Metropolitan Police soon produced possible suspects. At 2.30 a.m. on the night of the murder PC Peck had stopped a couple of young men about six miles north of Kingswood as they hurried towards London. They were conversing in a foreign language and tried to avoid his eye, but he stopped and searched them nonetheless. They were tired and had no money, and the taller of the two seemed very depressed and hung his head. Finding nothing on them, the constable let them go. It later transpired that two young foreigners of a similar description had been seen around Kingswood the day before the body was found, and in Reigate, where they had bought the unique type of twine with which Mrs Halliday had been tied.

Some inter-force difficulties soon began to emerge. After the body had been removed Met PC King found a pocketbook containing a passport and birth certificate in the name of Johann Carl Franz, an unaddressed begging letter and a letter to an Adolph Krohn signed by celebrated soprano Madam Teresa Tietjens, who was known for her kindness to distressed fellow Germans. The pocketbook, reported 'P' Division's Superintendent Payne, was taken from PC King by Surrey's Superintendent Coward.

Up in London Madam Tietjens told the detectives that on the previous Friday a young German had called asking for assistance to get back to Hamburg; she had passed him on to the proprietor of the Hamburg Hotel in the Minories but he had never arrived. They also called at steamship companies to enquire whether any Germans had recently left for Hamburg, and at the Austrian, Prussian and Hanseatic embassies and consulates to see whether they had had applications for replacement passports.

Soon, the detectives were being offered a bevy of young foreign suspects. One of them, Auguste Saltzmann, who had been arrested by the City police when found in a house for an unlawful purpose, was not identified by PC Peck or three other witnesses but Whicher, with his customary confidence, was convinced that Saltzmann was Franz. He had more witnesses brought up from Surrey, and two out of three of them said yes, this was one of the two men they had seen in the area.

The prisoner continued to deny he was Franz so photographic copies of the documents were sent to Germany. The reply was a long time in coming, and by the time it arrived Saltzmann had admitted to being Franz but was claiming that his papers had been stolen. The German police reported that Franz was considered to be a lazy and frivolous person and had served two years in prison for theft.

Whicher built up an impressive chain of evidence, bringing to court the manufacturer of the twine which had been used to bind Mrs Halliday and had also been found tied around one of Franz's shirts. It had been specially made for the Reigate shopkeeper, and he even claimed it was all from the same ball. Franz was committed for trial and the Reigate magistrates declared themselves pleased with the work of the Metropolitan Police.

They had a nail-biting time waiting for an identification witness to arrive from Germany. He did so just in time, but meanwhile a further pocketbook containing papers and a diary in the name of Franz was found in a wood near Banbury, and this tied in with some of his story about stolen papers. The twine-maker, it turned out, had his works in Whitechapel, where Franz claimed to have been staying and to have picked up the piece of string in the street.

Franz was found not guilty: another defeat for Whicher.

In his memoirs, prosecuting counsel Serjeant Ballantine reveals that he thought the evidence again Franz, although circumstantial, was 'conclusive' and that the not guilty verdict was largely down to the inexperience of the judge! In his summing up, Mr Justice Blackburn had given the impression that 'he was labouring under a sense of hesitation and doubt; and juries, always loath to inflict the penalty of death, were affected by his demeanour'.

It was the end of the line for Whicher, although he was to have a curious final adventure the following year when he and Chief Superintendent Walker, the Scotsman whom Dickens had mistaken for a detective, were sent to Warsaw to advise on the setting up of an English-style police force.

Mrs Carnell felt very ill so asked her friend Constance Wilson to go to the chemist to get her a soothing rhubarb cordial. But instead Constance brought back a black draught which burned Mrs Carnell's mouth, causing her to refuse to drink it down. Blisters quickly formed inside her mouth and holes appeared in the bed-sheet where the draught had spilled.

It was her lodger, George Graves, who noticed that the usually healthy Mrs Carnell tended to become ill only when visited by Mrs Wilson and he took the bed-sheet to the police. It was examined by the police surgeon, who declared that the holes must have been caused by sulphuric acid, commonly known as oil of vitriol. This would account for her complaining that the draught was too hot – a typical reaction when sulphuric acid was mixed with any other fluid.

PC Boden of 'D' Division tried to locate Mrs Wilson but she had left her lodgings. However, he bumped into her a few weeks later, arm in arm with *Mr* Carnell, whom she was supposedly attempting to reunite with his wife. She was charged with attempted murder and sent for trial. As this was a straightforward case it appears that it wasn't felt necessary to consult any Yard detectives.

Mrs Wilson's defence counsel implied an error on the part of the chemist and she was found not guilty. However, on her release Boden immediately stepped forward to re-arrest her. This time detectives had been involved in response to a number of letters which the police had received following the publicity about the alleged attempt on Mrs Carnell.

Their investigation revealed that Constance Wilson, alias Catherine Wilson, alias Turner, alias Taylor, had been a busy woman in the previous few years. Among those who had come to a sad end following acquaintance with her were a Mr Mawer of Boston, Lincolnshire, to whom she had been housekeeper. He died suddenly of an overdose of colchicum,[1] but since he was known to take small doses of this for gout she had escaped suspicion despite being left his property.

That was in 1854. In 1855 she and a Mr Dixon went to lodge with a Mrs Soames in London. Dixon died soon after. He had, Constance Wilson told Dr Whidborne, been in the habit of taking colchicum for his rheumatics.

Her landlady, Mrs Soames, fell ill next, dying in agony shortly after receiving the latest instalment of a legacy. Dr Whidborne had signed Mr Dixon's death certificate but refused to sign that of Mrs Soames. However, at the inquest, having carried out a postmortem in which he found only some inflammation of the bowel, he claimed that she had died from natural causes.

In 1860, Mrs Atkinson of Kirby Lonsdale made her annual trip to London to buy materials for her millinery and dressmaking business and took with her about £100 for that purpose. As usual, she stayed with her old friend Mrs Wilson. Oddly, however, though normally a healthy woman Mrs Atkinson fell ill quite quickly and died. Mrs

Wilson persuaded Mr Atkinson not to allow a postmortem on his wife, saying, 'All doctors are alike in London, always wanting to open dead people. I would not have her cut up, poor thing.'

It was with her murder that Catherine Wilson was charged when she appeared at Lambeth Police Court the day after her re-arrest. Three weeks later she appeared charged with the murder of Mrs Soames, and by the time she reached trial the charge read 'wilful murder of Mrs Soames and another'.

Attempts to control the availability of poisons in Britain had begun with various Acts of Parliament commencing with the Arsenic Act of 1851, but there remained various proprietary medicines which contained substances that were potentially poisonous if misused. The development of forensic medicine by the likes of Professor Alfred Swaine Taylor was also beginning to curtail this ancient means of murder. It was he who had examined the organs and the stomach contents of Mrs Soames after her body was exhumed, but he had to admit that, unsurprisingly, there were no signs of the vegetable drug colchicum in her body after all this time and to agree with Dr Whidborne that some inflammation to the bowel was possible without proof of poison.

Nonetheless, the circumstantial evidence was damning. The medical men also agreed that the victim's symptoms and rapid death were unlikely to have been as a result of the alleged pork pie culprit. Then there was the fact that Catherine Wilson had kept Mrs Soames's 'medicine' in her hands alone and had spread stories that she must have committed suicide after being let down by a man she had met on an omnibus – who had also bled her dry of money – and the various other murder accusations. She was found guilty and sentenced to death. Hers was the last public hanging of a woman in Britain and was attended by many thousands of spectators.

'The winter of 1862 was especially notable for garrotte robberies many of which were carried out with reckless brutality,' wrote Major Arthur Griffiths in his *Mysteries of Police and Crime* (Cassell,

Chief Inspector George Clarke, considered 'a "good sort" who was dependable (up to a point) and highly intelligent'

1898). These were partly due to the cessation of transportation and the large number of ticket-of-leave men[2] let loose on the capital. The thieves acted in pairs or more. The victim would be seized from behind and held in a choke hold, while an accomplice removed money, jewellery and even instruments from musicians returning home after a performance. On one occasion, Griffiths claimed, some miscreants intended to cut off a young lady's hair – which was long and fine and worth a considerable sum – but were disturbed before they could accomplish their task.

That same year, 1862, also saw the staging of another International Exhibition, held not in the Crystal Palace, which by now had been removed to Sydenham in south London, but in another specially erected building on the site in Kensington now occupied by the Science and Natural History Museums. Industry, technology and the arts from thirty-six counties were shown by 28,000 exhibitors. Their exhibits ranged from serious scientific machines such as Charles Babbage's analytical engine[3] and Bessemer's steel processors to decorative William Morris pottery.

Six million visitors attended between May and November. Again, also attracted were a great many pickpockets and thieves intent on stealing from exhibits and visitors alike. In turn they attracted the attentions of Detective Sergeants Tanner and Cole.

Tanner's notebook describes some of these arrests and his various duties at events where crowds gathered, from thanksgiving services in Westminster Abbey to the parade following the awarding of the Victoria Cross to Crimean War heroes in Hyde Park by Queen

The Penny Illustrated Paper *depicts a detective (who had covered himself in green baize 'like a statue') as he leaps out to catch a thief in the Austrian section of the International Exhibition in 1862*

Victoria. Refreshingly, he admits that not everything always went to his advantage. He was soundly kicked by a pickpocket whom he arrested on Derby Day and, at a fight 'got up between two toughs', one of the seconds, 'a pugilist . . . struck me on the nose and felled me to the ground insensible'.

One presumes he had a gentler time in his involvement with artists; these included a painter who wilfully damaged a picture belonging to Baroness Burdett Coutts; Raphael Monte, 'an artist and sculptor of great fame' (alas, not lasting) for fraudulent conversion of a marble bust, and an Italian artist who blackmailed a young lady sitter who had written him some indiscreet letters after falling in love with him.

In March 1864, Inspector Jonathan Whicher, last of the pioneer detectives, retired on pension, suffering from 'mental depression arising from congestion of the brain'. Inspector Stephen Thornton had died of apoplexy in 1861 while still in service. Frederick Williamson was promoted to inspector in his stead.

The following two or three years saw a flurry of new appointments, mostly of educated bilingual men, some of whom went directly into the branch on joining.

One of these was 27-year-old James Jacob Thomson, who had studied the new science of electricity, been an assistant secretary to an Indian prince, joined the Met in 1856, left to go to the Devon Constabulary six months later, then transferred to Hampshire. Not a steady work record, but he did speak French, Italian and Greek, having been born in the Middle East. Then there was the suave, smartly dressed Nathaniel Druscovitch, who was of Polish extraction and also fluent in several languages.

One of the oddest appointments was Edwin Coathupe, a 26-year-old surgeon who had been educated in Germany and studied medicine in Bristol.

These men were a far cry from the ex-labourers and butchers, such as Whicher and Smith, but two of the old-style men did gain entrance: ex-groom George Clarke and 24-year-old West Countryman

John Shore, who had already served two years in Bristol city police. Shore became known for his bad spelling, laboured reports, enormous physical strength and, according to two later branch chiefs, his unrivalled knowledge of 'the thieving fraternity' and remarkable memory for their names and faces. He and Clarke became the terror of race-course thieves and pickpockets.

Inspectors Williamson and Tanner were now the two senior men. The likeable Richard Tanner had come into the branch as a PC clerk after serving in uniform among the glitter, vice and corruption of 'C' or St James's Division. He was a favourite of Sir Richard Mayne and liked to 'keep a book' on the allocation of cases and the chances of promotion of his colleagues. He took to the work with great gusto, and one July evening in 1864 came the case which was to make his reputation.

15

And more . . .

Two young bank clerks entering a first-class railway carriage on the Highbury-bound North London Railway found the upholstery wet and sticky. On touching it their hands became red with blood. There was blood too on the door and its handle, on the silver-topped cane found under the seat and on the hat which lay on the floor.

The guard acted promptly. He locked the carriage door, asked the gentlemen for their names and addresses and telegraphed headquarters.

Ten minutes later the driver of a train heading in the opposite direction saw 'a dark mound' on the track ahead and just managed to stop his train within a few feet of the obstruction. The mound proved to be the body of a man. He was alive but unconscious and terribly battered about the head. In his pockets were four sovereigns, ten shillings and sixpence in silver, a silver snuff box and correspondence addressed to Thomas Briggs, Clapton Square, Hackney.

Identified as such by his son, who lived at the same address, Mr Briggs turned out to be the 69-year-old chief clerk at Robarts, Curtis and Co.'s bank in the City – the same establishment that employed the two young men who had raised the alarm. Mr Briggs junior also identified the walking stick and a small travelling bag. The hat he found a puzzle. His father always wore a tall silk topper made specially for him by Dignance, a high-class hatter in the City. This hat was stubby, oddly shaped and very much inferior in quality.

The fact that the victim still had money and valuables on him might have suggested that this was not a robbery murder, but what was missing was Mr Briggs's valuable gold watch.

The elderly bank clerk died without regaining consciousness and Britain had its first railway murder.

Inspector Richard Tanner was sent down from Scotland Yard and lost no time in having drawings of the unusual hat posted outside police and railway stations. A reward notice offering £100 for information joined them, and the bank and railway soon added another £100 each. Tanner also circulated pawnbrokers and jewellers with details of the watch and chain and sent men out visiting hatters.

Three days after the finding of the body a jeweller (by the curiously ominous name of Death) reported that the previous day a young foreign man (probably German) had asked him to value a gold watch-chain and exchange it for another. The son identified the swopped chain as belonging to his father. Unfortunately, the young man had stayed in the shadows of the shop so Mr Death's description of him was scant.

But Tanner was in luck when, a week later, a cab driver named Matthews came forward saying he had just learned about the crime and he recognized the name Death as being on a jewellers' box with which his daughter had been playing. It had been given to her by an acquaintance of his, a young German named Franz Muller who had been engaged to one of his daughters. Even more helpfully he recognized the description of the hat left at the scene as one he had acquired for Muller from Walker's – a firm on his cab route. What's more, he could give them Muller's address, and a photograph of him.

Alas, the bird had flown, as so many did then, across the Atlantic. But fortunately he had sent Mrs Blyth, his landlady, a letter posted just before he had left on the sailing ship *Victoria* four days earlier. Her mild-mannered, kind and affectionate lodger (who travelled to and from work on the North London line) had been talking about emigrating for at least two weeks, and on the day after the attack on Mr Briggs he was full of good spirits and told her he now had sufficient funds to do so.

There was no way of getting a message to the captain of the *Victoria* once she was at sea. But there was a faster vessel, the steam ship *City of Manchester*. Tanner boarded her armed with an extradition warrant and accompanied by Sergeant Clarke, Mr Death and Matthews the cabman. They arrived in New York nearly three weeks ahead of the *Victoria*. As usual, too much had been revealed to the press and New York became alive with excitement at the forthcoming confrontation, so much so that when the *Victoria* arrived sightseers began shouting out for 'Muller the murderer'. Fortunately he did not hear them.

He was identified by Mr Death and Mr Matthews and a hat and a watch similar to those belonging to Mr Briggs were found in his box. (The money for the passage had been obtained by a complex set of transactions with pawnbrokers.) Tanner charged Muller with the murder, but the extradition procedure became drawn out owing to anti-British feeling: there had been accusations that Britain aided the South in the American Civil War by running the North's shipping blockade and assisting raids on Northern vessels, and these, according to Muller's defence counsel, rendered the extradition treaty 'utterly inoperative'.

After a long rant on the subject, which drew cheers from the crowded room, he finally got around to challenging one aspect of the evidence by claiming that Muller's height (he was short) and general appearance did not tally with the description of either of the two men whom a belated witness had come forward to claim he had seen in the compartment with Mr Briggs.

But extradition was eventually allowed, and on 3 September the party set off back across the Atlantic on the steamship *Etna*. En route Muller was introduced to and enjoyed the books of Charles Dickens; he enjoyed the food, too, which he declared much better than that of a steerage passenger on the *Victoria*.

His arrival at Liverpool and in London was greeted with

extraordinary hysteria and the news that the German Legal Protection Society were coming forward to defend him.

The hat turned out to be a vital part of the chain of evidence. The hatters, Dignance, identified the one Muller had taken with him to America as the silk topper they had made for Mr Briggs, except that it was now an inch shorter. It had been neatly cut down by someone who could sew – and Muller was a tailor. Although several acquaintances claimed Muller was a good-natured and mild man it became evident that his was something of a split personality, for at times he could suddenly become overbearing, arrogant and rude. But like so many people at that time he was clearly frustrated by his own abject poverty.

Matthews the cabman was given a grilling by the defence counsel following a suspicion that he was somehow involved in the murder. But he had an alibi, so it was Muller alone who was found guilty and hanged. He persisted in claiming his innocence until the last minute, when he was claimed to have confessed by admitting, in German, 'I have done it.' Afterwards, 'Muller cut-downs' became all the rage.

While Muller was awaiting execution another young German was getting himself into trouble. (The influx of Germans into Britain was the result of economic failure following several disastrous harvests and political and religious intolerance in that country.) The intended ultimate destination of many German immigrants was the United States, but some of them remained in Britain and about half of the German incomers settled in London.

Early in the afternoon of Tuesday 8 November 1864, shipwright's apprentice Richard Harvey was out wildfowling with friends along the north side of the Thames between Victoria Dock and North Woolwich, to the east of London.

Richard ventured into some tall reeds to drive up the birds so his friends could shoot them, but he soon came running out, claiming there was a body in there. Further inspection did indeed reveal the headless body of a man, which had been partially eaten by rats.

Murder in the Railway Train.

Listen to my song, and I will not detain you
long,
And then I will tell you of what I've heard.
Of a murder that's been done, by some wicked
one,
And the place where it all occurred ;
Between Stepney and Bow they struck the
fatal blow,
To resist he tried all in vain,
Murdered by some prigs was poor Mr Briggs
Whilst riding in a railway train.

Muller is accused, at present we cannot refuse
To believe that he is the very one,
But all his actions, you see, have been so very
free,
Ever since the murder it was done ;
From his home he never went, but such a
happy time he spent,
He never looked troubled on the brain,
If he'd been the guilty man, he would have
hid all he can,
From the murder in the railway train.

Muller he did state that he was going to
emigrate
Long before this dreadful tragedy ;
He often used to talk, about travelling to
New York,
In the Victoria, that was going to sea.
Mr. Death, the jeweller, said, he was very
much afraid,
He might not know the same man again,
When he heard of the reward, he started out
abroad,
About the murder in the railway train.

If it's Muller, we can't deny, on the Cabman
keep your eye,
Remember what he said the other day,
That Muller a ticket sold for money, which
seems so very funny,
When he had no expenses for to pay.
They say his money he took, and his name
entered on the book,

Long before this tragedy he came ;
Like Muller's, the Cabman had a hat, and it
may be his, perhaps
That was found in the railway train.

Would a murderer have forgot, to have de-
stroyed the jeweller's box,
Or burnt up the sleeve of his coat,
Would he the chain ticket have sold, and
himself exposed so bold,
And to all his friends a letter wrote,
Before Muller went away, why did not the
cabman say,
And not give him so much start on the
main
If the cabman knew—it's very wrong—to
keep the secret up so long,
About the murder in the railway train.

When Muller does arrive, we shall not be
much surprised,
To hear that that's him on the trial ;
Give him time to repent, though he is not
innocent,
To hear the evidence give no denial.
Muller's got the watch, you see, so it proves
that he is guilty,
But like Townley don't prove that he's
insane
For if it should be him, on the gallows let
him swing,
For the murder on the railway train.

Now Muller's caught at last, tho' he's been
so very fast,
And on him they found the watch and hat,
Tho' across the ocean he did roam, he had
better stayed at home,
And hid himself in some little crack,
Tho' he pleads his innocence, but that is all
nonsense,
For they'll hang him as sure as he's a man,
For he got up to his rigs, and murdered Mr.
Briggs
While riding in a railway train.

London : Printed for the Vendors.

Crude verses about Britain's first railway murder cast suspicion
on the cab driver as well as the accused Franz Muller

He was clad in black cloth trousers and Wellington boots but only
the remnants of his shirt clung around his arm. In his pockets they
found a farthing and a scrap of paper on which some German words
were written.

The young men found a policeman and together they searched for but were unable to locate the missing head. The body was taken to the nearby Graving Dock Tavern where, newspapers later estimated, such was the extraordinary excitement created by the discovery that four thousand people turned up that evening to view it.

By the following day, *The Times* revealed, rumours and speculation abounded that the victim

was a foreign seafaring man recently arrived by one of the Hamburg vessels at Victoria Docks; that he had attended a pigeon shooting match held in the neighbourhood a few days ago, with notes and cash in his pocket, and that he was drugged, lured away, and despoiled of all he had. Another rumour is that he was a German employed in the district, and that he fell sacrifice to some quarrel with others among whom he lived.

Most of the spectators gathered that first evening were allowed to see the body in the hope that, despite the lack of the head, someone might recognize the man or his scant clothing.

And someone did. Shoemaker Heinrich Zutch recognized the Wellington boots. They were of a German make, the left sole was worn and, Zutch reported, the wearer had asked him if he might be able to repair them. Although the shoemaker did not know the owner's name he did know that he had arrived from Hamburg about five weeks earlier and had been lodging two doors from him with the unemployed sugar-baker[1] Karl Kohl.

He had last seen the man the previous Thursday when he had left the house with Kohl. Later that day Kohl had popped in to say he had lost his companion in the Commercial Road after he had gone into a sugar-baker's to ask about work. When he came out, the young man had gone.

The victim's name turned out to be Theodore Christian Fuhrop, whom everybody called John. John was a good-looking young man who dressed well in good clothes and had possessed several sovereigns, a silver watch, a gold chain and a gold ring

The newly married 26-year-old Ferdinand Edward Karl Kohl was short, thick-set, florid-faced and so hard up he had been constantly borrowing money and pawning his own and his wife's clothes.

When he had last seen him, Kohl declared, John had had £4 10s on him which he said he might spend on a girl. If he did so he would have nothing left and in that case, Kohl said, he would have turned him out. But Kohl also kept remarking that obviously John was gone and not coming back – which gave them the right to break into his box.

Superintendent Howie of 'K' Division thought this all very suspicious. Kohl and his wife were arrested and taken to Plaistow Police Station where they were joined by Detective Inspector George Clarke – promoted since his trip to the USA pursuing Muller.

The head was found the next day, buried in the mud about a foot down close to where the body had been. Clearly, it had been removed to prevent identification, but the murderer had been particularly unlucky. The reed bank was a lonely spot where few people ventured and at high tide became swamped with water which could easily have swept away the body and head when the tide receded.

A formidable case was soon built against Kohl for what was now known as 'the Murder in Plaistow Marshes'. Two witnesses had seen him and John out near the reed bank on the morning of the day John went missing, When Kohl got home that day he had been covered in pale mud from, he claimed, hitching a ride in a butcher's cart. But it was the kind of mud seen only by the river bank and it had been dry in town that day.

Kohl had twice been seen out by the reeds again a few days later (the head was thought to have been removed and buried some time after the death). Employees from the sugar-bakery in Commercial Road said he had never called there and Clarke proved that he had pawned what appeared to be John's clothes, ring and watch. One of his lodgers had loaned Kohl an axe, which the surgeon thought could be the murder weapon, and he had returned it after painting part of the shaft red (so the handle would fit better, he claimed). The police thought it was to hide the traces of blood which Dr Letheby had found there and on his clothes. Even more damning, shortly after John's disappearance the desperately poor Kohl was seen to be in possession of several sovereigns.

What the police did not have was a precise identification of the body and John's possessions, nor had they been able to notify next of kin. Kohl had put it about that John and he had been brought up together – practically as brothers. But he quickly admitted to police that he had met the trusting young man (who had very little grasp of English) on the boat when returning from a visit to Hamburg.

Someone needed to go there and Williamson thought it should be Detective Inspector George Clarke. By the tone of his report one gets the feeling that Superintendent Howie was not too pleased about handing over the victim's property to Clarke.

It was a busy trip taking ten days. In Hamburg John's brother identified the many possessions, and Clarke brought him back as a witness after going on to Spletau to check on Kohl's criminal record, which turned out to be 'generally bad'. He had done time for stealing from brother soldiers and absconded to England to avoid punishment for another offence. As usual, the claiming of his expenses on his return proved Clarke's most difficult task.

Kohl took advantage of his right to a jury composed half of foreigners and half of Englishmen but that did not save him. Kohl's young wife was released but Kohl was found guilty and executed.

Inspector Tanner's next big case after the Muller murder was a much sadder affair. It came to light on 10 August 1865, when Superintendent Searle of 'E' Division reported that a triple murder had been committed at the Star Coffee House, Red Lion Square, Holborn. Three little boys aged ten, eight and six had been found dead in bed – apparently poisoned.

They had been brought to the coffee house two nights previously by a man aged about thirty-five. He stayed with them on the first night but on the second he had merely seen them to bed, promising to return the following morning. He had not returned and the boys had not appeared for their breakfast. When their rooms were unlocked they were found dead but 'very placid as if they had not struggled'. The youngest, reported Superintendent Searle, had a penny in his groin 'no doubt given him by his murderer'.

There was no clue as to the identity of either the man or the children. His description was quickly circulated as being about five feet seven inches in height with a dark complexion and hair, dark grey eyes, no whiskers but a beard of several days' growth. His dark clothes were 'much worn' and included a buttoned-up waistcoat and a black and shabby scarf – 'no pin'.

Enquiries were initiated at coffee and lodging houses and aboard passenger ships. Inspector Tanner was busy taking descriptions of the boys when 64-year-old schoolmaster Mr Saltwood White appeared and saved him the trouble. They were his sons, he said, or at least he was 'the reputed father'. His second and much younger wife had left him several years earlier to go off with her paramour, Ernest Southey, 'a billiard marker'.[2]

His boys had been returned to him, but his school had not been doing too well lately and when Southey offered to take them off his hands so they could go with their mother to a new life in Australia, he had consented. They had been handed over to Southey two days earlier, just around the corner, by White's eldest son from his first large family – White said he couldn't bring himself to do it.

Tanner hastened back to the Yard to see Inspectors Williamson and Thomson, who would be able to identify Southey and supply further descriptive details. The man was no stranger to them nor to the Commissioner, Sir Richard Mayne. Southey had been warning them for some time that he would do something terrible.

Billiards was a popular game with the upper classes, and through his expertise Southey had mingled with them and made a lot of money playing for high stakes. On one occasion, he claimed, he won a wager with the Honourable Dudley Ward which should have netted him £1,172, but alas – Southey alleged – Dudley Ward proved to be honourable in name only and merely handed Southey a memo of the debt, promising to pay up the following day, then left the country.

Following this setback Southey's fortunes faded fast. Mrs White had tried but failed to support them by running a school and the boys had to be sent back to their father. At one stage she went to see their debtor's wealthy brother, Lord Dudley, but he threw her out. She brought a summons against him for assault, but the magistrates dismissed the case after Lord Dudley referred to her as a prostitute.

Southey then wrote to Earl Russell, the Foreign Secretary (who as Lord John Russell had been Home Secretary and was the nephew of the murdered Lord William Russell), telling him he had information to impart. Detective Inspector Thomson was sent down to Putney to see Southey, probably to find out how dangerous he seemed to be.

He saw a scene of dreadful poverty. The pair had been without heating, food and adequate clothing for some time, Thomson reported, and now, owing seven weeks' rent, faced the prospect of losing the roof over their heads. He found Southey, who was from a respectable family, 'had the appearance of a well-educated person' but had not so much information to impart as grievances to be aired. The 'want of ordinary necessities of life' had indeed, Thomson noted, brought the couple to the borders of insanity, but in his opinion Earl Russell could relax. The only people they seemed likely to harm were themselves.

On Christmas Day Thomson handed them a gift from Earl Russell – a sovereign, for which they were deeply grateful, as well they might be. The weekly wage of most constables at that time was exactly that amount.

On 30 December Southey turned up at Scotland Yard where he saw the now ageing and exhausted Mayne. He also wrote another long letter to Earl Russell, telling his tale again and informing him that the dread means of escaping their ruined and hopeless existence had already been purchased.

The 72-year-old Foreign Secretary had become one of Queen Victoria's 'two terrible old men' – the other was her prime minister, Lord Palmerston. Russell now exercised the same principle he employed regarding the American Civil War and the long-running territory dispute known as the Schleswig-Holstein Question: that of non-intervention. And there the matter rested. For the moment.

Southey re-entered Mayne's life in April 1865, when the Hon. Dudley Ward passed Mayne a letter from Southey with the comment 'I do not consider Mr E.W. Southey is in his right mind, or ought to be at large.'

Sir Richard scribbled his reply on the back of an envelope, saying that Southey's conduct had been enquired into by the police, who had found there were no grounds for proceedings against him either for any legal offences 'or confinement as a lunatic'. (Mayne may have also been distracted by the intensive flak being fired at police over the complicated Pellizzoni or Saffron Hill Affair. During a pub brawl between Italian and English workmen, one of the Italians had pulled a knife and stabbed three Englishmen, one of whom died. As with the Franz case, there was suspicion that Pellizzoni's countrymen may have deliberately confused the evidence, resulting in acquittal for one man and a short sentence for another.)

In mid-May Southey began writing to and calling upon other prominent persons, such as the Duke of Richmond and Tory MP and writer Sir Edward Bulmer Lytton. Concerned about his 'dark insinuations about some dreadful deed which might be averted' and more direct ones of shooting a nobleman and 'murdering his whole family of eight persons', they forwarded the matter to the Commissioner, who placated them as well.

But Southey was nothing if not determined. He even tricked his way into the presence of Prime Minister Palmerston while he was dressing for dinner, saying he was a messenger from Sir Richard

Mayne. Palmerston felt that the nobleman Southey referred to *and* Southey's own family should be put under protection.

Mayne saw Southey and gave him a stern warning. Next time he surfaced, police prevented Southey handing out letters to the Duke of Richmond and the Earl of Westmorland as they entered the peers' entrance at the House of Lords. Then he dropped out of sight.

Such people, not quite mad but not quite sane, teetering on the brink, full of threats and plots, were and still are a continuing police problem. Judging when it is safe to send them on their way or have them deemed to be of unsound mind and locked up is extremely difficult. The Commissioner, who found it impossible to delegate, had other problems on his mind and, since Southey had never deviated from his major line of complaint, may have believed the grievance was genuine and had some sympathy.

In August came the finding of the boys' bodies, the catalyst for which had been something the Commissioner could not have anticipated. Six weeks earlier Mrs White had left Southey, taking her daughter Annie with her. Consequently, when last seen he had been in great distress.

A notice offering £100 reward for Southey's capture was sent out. But it was too late. When Tanner filed an updated Detective Officer's Special Report the following day he was obliged to add a melancholy postscript: 'A telegram has just been received stating that "Southey" is in custody at Ramsgate having murdered Mrs White and the little girl alluded to.'

Tanner hastened to Ramsgate, where he discovered that as well as altering his appearance with the aid of a false beard and moustache Southey had drastically altered his *modus operandi*. No gentle poison for the females but sudden and violent death at close range with bullets to the head from a new five-barrelled revolver.

There was to be one final twist to this terrible tale. The Yard received a report that in fact a few weeks earlier a woman by the name of White, whose husband was a schoolmaster in Holborn, had left a little girl in the care of a Mrs Petty at 2 Cornelia Cottages, Lavender Road, Battersea – before she left for Australia.

It was Inspector Thomson, in at the start of the affair six months earlier, to whom the final surprise was to be revealed. He hurried over to Battersea where he saw Mrs Petty and Annie Elizabeth White, 'an exceedingly intelligent little girl of about seven years of age'. Her mother, Mrs White, had indeed left for Melbourne more than two weeks earlier, promising her daughter an early reunion. Southey had turned up ten days later and tried to take Annie Elizabeth away but Mrs Petty resisted him and he had left, saying 'something very dreadful would soon happen'.

So Mrs White had gone to Australia and her daughter Annie Elizabeth was safe in Battersea with Mrs Petty. Who, then, were the dead woman and child at Ramsgate?

They were his first wife, Mary Forward (Forward being Southey's real name) and eight-year-old daughter Emily, whom he had left several years earlier to go off with Mrs White.

16

'Quite a Road murder'

Shropshire's police committee begrudged every penny spent on their tiny force and were proud that their county police rate, at less than a penny in the pound, was the lowest in the land. They got their come-uppance in 1857 when the Home Office refused them the annual grant that had become available under the provisions of a new County and Borough Police Act because, the Inspector of

© West Mercia Constabulary

Shropshire Constabulary, 1868. In 1866 Inspector Tanner was called in to help the force solve the Duddlewick murder mystery

Constabulary reported, the force was 'inefficient in numbers'. They hurriedly took on another twenty-six men but declined to act on the suggestion that they employ a detective officer to handle the more serious crimes, despite the fact that the detection rate of this rural force was one of the lowest in the country. They could, if needed, the committee declared, always borrow a detective from London or elsewhere.

Thus it was that at 10 a.m. on Sunday 21 January 1866, Detective Inspector Richard Tanner left London en route for Duddlewick near Bridgnorth to give assistance in solving the mystery of the murder of 18-year-old Edward Edwards. Shropshire's first chief constable in 1840 had been Captain Dawson Mayne, Sir Richard's brother. He retired in 1859 and the force was now led by Chief Constable Lieutenant-Colonel Edward Burgoyne Cureton, veteran of the Crimea and Kaffir wars, who professed himself delighted that he was being sent 'an officer of such high repute'. However, he resigned that same month after only fifteen months in the post.

This case must have given Tanner a nasty feeling of _déjà vu_. There were so many similarities to the Constance Kent case and he would have been aware that the locals and the Shropshire police officers would not be quite so thrilled by his arrival as their chief claimed to be.

Duddlewick may sound like a children's book village but the murder which had taken place in that peaceful hamlet was a particularly terrible one. Edward Edwards was an orphan living with his uncle John Meredith, a farmer and miller. On the morning of Sunday 14 January at about 8 a.m. the boy had gone down to his uncle's mill, set two hundred yards below the farm, to feed some pigs and a horse. He was not seen again until 4 p.m. when a search party found him in the mill. He was unconscious, had twenty dreadful wounds to his head, one of them causing a piece of bone to be driven into the protruding brain, and numerous defensive injuries to his hands. The weapons used had probably been a heavy stick and a sharp-edged blacksmith's punch found at the horrific, bloodstained scene, where the boy had obviously put up tremendous resistance. He died the following morning without regaining consciousness.

The suspicions of the Shropshire Constabulary had quite quickly focused on farm labourer James Childe, who had been without money on the Saturday before the murder but had arrived at a Bridgnorth public house not short of money the following day. Robbery was thought to be the motive because the uncle claimed he had not yet received the mill's weekly takings. Moreover, Childe's white linen 'slop' or smock was bloodstained and, on being quizzed about this by the observant landlord, he claimed he had been in a fight.

The next day Childe bought some moleskin trousers and got rid of those he had been wearing. When the other pub customers began discussing the sensational crime Childe had shown no interest but had upped and left, saying he was off on the road to the Black Country[1] to look for work. The landlord told the Bridgnorth police his suspicions and a Sergeant Cox, 'wearing private clothes', set off in hot pursuit.

He found that his quarry had stopped at every public house en route to Wolverhampton, and it was in one that he arrested Childe on the Tuesday morning. However, Childe had an alibi. Witnesses came forward to say that on the morning in question he had been sleeping off the drink in a pub barn eight miles from the mill. The public and police, who were struggling to enforce the stringent new livestock movement regulations brought in to help stem the cattle plague raging through the country, lost interest in Childe.

Of course, by the time Tanner arrived the trail was cold, the story had been much gone over and elaborated on, alibis were set in stone and local partisanships established. He was soon writing to Sir Richard that he found himself thwarted by the local coroner, who was friends with vital witnesses.

Another familiar problem was the size and complexity of the Meredith household. Resident were Meredith's niece Mary, aged twenty-one, servant Elizabeth Harris, aged twenty-five, her brother Samuel, aged fourteen, and mill assistant Timothy Fletcher, aged eighteen. Non-resident servants and farm workers were in and out all the time and always referred to Meredith as 'my master'.

Tanner could find no motive for anyone to want to kill Edward.

> He was a poor boy (an orphan) solely dependent on his uncle John Meredith since seven years old. Was dressed in cord trousers and old clothes and not likely to attract the attention of any tramp, or stranger as being worth robbing. He was not entitled to any property, neither was it known that the deceased had quarrelled with any person as would be likely to commit such a crime. Duddlewick is a very small village and a stranger would almost sure to have been observed on the morning in question but none was seen.

As had Whicher, he therefore turned his attention to the victim's household and his suspicions were soon roused by the boy's uncle, John Meredith. He came to this conclusion, he wrote to Sir Richard Mayne, from Meredith's manner when he spoke to him on the case and his conduct on the day of the murder.

The farmer and mill-owner had risen at about nine o'clock, had his breakfast, then gone out for half an hour. One his return Mary Meredith had enquired if 'Ted' was coming home for his breakfast.

'I don't know,' he replied. 'I have been down to the mill but I cannot see anything of him. Give me my coat and vest, and a cup of ale; I shall go to church.'

Every Sunday morning the deceased brought the books from the mill to Meredith at the house so they could be settled before church. Yet now he went off without expressing any anxiety about this, and if he had been to the mill he must have seen the boy because he was found locked in the mill with the key in its usual place – above the door. On John's return from church at 1 p.m. the servant Elizabeth expressed uneasiness that Edward had not been back for breakfast and was now not back for dinner either (dinner could be at midday then), something that had never happened before. The uncle went out, was gone about half an hour and returned saying he had been to the mill and could see no sign of him.

'. . . and adds this', wrote Tanner, '(in my opinion) extraordinary remark, "but as the wind is blowing high he might have fell into the brook but we may as well have dinner and then, I will get William Dorrel (a neighbour) to go with me, and see if we can *track his footsteps*"' (Tanner's emphasis).

After dinner Meredith asked for a cup of ale, smoked his pipe for nearly an hour and diverted Dorrel's attention from the mill to the brook before finally going to the mill, where they found Edward 'insensible and nearly dead'.

Tanner had learned that there had been friction between the boy and his uncle due to the careless way the lad did the books, and this had led to frequent quarrels.

> My theory of the case is that on the Sunday morning in
> question the uncle, who is passionate, went to the mill, saw
> some further neglect in the books, probably struck him with
> a stick which was found broken alongside the deceased then
> finding perhaps that he had gone too far (as the deceased
> was also known to be very passionate and might have
> threatened proceedings) then he lost all control of himself
> and murdered the lad.

The difficulty was to prove all this. There had been bloody fingerprints on the mill stairs but there was no way of proving whose these were.

Meredith's clothes were taken to London 'for analysis'. Inspector Thomson suggested the well-known analytical chemist Dr Letheby for the task but Mayne consulted with an expert friend who recommended Professor Alfred Swaine Taylor, despite his reputation having suffered recently through that (admitted) mistake when testing for arsenic in another case.

The clothes were not obtained from the suspect until five days after the murder and then in quite a casual manner, allowing him to offer only what he had been wearing that day. Fortunately, Shropshire's Sergeants Cox and Christie had independently picked up a pair of bloodstained trousers from his bedside, although Meredith claimed the more than twenty spots on them had occurred when he helped carry the dying boy from the mill. The sergeants also retrieved a second overcoat, which appeared to have a great many blood spots on it, from a peg in the lobby.

'Surely you can't detect blood after it's washed?' Meredith had asked. (The trousers had been sponged.)

'We can,' Sergeant Cox had replied.

At least the inquest was moved from Meredith's farm, where it had begun, to the Cock Inn in Stottesden, the nearest village, but the coroner refused to comply with Tanner's request, supported by the magistrates, that very little evidence be taken and that the inquest soon be adjourned. Solicitor Mr R.O. Backhouse had been keeping a watching brief on behalf of the police but now changed sides. 'I told the police that if a certain course were pursued, I should appear on behalf of Mr Meredith and the family,' he told the coroner. And very useful his inside knowledge must have been to the accused.

He proceeded to question evidence, virtually cross-examine witnesses and correct the coroner. He even tried to put words into the mouths of witnesses and introduced another possible suspect, a boy named Thomas Childe (a common local surname) who had left Meredith's employ because he was suffering from a skin disease. Meanwhile, the police struggled on unrepresented, almost exactly mirroring the police court situation in the Road Hill House murder.

Tanner wrote disconsolately to Sir Richard, saying that he was sure he was on the right track and that the magistrates would issue a warrant for the arrest of Meredith, but the coroner (who commented that it was 'quite a Road murder') had continued thwarting him and he feared his witnesses had been tampered with.

But Meredith was arrested. *The Shrewsbury Chronicle* reported that Detective Tanner regretted that he had not been sent for earlier and that the local police had been going to arrest Mr Meredith before he came. They went over all the police case, ending up giving Meredith a splendid character reference. He was well known to be of a kind, hospitable and charitable disposition. He had been extremely fond of Edward, having cherished him from the age of six, and they were assured that, in the spirit of that affection, he had left the mill to his deceased nephew.

Tanner, they claimed, though recommending the arrest did not feel the evidence at present forthcoming was sufficient. 'Mystery, he believes, will long hang over this even as it hung over the Road murder.'

The truth was, Tanner obviously wanted out and thought this a good moment to go. 'The magistrates and also Col. Cureton all consider the prisoner to be guilty,' he advised Sir Richard Mayne, 'but see the difficulty of getting any evidence.'

Left to their own devices the Shropshire men did their best. At the resumed police court hearing Sergeant Cox caused a sensation by pointing out that the bloodstains on Meredith's trousers 'corresponded' with those on the mill walls (in other words, one presumes they were what we now regard as spatter stains) and that others who carried the body out had no bloodstains on them.

The defence counsel declared the evidence to be so weak and shadowy that he was sure the magistrates would agree that another hearing was unnecessary. They agreed and discharged the prisoner, to applause from the public gallery.

The inquest was resumed, and even *The Shropshire Chronicle* noticed that the unrepresented police were at a great disadvantage. Apparently Shropshire's civil authorities felt they had no appropriate funds for lawyers, which was also the reason Professor Taylor had not appeared at the police court. Despite objections from Meredith's solicitor and jurors who did not want to spend another market day in court, the inquest was adjourned – to a non-market day. Somehow the expenses were found for Professor Taylor's attendance and for the police to be represented. The coroner, doubtless now aware of criticisms about his disgraceful rolling over for defence counsel Backhouse, now assumed proper control.

Alas, Professor Taylor had to admit that there was no way 'in the present state of science' of telling whether the bloodstains were animal or human. The blood of a hare or a rabbit was very similar. But he did say that the stains on the trousers were caused by blood falling or dropping on them and those on the shirt by sprinkling in liquid state, which was in itself very pertinent – or would have been, had he been able to prove the blood was human.

A new witness, a journeyman miller who had done some work for Meredith since the murder, said that he had noticed that the farmer always grasped the stairs with his left hand as he was climbing them, his hand going to exactly the same spot where the bloody finger-marks were found. He also claimed that Meredith had told him that Edward had been an 'artful young dog' who would have resisted as long as he was able to rise, and that he had given him a graphic account of how the boy might have defended himself.

Edward's half-brother, a Bridgnorth butcher, also recalled how Meredith had talked him through how the murder must have played out:

> Here it commenced . . . they had a deuce of a fight
> here . . . He knocked him down here and then he
> knocked him against here; here is blood and hair, you
> see . . . He caught hold of the chains (for lifting flour
> bags) . . . Here he laid on him with a stick to make him
> loose causing the marks on his hands . . .

This chilling soliloquy had obviously become Meredith's dreadful party piece.

Nonetheless, the inquest jury brought in a verdict of murder by a person or persons unknown and the case was over. Cureton assured Sir Richard Mayne that Tanner had done his best to clear up the mystery and 'gave every satisfaction to the magistrates by his reports and advice'.

More to the point, he had escaped being burnt at the stake like Whicher.

By then, of course, Whicher had been vindicated when on 25 April 1865 Constance Kent turned up at Bow Street Police Court to confess to the murder of her stepbrother Francis Saville Kent.

Since the crime five years earlier she had been living in a French convent and, later, at a religious retreat in Brighton, where she had had time to contemplate her deeds. Williamson was called to take her confession, which must have been poignant for this man who had been deeply upset by the sad end to his mentor's career. At her trial Whicher is reported to have been a dignified though infirm figure.

Like Inspector Field, he was soon to be immortalized in print – as Sergeant Cuff in *The Moonstone* by Wilkie Collins, which was published in 1860. Cuff emerges on the scene, much trumpeted, a quarter of the way through, but dominates the narrative for another hundred pages. Although Dickens denied that Field was Bucket, there is no doubt that Whicher's experiences at Road influenced the writing of *The Moonstone*.

The plot revolves not around a murder but around the theft of a diamond and the consequences of that act, but the setting is a large country house teeming with family, servants and guests, all suspects. Pivotal to the plot are a teenage girl (the daughter of the house, whom Cuff soon suspects), the futile search for a nightdress (stained with paint rather than blood) and a bumbling provincial policeman. The case, as with the original, ends inconclusively, Cuff being sure the girl is the guilty party while she and her family successfully obstruct his proving this. The mystery is solved after Cuff is happily retired – and it proves not to be the girl after all. Cuff happily admits to his previous error, saying that it is only in books that officers of the detective force 'are superior to the weakness of making a mistake'.

What Inspector Whicher thought of all this is not on record, but one presumes it gave him some comfort. According to Major Griffiths in his *Mysteries of Police and Crime*, Whicher retired and died of a broken heart. This is not strictly true. In fact, he went on to be employed as a private detective for sixteen years, doing much good work, particularly on the famous Tichborne Claimant case.

In his *Memories of Famous Trials* (Sisley's, 1907) Evelyn Burnaby claimed a similar fate for Constance Kent when she was released after serving twenty years. After quoting the judge, Chief Baron Pollock, who predicted that Constance would be sent to the colonies and would make a good marriage, he then wrote: 'That prediction was, of course, not realized. I believe she died the very same year that she was liberated.'

In fact, she went to Australia under an assumed name with her brother, and died there soon after her hundredth birthday.

In April 1868, the Yard was consulted on what the *Warrington Guardian* termed a 'Shocking Accident'. This was the death of the widowed Mrs Brigham, who lived in Foxley Hall in Lymm near Warrington, Cheshire, caused when the pistol her son-in-law, Henri Perrau, was showing her went off.

Perrau's story had clearly not convinced someone in Cheshire so Williamson sent up one of his shrewdest men, Inspector George Clarke. Clarke arrived two weeks after the event and interviewed the household, which numbered seven: Mr and Mrs Perrau, her maid, the cook, the housemaid, the general maid and the coachman.

Henri Perrau was a Frenchman who had met Mrs Brigham and her daughter Henrietta when they had all stayed at the Langham Hotel in London the previous year. 'The acquaintance resulted in an engagement,' wrote Clarke – and a wedding in Paris at Christmas. Since then the pair had been travelling in Europe but had returned home to Foxley Hall only three weeks before the tragedy.

Perrau explained that Mrs Brigham had been sitting by the fire in the breakfast room reading a letter while he was cleaning his pistol.

'How is it managed?' she asked, and then, 'How is it loaded?' He showed her, and she took the gun and pulled the trigger four or five times, then handed it back to him 'with her left hand, the muzzle being towards her'. It went off and the bullet struck her on the left temple, killing her instantly.

The cook agreed about where they had been and what they were doing when she had brought in breakfast earlier, and claimed that the pair were 'on most friendly terms'. The trustees of Mrs Brigham's will (worth £40,000) and a solicitor acting for two cousins were less sanguine. As Clarke noted, 'They informed me that the whole of the property was left to *Madame Perrau on the death of her mother, who was the only existing obstacle to Mons*. *Perrau having absolute control over the property* – Madame Perrau being of weak intellect, and they suggest that by Mrs Brigham's death this obstacle would be removed.'

However, given that the 'very respectable' jury had returned a verdict of accidental death despite a gunsmith saying that in his opinion the pistol could not have been fired off in that manner (but, alas, refusing to swear that it could not), 'there is no matter at present', Clarke wrote, 'upon which further enquiry can be made except as to the antecedents of Monsr. Perrau'.

It was a case which was to come back and bite Clarke eight years later.

17

Travelling men

Sometimes the Yard detectives were called in to help solve crimes other than murders. Crimes such as the Great Stamp Office Robbery at Manchester.

Manchester police had their own detective superintendent, who may not have been pleased when the Chairman of the Board of Inland Revenue requested that Scotland Yard investigate the theft of £10,000 worth of stamps and money from their Manchester office. When Inspector Thomson arrived, Detective Superintendent Maybury informed him that there was no further evidence to be found, but Thomson insisted on examining the scene for himself.

He and Maybury deduced that the thieves must have gained entrance to the Stamp Office through the cellar wall of the adjacent warehouse, to which they had gained access through the floor of the offices above. Such a complex job involving a huge safe would have taken them a lot of time and effort and, Thomson claimed, in his experience thieves engaged in such big operations tended to suffer from looseness of the bowels. One can imagine Superintendent Maybury's bemusement when the man from the Yard set about looking for 'deposits' which might give them an idea how many men were involved. He found three, and also a page from a *Wright's Racing Calendar* for the month of May. Thomson also noted that two eggs had been broken on the outside steps but could make nothing of that.

Superintendent Maybury told Thomson about four possible

local suspects who he thought were currently living in London, and Thomson advised him on further local enquiries he should make to track down those who had been coming and going near the premises at the suspected time.

Back in London he persuaded Mayne to allow him to take the unusual step of forming a small team of divisional men who had shown some aptitude for detective work, and set them to search for the suspects Maybury had mentioned and to discover what the word on the street was about the robbery. Eventually they came back with the information that the robbers could not be the men mentioned by Maybury but were in fact two Londoners known as 'the Countrymen': brothers Tom and Bill Douglas. A little later the name Gleeson also came up. None of these men could be found so it was stalemate until 'a gentlemanly looking man' named Charles Batt presented a soiled twenty-shilling stamp at Somerset House, claiming that it had accidentally been spoiled.

Suspicions were aroused. Batt was arrested and charged with being in possession of stolen property. He turned out to be a returned convict, and one of the Manchester Stamp Office clerks identified him as having been hanging around at the time of the break-in.

Thomson got two of his team to keep watch when Batt appeared at police court the following day to see whether any of his friends turned up. There was no sign of any friends in court, but as Batt was being ushered into the prison van a one-legged man in the crowd surreptitiously passed him a screw of paper containing tobacco. The man turned out to be Richard Shaw, also known as Peg Leg Dick, who had lost his leg following an attempted prison escape.

Thomson approached Shaw and found him to be bitter because he was being treated as a has-been. He agreed to be an informant – as long as he was not obliged to give evidence in court.

Shaw proved to be the most trying man Thomson had ever met, as he related in his report to a Detective Police (Departmental) Commission in 1868: 'he was not truthful, he was seldom sober; he was never otherwise than filthy; and he persecuted me day and

The Hours of the Day & Night in London, George Augustus Sala (1859)

*There were opportunities to slip comforts to the convicted
as they were being loaded onto the prison van*

night by coming to my house, and even when I was not at home he
would lie dead drunk upon the doorstep, saying that he should be
sure to meet me at some time by doing so.'

And, of course, he was a constant drain on Thomson's purse.

Shaw told Thomson that the Countrymen were the smartest men
in England. Tom Douglas was 'a perfect gentleman', the owner of a
number of racehorses, frequenter of race meetings and on terms of
intimacy with many persons of distinction. His easy-going and more
retiring brother Bill was a civil engineer and a man of great muscular
strength. Shaw swore he had heard them and a man named Leeson
planning the robbery.

Thomson and Detective Sergeant Thomas finally caught up with
Tom and Bill at Doncaster Races and, taking a chance, arrested them

even though they still had very little evidence against them. Then they dashed back to London and the Islington homes of the brothers, where they found house-breaking implements and a number of *Wright's Racing Calendars* – with the month of May missing. They seized some of the proceeds of the robbery and pressured Peg Leg into giving evidence.

Despite, claimed Thomson, their using 'every trick and artifice' and 'even tampering with witnesses' the four men were found guilty. Batt received eight years' penal servitude and Leeson and the two Douglas brothers fifteen years each. After conviction they made overtures to Mr Howard, the Distributor of Stamps at Manchester, telling him that they had heard that no more convicts were being sent to Australia (which, one would imagine, would have pleased them) but if he would use his influence to get them sent there they would return the rest of the stolen property. The bargain was accepted.

Some time later Tom's wife approached Thomson. She told him that her husband had behaved himself in Australia, had been released and was doing very well. She wanted to take the family out to join him. Would he swear to the Emigration Commissioners that she was Tom's wife? He did.

Another unexpected outcome occurred when Superintendent Maybury retired: it was suggested to Thomson that he should apply for the post of detective superintendent and deputy chief constable at Manchester, but he preferred to stay in London. However, he told Coathupe (who had gone back to being a surgeon because he was tired of working for nothing as a detective) about the offer, and Coathupe applied and was accepted. Later he went on to become the chief constable of Bristol, his home city.

As for the eggs on the doorstep, Bill Douglas explained to Thomson that a group of lads and lasses had been congregating there to laugh and chat. They realized it would be dangerous if youngsters saw them coming and going – so they dropped the eggs to stop them sitting down. Some things you can never anticipate.

'We left Holborn Viaduct Station en route for Dover by the 7.35 a.m. train,' wrote Inspector Moser in *Stories from Scotland Yard* (George Routledge, 1890). He was describing how he escorted a French youth to Calais. This 'poor wretch' had stolen 5,000 francs from his Parisian employers, a firm of artificial flower makers, in revenge for the cruel way they had treated him. He had fled to Newhaven via Dieppe, and once across the Channel had attempted suicide by throwing himself off the cliffs but had ended up only with a severe wound under his chin.

Moser tracked the youth down and when he had recuperated took him before Bow Street magistrates on an extradition warrant; however, when going to his cell to collect him he found the lad hanging by a handkerchief tied through the ventilation holes. He was resuscitated but his wound had re-opened and he was sent back to hospital. Eventually, however, Moser and the boy left for Calais:

When on the journey, partaking of some refreshment, hard boiled eggs and sandwiches (I had obtained some coffee at the railway station), I asked my co-traveller whether he felt hungry, and would accept an egg. He took one, which of course was shelled, and then, to my utter astonishment, I saw him put the whole of it into his mouth at once. I first thought that it was simply ravenous hunger that made him do this, but soon I realised the exact position of affairs when I found that he was choking; then it struck me that it was another attempt on his part to do away with himself, which surmise proved correct. I had the greatest trouble to make him disgorge the egg, for he positively refused; and it was not until I used considerable personal violence by hitting him on the back of his neck, that a portion of the egg dropped out of his mouth.

Inspector Moser was right in presuming that had the lad been successful all the blame would have all been laid at his door 'and disinterested kindness would have received another serious check'.

Further extradition treaties had increased the number of overseas escort duties allotted to the Scotland Yard detectives, and although most of the difficulties regarding which crimes qualified had been ironed out, the duties themselves still had their problems and perils.

That suicide attempt was one of the rather more bizarre. Not so amusing was an extradition incident involving Inspector George Greenham. Through his own persistence and determination Greenham had ended up with two prisoners to escort back from Jersey rather than just one. He borrowed a Jersey policeman to help with the guarding, but this man turned out to be too seasick to be of any assistance. While Greenham tried to juggle his two charges, one of them, a Frenchman wanted for arson, robbery and attempted murder, hanged himself from a hat peg in his cabin. Desperate efforts to revive him failed. It was, Greenham said later, one of the most disagreeable experiences of his life.

The physical risk to officers themselves when escorting prisoners long distances was amply demonstrated when a City of London detective, Charles Thain, brought suspected thief Christian Sattler back from Hamburg on a steamship. Sattler was unhappy that Thain had handcuffed him while he was on board the ship, insisting that he had promised 'not to iron him' if he was compliant.

Thain had to leave his prisoner locked in a cabin for quarter of an hour while he went to the toilet. When he returned Sattler shot him in the chest at close range. Despite being handcuffed the prisoner had contrived to break open his box, remove the gun and load it, a gun he had acquired, he said, to shoot someone who owed him £25.

At first Thain's injuries did not appear life-threatening but he died twelve days later. Three pistol balls were extracted from his wound at postmortem. Sattler's reported attitude was that it served Thain right for 'breaking faith with me'. He would shoot like a dog anyone who did that. This, despite the fact that according to other passengers and crew the police officer had shown great kindness towards his prisoner.

Sattler was convicted of murder and hanged.

Inspector Moser (who, in 1894, was to write and illustrate an article on the subject for the *Strand Magazine*) preferred not to use handcuffs. He was particularly derisory about the British type, 'The Flexible', which were, he declared, 'heavy, unwieldy, awkward machines and at the best of times under the most favourable circumstances were extremely difficult of application. They weigh over a pound and have to be unlocked with a key in a manner not greatly differing from the operation of winding up the average eight-day-clock.' (He may have been exaggerating. He was a bit of a moaner.)

Furthermore, they could be used as weapons against the captor, as he himself had found. After he had forced his prisoner (a Russian rouble-forger) into a four-wheeler, the man had lifted his manacled wrists and brought them down heavily on Moser's head, 'completely crushing my bowler hat'. Pretty dastardly, that.

French and Belgian handcuffs (long, knobbly chains of steel piano wire or whipcord bound together) were more effective, he declared, because if the prisoner became difficult you could simply twist them, causing pain. But the 'perfected article' came from America. The US model was similar to the British (two solid metal snap bracelets joined by a short chain) but was lighter, less clumsy and more easily concealed and thus 'finds favour among the officers of Scotland Yard'.

Handcuffs, or lack of them, played a part in the suffering of another Yard man on extradition duty. Inspector Daniel Davey fell ill with typhus while in Naples. Even though a doctor thought him not yet fit enough to travel, he decided he would take his prisoner back. En route he relapsed, but was kindly treated by the prisoner so he could hardly refuse when the man asked that he be allowed the dignity of disembarking at Southampton without handcuffs. As soon as they left the ship the prisoner promptly fled. The inspector made feeble attempts to stop him then wandered, delirious, around Southampton, searching for him. When Davey was eventually found by his friend Greenham he was distraught, piteously moaning that he had lost his prisoner (a grave police sin) and was therefore ruined. He died shortly afterwards, but Greenham made sure the prisoner was recaptured and convicted.

That same year Inspector Druscovitch had a lucky escape. He and a prison warder escorted Leonard Aublin, a prisoner charged with a brutal double robbery murder, to Dover and handed him over to a Belgian gendarme who was to take him on to Brussels. Neither Gendarme Meeus nor the prisoner arrived at their destination. The gendarme was found dead beside the railway track which led to the Belgian capital. His prisoner was nowhere to be found.

First reports described their railway compartment as showing signs of a terrific struggle and 'deluged in blood' *à la* Muller. (The press quickly dubbed it 'the Belgian Railway Murder'.) Later reports speculated that the officer had in fact fallen asleep, woken up to find his prisoner gone and leaped on to the track in pursuit, but had not been as wise or agile as his quarry when taking the leap.

Of course, allowing a lone officer to escort such a dangerous prisoner was asking for trouble. At least there was no question that the escort of the *Flowery Land* mutineers needed to be done mob-handed.

On 28 July 1863, the barque *Flowery Land* left London for Singapore carrying wine, soft goods, British officers and a motley mixed-race crew. According to Evelyn Burnaby in his *Memories of Famous Trials* (reprinted Kessinger 2008), this consisted of six 'half-bred Spaniards from Manila', a Greek, a Turk, a Frenchman, a Norwegian, three Chinese, a Finn and a 'full-blooded negro'.

About three weeks out orders began to be disobeyed, and the Turk and some of the Spaniards began to answer back, for which they earned, wrote Burnaby, 'a sharp rope's-ending'. A witness not involved in the mutiny said that the captain did slap them sometimes and also that they wanted more fresh water to drink. Consequently, the Spaniards and the Greek hatched a plot. First they beat the first mate severely about the head with a capstan bar and threw him into the sea. Then they stabbed the captain and his brother (a passenger) to death.

The second mate, Taffir, barricaded himself into his cabin armed with a revolver but the mutineers offered to save his life if he would take them to Brazil, which he did. Once there, they boarded lifeboats and scuttled the ship, with the Chinese on board (they had already severely mutilated one of them). They told Brazilian authorities that they were from an American vessel which had foundered, but Taffir found someone who spoke English and the mutineers were soon rounded up and sent back to Britain.

Unsurprisingly, when five of these prisoners and two witnesses arrived at Southampton and another seven at Liverpool, the police escorts that were arranged were rather stronger than usual – eight to

The Trial of the Detectives, ed. by G. Dilnot (Geoffrey Bles, 1928)

Superintendent Williamson being examined at the Turf Fraud trial

each port. Seven of the accused were found guilty and sentenced to death, although two were reprieved and given life sentences.

A similar situation arose with the *Lennie* mutiny just over ten years later, but this had occurred much nearer home and the Scotland Yard detectives became involved in the actual investigation. The captain of the *Lennie* was a French-Canadian and his first and second mates were British. Again, the crew were a mixture of nationalities, most of whom did not understand English: Greeks, Turks, Austrians, a 16-year-old Dutch boy and a Belgian steward named Constant Von Hoydonck.

Again, the crew turned out to be very poor sailors, but despite this Captain Hatfield and his officers apparently treated them well enough, apart from shouting at them a lot, using some rough language and refusing to allow them spirits.

They were headed for New Orleans but had only reached the Bay of Biscay when some of the crew turned on the captain and his two officers, murdering them in a dreadful bloodbath. The captain was stabbed several times in the stomach and head, and the first mate was shot down from the rigging, which he had climbed in an effort to escape, then hacked to death and almost decapitated, as was the second mate.

The mutineers sought out the steward and informed him that he must navigate the ship to Gibraltar, from where they could get to Greece. They wanted to kill the boy in case he had seen too much and might blab, but Hoydonck refused to let them, locking the lad in a cabin instead, saying he intended to teach him a lesson. The lesson was to copy out distress messages in French and English, put them into empty bottles and throw them at intervals through the porthole.

The steward first headed the ship towards Bristol. When the crew realized what was happening he had to change course, but duped them again by heading for France and hoisting a 'ship in distress' flag, which the mutineers could not read although it did begin to arouse their suspicions.

Close to the French coast he encouraged six of the men to leave in a lifeboat, claiming it was safe to land there. Soon afterwards the French authorities became suspicious and a man-of-war approached the ship, which led to the arrest of the crew. The six who had left were caught soon afterwards.

Once extradition had been arranged, Williamson, Druscovitch and five others collected the eleven prisoners from Calais. Williamson was soon back across the Channel accompanied by the steward and a doctor to inspect and if possible identify a headless body and two heads found washed up there. He arrived to find that the body had been interred. He had it disinterred but it was in too advanced a state of decomposition. As for the two heads, the man who had found them had buried them in the sand 'below high water mark', Williamson reported, and 'the place could not afterwards be traced'.

Identification had therefore proved impossible, but he was able to examine the lifeboat in which the six had come ashore and its contents of knuckle-dusters, a spear and two revolvers. He was also able to interview the woman in whose house three of the mutineers had stayed the night after claiming that they were shipwrecked mariners, and to collect from her a picture and three 'stones' which they had given her – which turned out to be the captain's property. As further evidence he brought back one of the bottles that had contained the messages about the ship's plight.

The steward and the Dutch boy became vital trial witnesses and two other members of the crew who were not involved in the attacks, Lettis, an Austrian, and Peterson, a Dane, described the horrific murder scene. Four Greeks were convicted of the murder of the captain and were hanged. The steward, Constant Von Hoydonck, was complimented on his actions and awarded £50.

Naturally, the Yard men often escorted their own witnesses and prisoners around and about the British Isles. The discomforts of such tasks were complained of by Inspector Thomson, who had accompanied the nervous Great Stamp Robbery informer Peg Leg Shaw and his family to Edinburgh so they could escape the revenge of those he had ratted on: 'It was a terrible journey: Shaw was drunk for the whole of it and his family teemed with a foul stench.'

In the same case, where he and Sergeant Thomas arrested the Countrymen at the Doncaster Races, he had great difficulty getting them safely on to the Manchester-bound train. They handcuffed the pair together and eventually found a compartment to themselves, but it was unlit, and so they wouldn't have to spend the journey in darkness he got a porter to find a couple of ginger beer bottles and buy some candles to put in them. When there was lighting in those early trains it usually emanated from one dim and inefficient oil lamp set in the roof; passengers often took candles with them.

Another discomfort of rail travel was the lack of refreshment facilities and lavatories, resulting in a dash for the tea-rooms and the toilets on reaching certain stations. To help cope with this you could buy a Walters Railway Convenience, which was 'worn imperceptibly with greatest comfort and security'. And in winter the carriages were very cold. Sixpence would get you a hot-water-filled foot-warmer, but these soon lost heat and became useless clutter on the floor.

Added to all of this was the soot and smoke from the engines and the constant threat of accident. Train conditions did vary from company to company but the one most used by the detectives, the London, Chatham and Dover Railway, was known for its shabby rolling stock, a motley collection of cast-offs from other companies, although the LCDR did make a bit more effort with its boat trains.

The detectives also ranged far and wide following up their own investigations. On their initial meeting with Charles Dickens, the ruddy-faced, soldierly-looking Sergeant Thornton described events which led up to an incident in New York.

He had been following 'Meshek, a Jew' who had 'been carrying on, pretty heavily in a bill stealing way', across the country from Chatham, to Cheltenham, to Birmingham and Liverpool, by tracking sightings of his carpet bag on the side of which, 'worked in worsted', was a green parrot on a stand.

At Liverpool he lost Meshek, who had sailed for America.

About a year later Thornton too was in the United States tracing an Irish bank robber. He described to Dickens how he had caught up with and arrested the man: 'I took him, and lodged him in a New York prison called the Tombs; which I dare say you know, sir?' (Dickens, who made a habit of visiting prisons wherever he went, acknowledged that he did.)

The following morning Thornton had been passing through the magistrates' room for the examination of his extradition case when, in a corner, he spotted a carpet bag. *The* carpet bag. As he told the author:

'That Carpet Bag, with the representation of a green parrot
on a stand,' said I, 'belongs to an English Jew, name of
Aaron Meshek, and to no other man, alive or dead!'
I give you my word the New York Police Officers were
doubled up with surprise.
'How did you ever come to know that?' said they.

It turned out that Meshek was in custody for another offence and that inside the carpet bag were 'some memoranda relating to the fraud for which I had vainly endeavoured to take him'.

The Yard men were eventually to range as far as New Zealand and Argentina in pursuit of suspects. The traffic was, of course, two-way.

One of the oddest of the reverse cases began one night early in January 1870, when a 47-year-old clerk named George Dyer called in to an 'E' Division police station to confess to a murder he had committed at Mia Mia Creek, a gold-digging site in the Australian outback, thirteen years earlier. The deed, he claimed, had since preyed hourly on his mind. Inspector Hubbard, doubtless somewhat startled, took Dyer to see his newly appointed superintendent, James Jacob Thomson.

Apparently for his first six months at Mia Mia Creek Dyer had worked on his own, but since it made more sense to share the tasks and the protection of your property he teemed up with another loner, George Wilson. The pair got on pretty well for about a month but then there was a quarrel about the amount of gold realized. Both became very angry. Wilson drew out his sheath knife (Dyer claimed) whereupon Dyer 'took up a spade and cut him down with it. He dropped down dead in a moment. I cut his head clean open.' He dumped the body down a well, and when others enquired where his mate had gone he told them he had had gone off to a new digging, 'the Inglewood Rush'.

Three years later Dyer came back to England but, he admitted, had had no peace of mind since. Messages were sent to Australia but the time lag (two months) and initial scant response led to numerous remands and release on bail, the thinking now being that Dyer had probably confessed in a fit of insanity. And, indeed, he himself now made this claim and was declaring that he had never killed Wilson or anybody else.

Unfortunately for him the doctor at the House of Detention had certified that he had 'shown no symptoms of insanity since his admission'.

Scotland Yard began to receive letters from friends and relatives of men named Wilson who had gone out to Australia and not been heard from since. An anxious Emma Wilson of Macclesfield wrote that her husband had a very fair complexion, was good-looking, five feet nine inches and had brown hair. He also had four toes on one foot, but she couldn't remember which one. Clearly her husband was not the George Wilson Dyer described, who was thick-set, about five feet four or five inches, with a swarthy complexion and dark hair, whiskers, moustache and beard.

News eventually arrived saying that a body had been found at Mia Mia several years earlier; the victim had been killed in the manner claimed except there appeared to have been many blows (and to the back of the skull), not just the one. A warrant was taken out and Sergeant Robert Fulton Holmes of the Victoria Police made the voyage to England to collect Dyer.

Judging by his letter to Sir Richard Mayne, Sergeant Holmes was an opportunist. He requested permission 'after making the arrangements' for a few weeks' leave so he could visit Ireland 'to see my friends whom I have not seen for nearly thirteen years and whom in all probability I may never again have the opportunity of seeing', and also to allow him to recuperate a little 'before re-embarking upon such a long sea voyage'.

He got his leave, then took Dyer back to Melbourne, where he was found guilty of manslaughter and sentenced to eight years' hard labour.

18

Double trouble

The Home Office and the police were expecting acts of political violence to be committed some time soon, and in 1867 they were. Not by the Chartists, who were a spent force, but by the Fenians and the Irish Republican Brotherhood (IRB). The IRB had been founded in Dublin in 1858 and the Fenian Brotherhood (of Irish-American immigrants) in New York at around the same time.

Shortly afterwards the US Civil War gave the Fenians (who fought on both sides) the opportunity to gain some expertise in the handling of weapons and explosives. In 1865 they backed an abortive uprising in Dublin (the plans had fallen into the hands of the Dublin police after an emissary got drunk and lost them) and the following year they attempted to set up a base in Canada from which to attack British shipping.

Another Dublin uprising was expected by the British authorities because they had spies in both the Fenian and IRB camps. To gather arms for this uprising, rebels decided to raid the poorly guarded arsenal at Chester Castle on the British mainland. The plan failed because of the startling influx of Irishmen which alerted that sedate city, because the train caught by the man who was to lead the raid was late, and because an informer, John Corydon, had given the game away anyway.

The Dublin rising was rescheduled but this one also failed and the leaders went underground in England. One of them, Colonel Thomas J. Kelly, was captured accidentally in September 1867 as he tried to settle an internal quarrel. John Corydon identified Kelly and picked out another Fenian, named Deasy.

A fellow-Fenian colonel, Ricard O'Sullivan Burke (thought to be the chief Fenian arms agent in England) decided to rescue Kelly, a decision that was to have far-reaching and tragic results.

The prison van carrying Kelly was ambushed, and a pistol shot fired through the keyhole killed the police sergeant inside. (Versions of the story vary. Some claim it was a deliberate act of murder, others that it was accidental.) A woman prisoner got hold of the keys and handed them out and Kelly was released.

Many arrests followed this 'outrage'. Three of those charged with the murder of Sergeant Brett were found guilty and publicly hanged in November 1867. They became known as the Manchester Martyrs.

However, Kelly and his rescuer, O'Sullivan Burke, remained elusive, even though Scotland Yard were called in to assist in finding them. But the scene of action was switching to London anyway.

Already one rather strange Fenian-related incident had occurred in the capital, even as the Manchester Martyrs were awaiting trial. As three military bandsmen walked home after their performances at London theatres, a couple of men lounging on a corner made honking noises after them and called them pigs, then jostled them. There was a bang and a flash and Life Guardsman Eddie M'Donnell fell to the ground exclaiming, 'I've been shot!'

At first it seemed that M'Donnell might survive, but several days later he died of pneumonia, the bullet having passed right through his chest. The case was now one of murder but, curiously enough, although Fenians or the IRB were suspected of involvement, it was soon being suggested that he had been shot not merely because he was a British soldier but probably because he resembled a Fenian informer thought to be in the area under the guard of two detectives, who had left the pub about the same time as the bandsmen. It was a case of mistaken identity.

'These Irishmen,' *The Times* speculated, 'probably imagining by their upright walk that the bandsmen were detective policemen in plain clothes, attacked them.' (Elements of the press and public believed they could always recognize a policeman in plain clothes by his rigid and upright walk, acquired while pounding the beat in his heavy boots and stiff uniform.)

Inspector Thomson arrested a clerk named Groves, who admitted to being in the area at the time. This man had Fenian papers and a pistol among his belongings, and an informer identified him as a man who had been following him and threatening to shoot him.

Not surprisingly, the numerous officers escorting the horse-drawn prison van taking Groves to the Middlesex House of Detention in

Examination at Bow Street of M'Donnell
murder suspect, John Groves

Clerkenwell were equipped with enough cutlasses and revolvers to repel an army.

But the case against Groves was thin and fell apart when a sensational new witness showed signs of being deranged and the bullet which had killed M'Donnell and had fitted in the pistol's chamber refused to exit through the barrel.

However, Thomson was soon to make a spectacular arrest at the very time when desperate last-minute attempts to gain clemency were being made on behalf of the three men awaiting execution for the Manchester rescue. Intelligence had been emerging that serious arms-buying was going on in Birmingham, supposedly on behalf of the Chilean government. The buyers bore a curious resemblance to the Fenian leader who had planned the Manchester prison van rescue, Colonel O'Sullivan Burke, and his aide, Casey. Then an informer named Devaney told Thomson that O'Sullivan Burke was staying in the same lodgings as him in Tavistock Street near Tottenham Court Road.

Thomson and Devaney found O'Sullivan Burke and Casey out walking and called upon a passing PC to help arrest them. In the scuffle Burke broke away, whereupon Thomson pulled out a revolver and shouted, 'By God, Burke, if you don't stop I will fire on you!'

Burke, who was said to be a light-hearted, humorous fellow, stopped in his tracks and said, 'Don't do anything desperate.'

Eventually the policemen managed to hail two cabs to take them to Bow Street Police Station. The pair were charged with treason felony and sent on remand to the Middlesex House of Detention in Clerkenwell. There must have been a less vulnerable place to send them: the area had a big Irish population and was historically radical, and meetings supporting clemency for the Manchester Martyrs had recently been held on Clerkenwell Green.

Two or three policemen were put on guard around the perimeter wall. But Thomson suspected that Kelly, the man who had been rescued from the prison van, would want to return the favour and try to break out O'Sullivan Burke.

For several days and nights Thomson dragged the informer Corydon around the prison walls in the hope of identifying Kelly and other Irishmen he was sure would be lurking about, but after a few nights the watch was stood down because the informer was tired. In fact, it was not Kelly (who was probably in the US by then) but another Fenian, James Murphy, who with a team of fifteen IRB men was to attempt the rescue.

The plan was simple: lean a barrel of gunpowder up against the prison wall at the time when the prisoner, Burke, would be exercising in the yard on the other side. Burke would be alerted by means of a white ball thrown over the wall. Friends would be waiting with horses to get them away from the area quickly.

The escape was planned for 12 December, but the fuse refused to light so the barrel was trundled away and brought back again the next day. By then, Mayne had received information of the plot but not the expected date. He sent Inspector Thomson to warn the governor, who altered exercise times so that Burke would not be in the yard when expected, but refused to believe that an attack was possible or to take any further precautions.

The second time the fuse did light, the white ball was thrown over the wall and the gunpowder, all 548 pounds of it, exploded with a noise that made horses bolt and that could be heard forty miles away. Unfortunately, it demolished not only the prison wall but the block of tenements opposite, killing six people, two of them children, and horribly maiming many others, six of whom later died.

Eventually, six men were charged with causing the explosion, two of whom, both Irish Republican Brotherhood members, turned Queen's evidence. Three more were acquitted of murder but found guilty of lesser charges. Only one, a Glaswegian named Michael Barrett, was convicted of wilful murder and hanged. It was the last public hanging to take place in England. He too became a martyr to be sung about; he always protested his innocence.

After that there was a lull in Fenian and IRB activities on the British mainland, but they began again in earnest early in the

*The aftermath of the Clerkenwell prison explosion, which
was intended to release a Fenian prisoner in 1867*

1880s and were given extra strength by the new wonder explosive: dynamite. Included in the targets were several railway stations to be hit at the same time (not unlike 7/7 but without the loss of life), the Tower of London, the Houses of Parliament and even Scotland Yard itself.

Meanwhile, in 1867 Thomson was employed on the newly formed, short-lived (1867–8) Secret Service, which was followed in 1883 by the Yard's Special (Irish) Branch, led by Williamson and Inspector Littlechild.

Mayne and the Metropolitan Police had come under savage attack following the Clerkenwell bombing, and the criticism – of Sir Richard in particular – became continuous and insulting.

On Boxing Day 1868, Mayne died. He had kept an increasingly

iron grip on the force for thirty-nine years (on his own since 1850, when Rowan retired).

In his place came Colonel Sir Edmund Henderson, a professional soldier but one who had dealt with convicts both in Australia and for the Home Office. His first year in office turned out to be a particularly murderous one.

Most of the violence centred on the East End of London, the scene of great deprivation following a slump brought about by over-speculation.

Two of that year's murders were curiously alike. Both occurred in Poplar and both were double murders of a young woman and an older person. The cause of death was the same in both cases, as was the final outcome. In neither case was there any real mystery as to the identity of the murderers, but the hunt for one of them became a protracted affair. Inspector Thomson, then still an inspector in the branch, handled both cases.

Most of the inhabitants lived in Poplar New Town, which straddled the top of the loop of the Isle of Dogs where lay the East India and huge West India and Millwall Docks. In his *London Labour and the London Poor* (Griffin, 1861), Henry Mayhew spoke of these docks as 'the very focus of metropolitan wealth . . . and yet you have but to visit the hovels grouped round about all this amazing excess of riches to witness the same amazing excess of poverty'.

Some Poplar inhabitants lived a little further into the loop, in the short streets sandwiched between the high-walled docks and a ribbon of tall, Thames-side taverns and lodging houses. It was in one of these curious isolated islands of tiny terraced houses that the first of these terrible crimes occurred.

When Eliza and George Taffe returned from visiting a relative on 7 February 1869 they found themselves unable to gain access to their home, 2 Russell Place, Prestons Road. A neighbour and Eliza's brother-in-law climbed over the rear wall and forced the back door. Inside, the Taffes found the bodies of their daughter, 26-year-old

Sarah Ann Cooper, and her 86-year-old blind grandfather, Peter Pearson. Their throats had been cut.

Sarah's husband, John William Cooper, a 26-year-old unemployed marine engineer, was nowhere to be found. According to 'K' Division's Superintendent Worels, Cooper 'bore but an indifferent character' and *The Times* soon discovered that he 'lived on very bad terms with his wife and family'. Worels also found that two photographs of Cooper were missing from an album. 'It is supposed that Cooper tore them out of the book,' he reported, 'to prevent copies being multiplied.' However, police obviously acquired another picture of him, looking very young, which I discovered in the case file at the National Archives. It is very small and faded, and was taken by the London Stereoscopic and Photographic Company, photographers to HRH the Prince of Wales. Police also built up a description of Cooper as being five feet six inches in height, with brown hair and whiskers – the latter worn around his chin – and a florid complexion. Most importantly, he had no left thumb.

In the days before health and safety legislation, when medical knowledge and facilities were limited, scars, missing digits and even wooden legs were quite common and could be useful aids to identification. At first this missing digit seemed to be just that.

Details of possible suspects soon began to come in. A railway policeman at Farringdon Street Station had seen a man of similar description to Cooper. Like Cooper he had lost his left thumb, and he wore a blue cloth cap with a French peak. The man had enquired about the first train to Chippenham the next day, and had come back in the morning for a ticket to Paddington to board it. An Aldershot grocer reported that a man of that description had asked him for relief but he couldn't say which of his thumbs was missing (Aldershot is on the way to Chippenham). A PC at Emsworth, a coastal village south of Aldershot, found that such a man had stayed at the Locomotive Inn and been trying to get a ship nearby. Police at Loughborough in Leicestershire had arrested a one-thumbed tramp. Dover police reported that a man 'deficient of his left thumb' had been trying to sign on to a Rotterdam steamer; the governor of Maidstone Gaol had a one-thumbed bacon-stealer in his custody – and so it went on. None of them were Cooper.

Seamen were always particularly difficult to pursue when there were so many ships harboured in the Thames and at the various southern ports where they might get work and thus transport out of the country. Cooper also had a widespread network of relations, which complicated matters further.

Then came the writing on the wall – in fact, the toilet wall at London Bridge Railway Station. It read:

My name is John Cooper the murderer No 2 Russel Place
if you will look in the East India Dock you will find I have
been sleeping in the inside of one of the iron tanks but this
night I am going drown myself and put an end to all my
sorrows. I hope my mother is quite well.
John Cooper Murderer Poplar.

The handwriting proved not to be Cooper's, and it turned out that all the East India Dock tanks were full of water. Someone was amusing himself at police expense.

Several days later a lighterman navigating his way into the London Dock spied a floating body by Shadwell Dock Stairs – it was Cooper's.

Only the previous day Superintendent Worels had reported Poplar's second double murder while Thomson, who had been dashing about following false trails to Emsworth and Loughborough, was now fielding cryptic enquiries from Assistant Commissioner Labalmondière as to how certain information had got into the newspapers and the fall-out from a mistake in Cooper's reward notices. They had given his address as 2 Russell Street instead of 2 Russell Place, thus, claimed the landlord of the former via his solicitor, putting a stigma on his house which he was currently trying to sell.

Thomson was uncowed, pointing out that he was not familiar with the area and that they had been in a rush to get the notices out and were inundated with so many enquiries still to be made on the case. These thing happen occasionally, was his stance.

As for the second murder: Robert George Still had been unable to get a reply from repeated knockings on the door of his sister-in-law, Mary Brown, who lived behind the tobacconist's shop she managed in Poplar High Street. Climbing in through the back window, he found the body of Ann Brown, his 23-year-old niece, draped 'undressed' across the bed. Nearby was that of her 50-year-old mother, Mary Brown. Both had had their throats cut – as with the previous murder, with a knife rather than a cut-throat razor.

The efficient Superintendent Worels, although tactfully requesting the assistance of a Yard detective, already had the job half done. Inspector Thomson and a sergeant were sent.

Worels reported:

Suspicion is at present attached to a man named John
William Bradshaw (an unemployed engineer) who formerly
lodged with the deceased but left about five weeks since,
and removed to No. 8 Archibald Street, Bromley, at which
place he has committed suicide by cutting his throat about
8 a.m. on the 3rd inst . . . he was seen passing the shop kept
by the murdered woman at about noon on the 2nd inst.

The surgeon thought the women had been dead at least twenty-four hours, therefore Bradshaw could have done the deed.

Thomson verified all this. He discovered that it seemed the suspect had made overtures to Ann Brown and had been resisted and that, according to his own brother, he was 'a man of violent and irritable temper'. The inquest jury, who praised the police for their service in elucidating the facts of the case, agreed that he must be the perpetrator. Oddly, Harriet Emberson, the woman he was lodging with in Bromley, had expected to marry him that very Tuesday.

Thomson, the Commissioner and the Home Office were now embroiled in sorting out protracted quarrels about which of the watermen who handled Cooper's body should get the reward and how much the undertaker should receive. Such was the state of affairs Mayne's lack of delegation had left behind: the chief of police of the world's busiest city dealing with trivial financial matters.

Soon, however, the Yard was back to more complicated murders committed by those dastardly foreigners.

Mme Maria Caroline Besant Riel, the 42-year-old mistress of Lord Lucan, the general who had passed on the disastrous Charge of the Light Brigade order, had not been seen in her Park Lane house since the previous day, Sunday 7 April 1872.

When her daughter Julie returned from a trip to Paris on the Monday, the maid told her that she had last seen her mistress the day before, when she was preparing for a morning walk in Hyde Park, but given that the maid spoke no French and Mme Riel and her cook spoke little English she was used to not knowing what was going on.

Mme Riel could not be found at Lord Lucan's place either, so the two women set about searching the Park Lane premises. The search proved fruitless until they came to the pantry, which was locked. Inside, they found the battered body of the mistress of the house.

'The features were much distorted,' reported Superintendent Dunlap of 'C' Division, 'the hands clenched and deeply scratched, and the nails broken. The whole appearance of the body,' he continued, 'is that of having been subjected to great violence.' Furthermore, the victim had a rope around her neck which had obviously been pulled very tightly. In the surgeon's opinion the death had occurred at least fifteen hours earlier.

Also missing since 8 p.m. the previous evening was the French cook, 28-year-old Mme Marguerite Dixblanc, together with two railway bonds and some Bank of England notes. The Yard's newly appointed Detective Inspector James Pay set about tracing the dark-haired, sturdily built French cook, who had been last seen wearing a green satin-cloth dress, a grey waterproof cloak and a black velvet bonnet with a hanging rose.

Warning telegrams (some of them 'submarine', made possible by the underwater cabling now straddling both the Channel and the Atlantic) were sent out to many ports, and soon possible sightings were coming in. One suggested Mme Dixblanc had been in Hull and was now making her way to Liverpool and thence to America.

The most promising lead came, once again, via a humble cab driver. John Turner, badge number 8149, had taken a woman answering the cook's description and with no luggage whatsoever from Park Lane to Victoria Station at around 8 p.m. on the day in question. Because she had 'the appearance of a servant' the interpreter for the London, Chatham and Dover Railway presumed she would want a seat on the daily cheap service train and told her

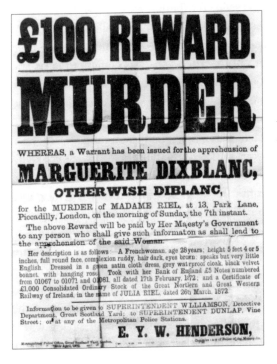

Marguerite Dixblanc was a cook who murdered her mistress following a dispute over her dismissal

she was out of luck: it had left two hours ago. She assured him that the first-class-only express leaving in fifteen minutes would do her nicely, thank you. She paid with a £5 Bank of England note, and the company was not only able to tell Druscovitch her ticket number but confirmed that she had arrived in Calais, where that portion of her ticket had been collected.

A telegram to the Paris police was swiftly followed by Chief Inspector Druscovitch and Inspector Pay, who also travelled by the overnight express. They were armed with the name and address of an acquaintance of the missing cook, Mme Guerin, with whom she had lodged during the Commune revolt of the previous year. Friendships formed during that dangerous time were likely to be strong. (*The Times* had already informed its readers that Mme Dixblanc had been one of the rebels, had developed a 'taste for the terrible', had boasted of the deeds she had committed during that awful time and had come to London to escape retribution.)

Another friend was traced – a Madame Bouillion, who hailed from the same village. She admitted to receiving a letter from Dixblanc, advising her not to write as she was coming to Paris and would pay her the money she owed her, but 'subsequently written' on the second page was the news that she would not see her friend again as she was off to America. Warning telegrams were fired off to Brest, Le Havre, St Nazaire, Bordeaux and Cherbourg.

'I must beg of you to keep this information to yourself,' Druscovitch wrote to Superintendent Williamson in a letter dashed off from the hotel that first evening, 'so as to prevent it getting into the newspapers as the French papers copy everything connected with this case.'

The detectives must have been exhausted, but their first day in Paris was not yet over. With a French police inspector they returned to the Bouillion residence to speak to the husband, who admitted that in fact Dixblanc had slept in the home after her arrival on the Monday but had left the following morning without saying where she was going. He seemed annoyed with his wife for not having told them the truth and divulged the name of Dixblanc's sweetheart, who worked for the Paris Omnibus Company. They went in search of him, without success. Druscovitch got the impression that the husband still knew more than he was telling.

But the French police were not about to put up with any procrastination: at five the following morning they raided the Bouillion house and arrested him, followed, two days later, by his wife. On the premises they found Mme Dixblanc's green dress, eight £5 Bank of England notes, some English gold and a ring set (in Druscovitch's opinion) with imitation diamonds and emeralds.

Another letter to Williamson – they couldn't risk a telegraph: 'secrecy is now everything' – reported that the husband now declared that he would rather die than give any more information but, Druscovitch assured Williamson, 'we have other means at our disposal upon which enquiry may be made and perhaps with some chance of success'.

These 'means' probably referred to the addresses which the heavily pregnant Madame Bouillion and her family were now suddenly remembering. British and French officers fanned out over Paris, picking up Dixblanc's trail but not the woman herself. (The Bouillions were kept in custody for several weeks and she gave birth in Saint-Lazare Prison.)

'Nothing fresh since yesterday,' telegraphed Druscovitch on Saturday 13 April 1872. 'Send me bill offering reward by tonight's post.' Sunday's telegraph home told a different story: 'Marguerite Dixblanc has been apprehended here.'

On his second visit to a coal merchant – one of the addresses gleaned – a French inspector had found the missing cook sitting on the doorstep and recognized her immediately, having just been shown her photograph.

Druscovitch's next letter, giving details of the arrest, carried a postscript: 'I may mention that on neither occasion has sufficient postage been paid on your letters; on the first occasion I had to pay 90c and the last 1.50c.'

Once in custody Marguerite Dixblanc freely admitted her guilt, explaining that Julie Riel had sacked her but only given her a week's notice, which left her in a desperate situation. Then, on the Sunday morning, she and Madame Riel had quarrelled violently and in the process her mistress had accidentally been killed. She insisted that the rope around the victim's neck had only been used to drag her body to the pantry. The man who examined the body disagreed. Given the damage to the woman's throat, the act must have been much more deliberate.

The extradition proceedings were complicated by the fact that Mme Dixblanc turned out to be not French but Belgian. However, when the case finally came to trial the idea that these were two passionate foreigners locked in battle was helpful to her defence, despite the fact that there was some evidence the crime may have been premeditated.

The Times assured its readers that the features of the accused were 'not as hideous as has been pretended' but that she was a strongly built woman, with powerful neck and shoulders, thick black hair, a clear complexion, large sensual mouth, slightly dilated nostrils, cold blue eyes and a low, broad forehead. They added a titillating revelation. Her hands – which, they said, she tried to conceal behind the folds of her skirt – 'are those of a man'.

The English maid told the court that Mme Riel was very excitable, gesticulated a great deal and was often unjust, while Lord Lucan admitted that, 'like a good many French ladies, she was a little *vive*. I do not know an English word which would describe it better . . . she was hasty.'

The defendant was found guilty but the jury found the premeditation not proven and gave a strong recommendation to mercy, which was shown when her death sentence was commuted to penal servitude for life.

In 1868, the Home Office had set up a departmental committee on the organization of the force. Among its recommendations was that the force itself should be increased in size, and also the number of detectives. They had started out as ten in 1842 (eight sergeants and two inspectors) and by now, when force numbers had risen to 8,000 from an original 3,000, were only up to fifteen: a chief inspector (Williamson), three inspectors and eleven sergeants.

It had also become clear that operating centrally as a separate department was not ideal, that the lack of promotional opportunities within the branch had cost them several good men, and that poor pay and great difficulties in getting expenses reimbursed were a constant irritation to the detectives and a strain on their pockets.

Henderson quickly put some of the committee's recommendations into effect, raising the Detective Branch numbers to twenty-seven, promoting Williamson to superintendent, creating two more posts of chief inspector and improving pay and allowances. Even more important, he introduced divisional detectives to operate separately under divisional superintendents.

19

Changes

The infant mortality rate in Victorian times was notoriously high, due not only to natural causes but also to unnatural ones.

Jonathan Whicher, whose downfall in the branch was brought about by his investigation into the murder of little Francis Saville Kent, had previously investigated two suspected child murders.

The first was the very strange case in which a man in Nottingham had received a parcel containing the corpse of a little boy and some clothing, including an apron marked 'S. Drake'.

His wife's sister, Sarah Drake, worked as a cook housekeeper in Upper Harley Street in London. Whicher and the Nottingham Superintendent, who had called in at the Yard for some assistance, went to the address and arrested her. She seemed surprised that they knew and wondered why. When they told her, she cried.

It turned out that for two years she had been paying a Mrs Johnson five shillings a week to look after her illegitimate boy, Louis. But she had fallen behind with her payments to the tune of £9 10s so Mrs Johnson had returned the boy. Sarah, who had just taken up a new post, pleaded that she keep him another week but Mrs Johnson refused: Sarah had defaulted too often on her payments.

Fearful of losing her new place, Sarah strangled the boy with a silk handkerchief. She confessed to the searcher at the police station that she had 'hung' him but the surgeon who carried out the postmortem thought a joint cause of death was the strangulation plus injuries to the child's head.

She had packed the body in a box, asked the butler to address it and sent it off to her sister and her husband in the hope they would bury him. One imagines that Sarah was a fairly simple-minded soul, and at her trial she showed great anguish, rocking back and forth – a classic sign of mental disturbance. However, the many fanciful reasons she wrote to Mrs Johnson to excuse non-payment and not coming to see the child suggest she may have also been quite devious. She hinted that the father was French and she was fearful that his family might try to claim the boy.

The trial judge gave the jury a way out, suggesting they might decide that the shock and terror of the child being suddenly left on her hands might have unbalanced Sarah. They took it, and found her not guilty on grounds of temporary insanity. She promptly fainted.

Ten years later, Whicher investigated whether the Reverend Bonwell and his lover had killed their illegitimate son before arranging to have his body slipped into someone else's coffin. The inquest jury found against a murder verdict but criticized their behaviour, and later Bonwell was defrocked.

During the late 1860s and early 1870s there was an epidemic of baby deaths, judging by the increasing number of bodies found deposited around the capital: behind walls, in parks and gardens, even in cab racks and omnibuses. Headlines such as 'Two More Child Murders', 'More Infanticide', 'Murdered Child Found in Cab' regularly featured in the *Islington Gazette*. It was not that Islington was worse than other areas but that the local coroner, Dr Lankester, insisted on postmortems and proper inquests and encouraged murder verdicts where evidence suggested it.

'Baby-dropping' incidents were not new and not necessarily sinister. Many involved stillborn babies born to poor women who couldn't afford burial fees. But now more babies appeared to have died of neglect or to have been suffocated or even strangled, and these deaths were increasingly laid at the doors of baby farmers.

Baby farms were merely private nurseries operating without controls and run by untrained women in their own homes. And there was a need for such places. Working-class unmarried mothers still had to earn their own living, usually in service, so were unable to look after the babies themselves. Better-off women used baby farms and lying-in offshoots to hide guilty secrets.

The reason for the high number of deaths in baby farms was overcrowding (sometimes ten children to a room) and unsanitary conditions which encouraged the spread of the many lethal infections about in those days. Poor feeding – sometimes merely arrowroot and water instead of expensive milk – also made the babies more vulnerable.

The bodies were dumped, both to avoid the expense and bother of burials and also to avoid drawing attention to certain establishments. And, of course, some of the babies *had* been deliberately neglected or even murdered. A lump sum rather than a weekly arrangement would be paid just to get rid of the baby. Dr Lankester accused the police of being apathetic about the problem but admitted that lack of control and irregularities in the law didn't help.

Matters reached a height in June 1870, when in the space of a few weeks no fewer than sixteen babies' bodies were found scattered around – not in Islington, but south of the river in Camberwell. The Yard detectives had made some efforts in this direction but it was two divisional officers, Sergeant Relf and Constable Tyers, who tracked down Brixton baby farmer Mrs Waters, who was responsible for the dropping of some of the Camberwell bodies. She was tried for murder and hanged. Her sister was sentenced to eighteen months' hard labour.

The subject now became a hot topic, and the suave and intelligent Inspector Druscovitch and Sergeant Meiklejohn, a Scot already mired in the criminal activities that were to bring the branch down, were given the task of chasing up some of the suspect premises by following Relf's example of answering baby-farming advertisements.

They pinpointed a baby farm worth watching in Islington and also homed in on Mrs Hall of Coldharbour Lane, who accommodated young ladies during their confinement 'and it is believed that occasionally, by a certain process, succeeds in bringing the children into the world stillborn'. However, having discovered that Relf and Tyers had beaten them to it, Druscovitch 'begged to be permitted to withdraw . . . as two persons endeavouring to obtain evidence against the same party and at the same time would in all probability frustrate their common object'.

But Yard detectives did become involved in what must surely be one of the strangest of their cases, which came to light in April 1872. Sergeant Mullard, one of the new divisional detectives, had attracted some adverse publicity when he gave evidence regarding a baby who had apparently died of suffocation. He seemed to be suggesting, the press claimed, that Agnes Norman, the baby's nurse, was responsible not only for that tragedy but for other similar occurrences as well. Thus he was making accusations against a poor undefended woman. (Some felt that Mrs Waters, the recently hanged baby farmer, was not a murderess but rather a poor and ignorant woman who had merely been a scapegoat pounced upon in a typically British fit of moral indignation.)

The 42-year-old ex-grocer Inspector James Pay of Scotland Yard was given the task of looking further into the matter, and he had to agree with Mullard that the mortality rate of Agnes's charges did seem oddly high, even by the current standards.

Back in January 1869, Agnes had been employed by the Milners in Kennington. Soon after her arrival, the arm of ten-month-old Thomas was found to be severely bruised and the eldest boy, eight-year-old Alfred, told his father that the nursemaid had let the baby fall off the table and given him a penny not to tell. Within a short time baby Thomas was dead. The inquest jury brought in a verdict of natural causes due to teething convulsions.

Two weeks later, Agnes was left in charge of the other three Milner children (from ten in the morning until ten at night) and when the parents returned they found that delicate three-year-old Amelia had died. No inquest was held, despite the fact that young

Alfred had disclosed that Agnes had put Amelia in the wardrobe at one point and had given him a halfpenny not to tell.

A couple of months later, when Agnes was employed by the Gardners, their family friend Mrs Taylor called to see them, bringing along her five-month-old baby, which she left with the nursemaid for a couple of hours. When she went to collect him the baby was dead. The inquest verdict was natural causes due to spasms of the glottis. Less than three weeks later the previously weak and sickly one-year-old Gardner baby was also dead. The family doctor issued a certificate stating that the death was due to convulsions.

However, a much stranger element was emerging, as Pay reported: 'During the six weeks that Agnes Norman was in the service of Mr Gardner three dogs, a cat, a parrot, twelve canaries and linnets and some goldfish, died very mysteriously.'

While Agnes was with her next family, the Browns, a cat, a canary, a linnet and some goldfish died, and the parrot was thought to be in extremis because of a swollen neck which looked as if it had been pinched. The grandson, Charles Parfitt, complained of waking up suffocating to find Agnes with her hands over his mouth and throat. He screamed and she gave him a sweet not to tell.

In her next post all the animals died, but no children. Finally came the case which had roused Sergeant Mullard's suspicions. The tempo had now increased. After only two days with the Beer family (and Agnes having been left in charge of the three children for nine hours, from 3 p.m. to half past midnight) fourteen-month-old Jessie Beer succumbed and the cat and the canary also died 'mysteriously', as Pay was again to put it.

Of course, a great many babies died mysteriously then (and some still do) and medical knowledge on the subject was woefully inadequate. But Jessie was found to have marks of her upper teeth on her lower lip, which it was felt could not have been made by the child herself lying on anything – outside pressure must have been brought to bear.

Agnes was charged with murder, attempted murder, manslaughter and assault, but the conflicting opinions of medical experts caused the judge to halt the first case – that of the murder of Jessie Beer. She was, however, found guilty of the attempted murder of Charles Parfitt and sentenced to ten years' penal servitude.

In August 1876, George Clarke, now a chief inspector, received a bombshell letter from a Mr Oldfield of Trafford House, Old Trafford, Manchester. It informed him that Henri de Tourville, who had recently suffered what the *Manchester Evening Mail* called 'a Strange Tragedy', was none other than Henri Perrau, the convenient death of whose mother-in-law Clarke had investigated eight years earlier.

It seemed that de Tourville's second wife had fallen to her death from a Tyrolean mountainside. Mr Oldfield had told his local police about it but they did not seem interested. No doubt he (Clarke) would be.

It transpired that de Tourville had returned from a sightseeing expedition to Stelvio Pass, casually saying that his wife had been injured and that four men should come with him to get her. While the horses and carriage were being got ready he settled down to enjoy his dinner. The men found Mrs de Tourville dead at the bottom of a ravine. Suspicions were aroused and an inquiry was held, after which de Tourville was set free and rapidly left for England.

Clarke felt this matter should be gone into and this time pursued the matter. The Austrian authorities did not appear pleased with this development, the Austro-Hungarian Consul General writing to Monsieur le Colonel (Henderson) enquiring why they wanted to proceed for the second time against Mr Heinrich von Tourville, who had been accused in July last of causing the death of his wife, and gave a list of questions he wanted answered. The first was: 'Which motives have induced the detective office to investigate this matter and on what suspicions?'

The victim's reputed fortune of £70,000 and the facts that she was stout, ten years older than the suspect and that they did not get on made a good start for motives, and Clarke's report on Mrs Brigham's 'most suspicious' death was forwarded to Austria.

Eventually, the Austrians applied for de Tourville's extradition. Now much correspondence passed to and fro among the British authorities and many opinions were sought as to whether the Extradition Act covered the case of a British subject (he had become naturalized) for the murder of an Englishwoman abroad. Could the case not be heard in Britain?

Permission to proceed was finally granted and extradition proceedings began at Bow Street. Photographs of the approaches to the Pass and the scene where the body had been found were produced, as were depositions from witnesses. These included one from interpreter Adolph Schmidt, which said that he had noticed that the Austrian district judge had kept changing the answers given by the victim's maid to give a different impression, more favourable to de Tourville.

The accused had kept changing his story (one version held that his wife had committed suicide) and his casual, uncaring stance at the time was much commented on, including the fact that after her death he held dinner parties at the hotel.

Mr Thomas Bond, a Fellow of the Royal College of Surgeons, gave his opinion that the victim's many head injuries, as described, could not have been caused by a fall.

Extradition was granted and the accused, who, claimed *The Times*, 'had assumed a jaunty, flippant manner throughout sometimes laughing out loud at the proceedings', suddenly became serious. Clarke and German-speaking Sergeant von Tornow escorted him to Vienna, where they stayed to watch the case despite the court president wanting to know on whose authority they were there.

The two Austrian doctors who had previously agreed with the suicide claim now – after consultation with experts – firmly changed their opinions to the cause of death being murder. (One of these doctors had been among the guests at a de Tourville dinner party, as had the son of the other and two sons of the judge.)

The jury found him guilty by nine votes to three, and Henri Dieudonne Perrau de Tourville was sentenced to death. In a leader *The Times* found it very curious that after 'the scandalous laxity' of their original enquiry the Austrians should then have demanded de Tourville's extradition. Clearly they were unaware that the impetus had come from the other direction, perhaps encouraged by feelings of guilt about Mrs Brigham.

The 35-year-old Sergeant John Meiklejohn from Dunblane on the edge of the Scottish Highlands may have been corrupt before he entered the Detective Branch in 1866, but by the early 1870s he was definitely supplying warnings of police interest in their scams to a gang of turf fraudsters.

As well as handling extradition matters, keeping a lookout for Fenians and baby farmers and taking charge of the more serious or complicated murder enquiries, the Yard detectives also investigated cases of fraud, particularly those associated with horse racing.

Chief Inspector Clarke was the accepted authority on these and inevitably the others also took a hand in breaking up the gangs who were always thinking up new and crooked ways to part the public from their money. The detectives had increasingly been called upon to help police race meetings to catch members of the swell mob who picked pockets, rigged gambling games and gammoned countrymen, not to mention cheating bookmakers, horse dopers, shofulmen (who passed dud coins) and gangs who demanded protection money from stall-holders. Thus the detectives inevitably became familiar with the racing fraternity.

In 1873 a William Kurr and two accomplices set up a betting agency in Edinburgh and its methods soon came under police scrutiny. One of the partners was arrested but Meiklejohn tipped off Kurr, who fled to America. Six months later he was back and calling on Meiklejohn to bribe him for further tip-offs about Yard interest in the various frauds committed by him and his associates.

At that time Chief Inspector Druscovitch found himself in need of £60, having backed a bill for his brother which he now could not meet. Meiklejohn, despite being flush with bribes, was unable to help but he knew a man who could: Kurr.

Meanwhile, the branch was handling various serious crimes. In 1871 there was the vicious murder of pregnant housemaid Jane Clouson in Eltham, very possibly by the son of her previous master. In 1872 came the murder of Hoxton print shopkeepers Mrs Squires and her daughter, in which were found bloody thumbprints on a map, hairs grasped in the fingers of the daughter and a blood-soaked apron and duster. But, as ever, these clues were of no real help, and like those of prostitutes the murders of shopkeepers were difficult to solve because of the number of possible suspects. Also in 1872 came the murder of prostitute Harriett Buswell, which threw up severe identification problems. In 1873, there was a case in which body parts were found in the Thames, and in 1874 and 1875 two very high-value jewellery thefts from luggage at Paddington railway station.

The following year brought the latest sensational case: the mysterious end of young barrister Charles Bravo, who died in agony in his Balham home only four months after his marriage to an attractive widow. Was it suicide or murder?

All of these cases ended without convictions, leading to the branch yet again being subject to heavy criticism. Some was deserved, some not.

The *Daily Telegraph* complained that Inspector Bucket of *Bleak House* and the detective heroes of Mr Wilkie Collins 'have created an utterly false impression as to the capabilities of our police force'. But the paper did point out that when, after six months, two bodies of murdered women recovered from the Regent's Canal remained unidentified, the detective force was 'all but powerless'.

The Yard detectives themselves felt particularly hampered by the new divisional detective system, which did not appear to be working. Not only were the chosen men uneducated, they were often selected to get them out of the way because they were a liability on the streets. Worse, no-one seemed to be in charge of them. This resulted in the bungling of the early stages of enquiries. Also, it was later admitted, the divisional detectives would often hold back information through jealousy and the suspicion that were a case solved all the credit would go to the Yard men.

By July 1876 the Turf Fraud gang were ready for their biggest scam.

They had printed a racing journal, the *Sport*, only in sufficient numbers to send out to wealthy French betting enthusiasts. The leader in the first issue declared the intention of the owner to thwart British bookmakers who, because he was so successful, were refusing to take his bets. He would get agents abroad to place them for him – in their own names and using their own money – then he would reimburse them, plus 5 per cent of his winnings, thus helping them become rich like him.

© *The Graphic*

In the dock at Bow Street: those accused of the Turf Fraud conspiracy.
Left to right: Inspector Meiklejohn, Chief Inspectors Druscovitch
and Palmer, and solicitor Mr Froggatt. Chief Inspector
Clarke joined them later

BULL'S EYE ON BOBBY

Mr Bull (takes Policeman's lantern). 'THANK YOU. I'LL JUST HAVE A LOOK ROUND MYSELF. STRIKES
ME THE PREMISES AIN'T AS CLEAN AS THEY MIGHT BE!'

[*Punch*, Aug. 25, 18]

*The reaction of
Punch to the Turf
Fraud Scandal*

But the gang were going to need to be warned if and when any
complaints came in, and since most of the foreign correspondence
passed through the hands of Chief Inspector Druscovitch it was
time to haul in their catch. They assured him that what they were
involved in was nothing more than a technical evasion of the betting
laws – nothing criminal – and asked him to warn them. He agreed
but refused to take any money, although it was later claimed that the
£25 offered had been tucked into his pocket.

Crises came after the gang netted £10,000 from a French
aristocrat, the Comtesse de Goncourt. She found she required
more money to release her winnings, so consulted her lawyer. He
immediately realized she was being duped and alerted a London
solicitor, who went to Scotland Yard. Williamson put his trusted
aide Druscovitch on the case.

Eventually, puzzled by the lack of progress, Williamson took over the case himself and sent Druscovitch and several other officers over to Holland to bring back one of the gang who had been arrested over there. Meanwhile, Sergeant John George Littlechild went to arrest Kurr and found himself looking down the barrel of Kurr's revolver, giving chase to him and his companions down a long dark road in Islington, but ending up getting his man.

Once arrested the gang began squealing on the detectives who had covered up for them: these, they claimed, were Meiklejohn and Chief Inspectors Druscovitch, Palmer and Clarke. The Turf Fraud Scandal, which came to fruition in 1877, saw these men in dock charged with conspiring to obstruct the course of justice. The first three were found guilty and given two years' hard labour. The sixty-year-old Clarke was acquitted, possibly because Williamson spoke up for him or maybe because the jury believed his defence counsel, who claimed that the gang had cooked up a case because of his past successes against them. He retired shortly afterwards.

In his book *The Mainspring of Murder* (John Long, 1958), Philip Lindsay claims that the Scotland Yard detective investigating the murder of Mrs Brigham in Manchester 'proved surprisingly venal and, after receiving a small present, he closed the investigations'. But since the author does not reveal his source (and is wrong in claiming it was the Swiss who pursued de Tourville) it may be that this accusation was merely supposition in the light of Clarke's arrest in the Turf Fraud case.

When asked how he kept an eye on a man while he was making his enquiries, Williamson was to tell the subsequent Departmental Commission: 'When he leaves the office I have really no check upon him.'

From the Commission's findings emerged a new system, the CID, based on that of the French, which its new director, lawyer Howard Vincent, had studied and recommended to them. How ironic, when many of the problems encountered by the Detective Branch had been due to the insistence that they should *never* operate in the spying, tyrannical manner of the French.

20

The CID

The man appointed to be the director of the Criminal Investigation Department was 29-year-old Charles Edward Howard Vincent, the younger son of a baronet. He had served as a lieutenant in the Royal Welsh Fusiliers, studied military organization in Russia, trained in law then, in 1876, been called to the bar. The following year he began to study Continental police systems, particularly those of the French, and it was his report on these to the Home Office Departmental Commission on the Detective Force which won him the post of CID director.

Howard Vincent, the lawyer who became the director of the new CID

The press soon expressed fears that the young barrister might introduce some of the illiberal French methods – methods such as the use of police spies and *agents provocateurs*, long spells in custody to extract confessions and the searching of premises without warrants. But Williamson helped keep him on the straight and narrow as regards what was permissible here, as did his slightly anomalous position. The director of the CID had been given the status of an assistant commissioner but not the position, and he was directly answerable to the Home Office but not actually in full command of the detectives.

What he was able to do was reorganize, and he set about this with energy and enthusiasm: he secured pay rises and increased allowances for the detectives; greatly improved the *Police Gazette* (a descriptive catalogue of known and wanted offenders which had become so badly produced as to be ineffective); established the Convict Supervision Office with its gallery of rogues to aid identification; gradually increased detective numbers to 800; set up the Special Irish Branch to cope with the growing Fenian problem; and wrote the Police Code, which summarized all the laws officers needed to know about and which remained in use, with regular updates, for eighty years.

The new department was allotted 280 officers, 254 of these on division. The divisional detectives were led by 15 detective inspectors known as local inspectors under the overall supervision of the Yard. This supervisory role soon became extended to include the divisional superintendents who suddenly discovered an interest in detective work.

At Scotland Yard detective numbers rose to twenty inspectors and three chief inspectors (the uneducated but honest Shore promoted to be one of the latter) and despite the Turf Fraud problems having occurred on his watch, Williamson was promoted to be chief superintendent.

One of the Yard inspectors, 38-year-old Edward Sayer, died of pleurisy soon after the changes, as did a new divisional detective,

Sergeant Allday of 'G' Division. Press reports claimed that Allday had been forced back on duty while in feeble health but in fact he had been off sick for six months and had resumed duty against advice – possibly to hold on to his newly desirable detective position. The death rate from tuberculosis and other pulmonary diseases and infectious diseases was high: thirty-six of the former and seven of the latter in the sixty-four noted in the 1878 Return of Deaths for the London and Woolwich Dockyard divisions.

Of course, instant success did not come the way of the new department. Results, as always, were mixed. The first three murders, which occurred over a short period between 1878 and 1879, were oddly similar and yet again demonstrated the perils of employing servants. This time they were *mistress*/servant murders, or at least were suspected to be. Each case was investigated by a pairing of a local inspector and a Yard detective.

The first victim was the wealthy, elderly and reputedly parsimonious widow Mrs Rachel Samuels, whose body was found in the kitchen of her large house in Bloomsbury at midnight by her lodger, a man *The Times* described as 'a Bohemian musician'. She had no live-in servant; a girl came in each morning to clean. But it was an ex-servant, Mary Donovan, who had left on her marriage, who captured the attention of local Inspector Kerley and Yard Inspector Andrew Lansdowne.

Mary still visited Mrs Samuels two or three times a week to do odd jobs, meanwhile complaining that the old lady worked her too hard, paid her badly and fed her little. Mary had been seen on the premises at 8.30 p.m. on the evening in question, and Mary's own landlady assured police she had not returned home at all that evening but came back early the following morning in a disturbed and disorderly state and carrying a bundle. The telltale sudden acquisition of a little ready cash, 'bloodstains' on her clothes and a motive of jealousy that her own sister had been invited to live with Mrs Samuels added to suspicions, as did her new boots and her recent pawning of a wedding ring. A pair of new boots and a wedding ring were missing from the house. She was arrested, but the case fell apart when the boots were found not to be the stolen ones and the pawnbroker's assistant admitted he had been mistaken when identifying her as the person who had pawned the ring.

Early one morning a few weeks later a coalman spotted a wooden box floating half-submerged in the Thames near Barnes in west London. Inside he found what looked like 'a lot of cooked meat'. Some of the meat looked fresher and vaguely human. It turned out to be the partial remains (some boiled) of a fifty- to sixty-year-old woman. There was no head and none was ever found, although a foot turned up on a dung heap five days later. Not an easy one for local Inspector Henry Jones and the Yard man, stocky, ex-Wiltshire labourer Inspector John Dowdall, to solve.

Two and a half weeks later three men turned up at Richmond Police Station to reveal their suspicions about an old friend, 29-year-old Katherine Webster, who had suddenly visited one of them, Henry Porter, on the day before the box was found. Kate, as she was known, had been better dressed and more confident than previously and was showing off rings, trinkets and photographs of relatives, telling them she was now a widow, Mrs Thomas, and had come into some property from an aunt in Richmond. Could Porter help her clear the house? He could.

Meanwhile, Porter and his son helped Kate carry a heavy bag as far as the River Thames, where she left them to have a drink while she popped off to take the bag to a friend. The young Porter then saw Kate home, at which point she asked him to help her carry a large corded box down to the riverside where she was to meet another friend. After the boy left her he heard a loud splash; then Kate soon caught up with him – minus the box.

Another man, John Church, helped with the house clearance, and while they were so engaged a neighbour popped in to enquire about the whereabouts of Mrs Thomas and ask why they were removing her property. Of course, the men thought Kate Webster was Mrs Thomas, but by the time they went to the police Kate had flown – back to Wexford in Ireland. Dowdall and Jones went over to bring her back.

At the house in Richmond they found charred human remains under the boiler and inside it a great deal of grease. (It was rumoured that she sold jars of human dripping to a nearby pub.) Kate tried to implicate Church but he was dismissed from the case and she alone was found guilty and hanged, after confessing that Mrs Thomas had sacked her so she had killed her with a cleaver.

This case and another concurrently being heard at the Old Bailey must have caused many mistresses to glance more warily at their servants. Again, the victim was an elderly woman, quarrelsome spinster Miss Matilda Hacker, who had rather mysteriously gone missing from her lodgings at 4 Euston Square (coincidentally only five minutes from the home of the first victim, Mrs Samuels).

Six months after 25-year-old Hannah Dobbs, the servant who looked after the lodgers, claimed to have last seen Miss Hacker, her decomposed body was found in the coal cellar. Hannah had been seen with a watch and chain and a sum of money, both of which she said had been left to her by a relative. Like Kate Webster, Hannah Dobbs was already a convicted thief.

Local Inspector Gatland and Yard Inspector the tall, Prussian-born Carl Max Hagen were put in charge of this enquiry. Hannah claimed the forced cash box found in her possession was her own but could not explain away the large stain on Miss Hacker's carpet. Inspector Hagen cut out the stain and took it to court; he also traced the watch and chain (identified as Miss Hacker's) to a pawnbroker's where it had been deposited as soon as questions had begun to be asked.

In his book *The Bench and the Dock* (Stanley Paul, 1925), Charles Kingston points out that the case against Hannah was very strong and that when found not guilty she was the 'luckiest prisoner ever' to have stood in the Old Bailey dock. This was due, he claimed, to her defence counsel convincing the judge and jury that a young woman could not have done the deed or carried the body down to the cellar.

The feared 'un-English' moves were made by the branch when, to catch a chemist named Titley who was known to be selling concoctions for procuring abortions, an ex-policeman's wife and Bow Street searcher was sent to buy some potions for her daughter, the story being that she had been got into trouble by a toff. Titley was suspicious and demanded to see the daughter or the young toff, so a detective sergeant was duly dressed up in frock coat and top hat to play the gentleman seducer. Titley handed over the drugs, was arrested and sent down for eighteen months.

This provoked an instant outcry about the use of *agents provocateurs* and resulted in three detectives and the hapless lady searcher ending up in dock themselves, accused of incitement to commit a crime. But the charge was dropped on technical grounds.

Vincent also attempted to revive the practice of side-stepping the branch's physical requirements to allow direct entry of gentlemen candidates on the grounds of their greater intelligence, education and linguistic ability, even though most previous such experiments had failed. This one also did. Of the half-dozen 'retired army officers and younger sons of gentlemen' taken on, five were dismissed and the other one made to resign.

In 1881 the second railway murder occurred. The victim was Frederick Isaac Gold, again a late-middle-aged man, whose battered body was found near the entrance to Balcombe Tunnel on the London–Brighton line. Again there was a bloody scene, and a watch and chain and a hat were prominent elements of the evidence. The murderer (a very strange and desperately poor young man named Percy Lefroy) was caught and hanged, but police came in for a great deal of press criticism over the handling of the case and by now the comments directed at Vincent were becoming as insulting as those suffered by Mayne. After six years he decided he had had enough and left to stand for Parliament.

Illustrated London News, 1883

Visitors are shown exhibits at Scotland Yard's Crime Museum
(later dubbed The Black Museum) which was founded in 1875

The CID's next challenge was the Fenian 'dynamite outrages'. These included the bombing of Scotland Yard itself. Their handling by Williamson and Littlechild brought some press approval but the Ripper murder enquiries set them back again, as did police tactics during the unemployment marches and riots of the late 1880s.

Several officers who began as local inspectors were to gain later prominence. Among these were the much commended Frederick Porter Wensley, who was successful in several important cases and rose to be chief constable (CID), and Frederick George Abberline, whose scrapbook of newspaper cuttings shows him to have been a very busy and enthusiastic 'H' Division local inspector. In 1885 his prompt action resulted in the capture of the Fenians who had placed bombs in the Tower of London, and after his transfer to the Yard his East End expertise was called upon for the Ripper enquiries.

Then there was Inspector Edmund John James Reid, who followed

Abberline on to 'H' Division and was, according to the *Weekly Dispatch*, one of the most remarkable men of the century – record-height balloonist, parachutist, leading Druid (Masonic), actor, singer, conjurer and model for Detective Dier (Reid backwards) in novels by Charles Gibbons. However, in his *Jack the Ripper Encyclopedia* (Metro Books, 2001) John J. Eddleston finds Reid a somewhat unreliable policeman. Too up in the air, perhaps?

It is true that some Metropolitan Police methods continued to lag behind those of some Continental and British forces. (There was resistance to the widespread installation of telephones, partly due to cost but also to the fear that if it happened the public would start ringing them direct!)

However, fingerprinting was coming into use and it was the Yard which pioneered the classification essential to its usefulness. In 1903 a Fingerprint Bureau was formed, later followed by a Photographic and Graphic Branch. This, plus the emergence of notable forensic advisors such as Bernard Spilsbury and firearms expert Robert Churchill, caused Scotland Yard's crime-solving reputation to grow.

In 1907 the Home Secretary appointed a clutch of leading Scotland Yard detectives to act as a mobile Murder Squad which could be offered to smaller forces confronted with major cases. Calling in the Yard had become official. The Bow Street Runners were laid to rest at last.

Endnotes

Chapter 1
[1] A light open carriage.

[2] 'Public offices', where magistrates and policemen were based, were also referred to as 'police offices'.

Chapter 2
[1] Handkerchiefs were often large and something of a fashion statement.

Chapter 4
[1] By means of a warming pan filled with hot coals.

[2] Blacked out on three sides to make it less visible when being carried.

Chapter 5
[1] Frock coat.

[2] A stiff band worn as a cravat.

[3] Actually in the name of John Mott.

Chapter 6
[1] Waylaying a child and stealing its clothes.

[2] A man who drove a cart.

[3] A French stage coach.

[4] Not a gypsy, but a wealthy gentleman seeing the world.

[5] Another term for a wallet.

Chapter 7
[1] A rod was about 5.5 yards, so he is indicating 100 yards (roughly 100 metres).

[2] At that time, Wellingtons were high boots made of leather or hessian.

[3] Footprints or 'footmarks' were recognized as useful evidence. Where practical, plaster casts were taken.

[4] Marrs and Mrs Williamson were victims of the brutal Ratcliffe Highway Murders of 1811.

Chapter 8
[1] Active in England until 1933. A jury that could decide whether there was sufficient evidence to send a case to trial. If there was, they would return a 'True Bill' against the accused.

Chapter 9
[1] As named by the *Quarterly Review*, June 1854.

[2] A term used by the press for plain clothes officers who were unofficial divisional detectives.

Chapter 10
[1] In some collections this is entitled 'The Detective Police'.

[2] In 1841 the Metropolitan Police had taken over the security of the Deptford and Woolwich Royal Dockyards.

[3] Confidence trickster.

[4] The term used for suspected murder or unexplained sudden death.

[5] As we shall see later, the detective in *Bleak House*.

Chapter 11
[1] Since they were also police chiefs, inspectors were sometimes called superintendents.

[2] An endorsement that there is sufficient evidence for the case to be tried.

Chapter 14
[1] Distilled from the corms and seeds of *Colchicum autumna*, used in some quack medicines, particularly for gout.

[2] Those out on licence before serving their full prison terms.

[3] Regarded as the essential germ of the modern computer.

Chapter 15
[1] Sugar refiner or confectioner.

[2] A person who marks down the points made by players.

Chapter 16
[1] The industrial Midlands.

Sources

The National Archives

Metropolitan Police case files:
MEPO 3.
Records of the Offices of the
Commissioner: correspondence,
paper, letter books and registers:
MEPO 1, 2, 3.
Metropolitan Police officers' records
1830–1933: MEPO 4.
Home Office correspondence: HO 45.
Problems over the extradition treaty
with France: HO 45/398.
De la Tourville murder and
extradition and Mrs Brigham's
suspected murder: HO 45
9419/58406.

Online

Old Bailey Online (www.
oldbaileyonline.org) – trial
transcripts.
Surrey Police website (www.surrey.
police.uk/about/history.asp) – history
of Surrey Police.

Metropolitan Police Historical Collection

Police Orders
Divisional registers
Richard Tanner's notebook

Newspapers and journals

Daily Telegraph
Fun
Household Words
The Illustrated London News
Islington Gazette
Journal of the Police History Society
Lloyd's Weekly Newspaper
Morning Advertiser
Morning Chronicle
Observer
Police Review and Parade Gossip
Punch
The Penny Illustrated Paper
The Times
The Shrewsbury Chronicle

Select bibliography

The Annual Register (Baldwin & Co.)

Ackroyd, Peter, *Dickens* (Minerva, 1991)

Ballantine, Mr Serjeant (William), *Some Experiences of a Barrister's Life* (Richard Bentley, 1882)

Browne, Douglas G, *The Rise of Scotland Yard* (Harrap, 1956)

Bunker, John, *From Rattle to Radio* (K.A.F. Brewin Books, 1988)

Burnaby, Evelyn, *Memories of Famous Trials* (Sisley's, 1907)

Campbell, Christy, *Fenian Fire* (HarperCollins, 2003)

Cavanagh, Ex-Chief Inspector (Timothy), *Scotland Yard Past and Present* (Chatto & Windus, 1893)

Cobb, Belton, *The First Detectives* (Faber & Faber, 1957)

Cobb, Belton, *Critical Years at the Yard* (Faber & Faber 1956)

Dickens, Charles, *Miscellaneous Papers/Edwin Drood* (Hazel, Watson & Viney, 1933)

Dilnot, George, *The Trial of the Detectives* (Geoffrey Bles, 1928)

Elliott, Douglas J., *Policing Shropshire, 1836–1967* (K.A.F. Brewin Books, 1984)

Fido, Martin and Skinner, Keith, *The Official Enclyclopedia of Scotland Yard* (Virgin Books, 1999)

Goddard, Henry, *Memoirs of a Bow Street Runner* (Museum Press, 1956)

Griffiths, Major Arthur, *Mysteries of Police and Crime* (Cassell, 1898)

Le Caron, Henri, *Twenty-five Years in the Secret Service* (William Heinemann, 1893)

Littlechild, John, *The Reminiscences of Chief Inspector Littlechild* (The Leadenhall Press, 1894)

Lock, Joan, *Marlborough Street: The Story of a London Court* (Robert Hale,1980)

Lock, Joan, *Tales from Bow Street* (Robert Hale, 1982)

Lock, Joan, *Blue Murder* (Robert Hale, 1986)

Lock, Joan, *Dreadful Deeds and Awful Murders* (Barn Owl Books, Taunton,1990)

Lock, Joan, *Scotland Yard Casebook* (Robert Hale, 1993)

Moser, Inspector Maurice and Rideal, Charles F., *Stories from Scotland Yard* (Routledge, 1890)

Quinlivian, Patrick and Rose, Paul, *The Fenians in England 1865–1872* (John Calder, 1982)

Rhodes, Linda; Shelden, Lee, and Abnett, Katherine, *The Dagenham Murder* (The London Borough of Barking and Dagenham, 2005)

Rose, Lionel, *Massacre of the Innocents: Infanticide in Great Britain 1800–1939* (Routledge and Kegan Paul, 1986)

Rumbelow, Donald, *I Spy Blue* (Macmillan, 1971)

St John Packe, Michael, *The Bombs of Orsini* (Secker & Warburg, 1957)

Stead, Philip John, *Vidocq: A Biography* (Staples, 1953)

Summerscale, Kate, *The Suspicions of Mr Whicher* (Bloomsbury, 2008)

Taylor, Bernard, *Cruelly Murdered: Constance Kent and the Killing at Road Hill House* (Grafton, 1989)

Index

Abberline, Inspector Frederick George, 246
Agar, Ted, 148-9
Aggs, Inspector William, 17-19, 156-7
Albert, Prince, 72, 74
Allday, Sergeant, 242
Allen, PC John James, 84, 86
Allsop, Thomas, 153, 155
Armstrong, William, 131
Arundel and Surrey, Earl of, 121
Atkinson, Mr, 168
Atkinson, Mrs, 167-8
Aublin, Leonard, 204

Backhouse, Mr R.O., 191, 193
Baden-Powell, Lord, 117
Baker, Superintendent Thomas, 32, 35, 42
Baldock, PC, 78-9, 83
Baldwin, PC, 42
Ballantine, Serjeant, 50
Baring Brothers, 117
Barnes, PC Henry, 109-10
Barrett, Michael, 216
Barton, Inspector, 74
Batt, Charles, 198, 200
Bean, John William, 72
Beckwell, Mrs, 78
Bedford, Duke of, 41
Beer, Jessie, 232
Bellany, James Cockburn, 62-3
Bellany, Rachel, 62-3
Beresford, Inspector Henry, 32, 34-6, 38-9,
    42-4
Berg, Robert, 75
Bernard, Dr Simon, 153-6
Biddlecombe, Inspector William Henry,
    127-31
Bird, William, 135
Blackburn, Mr Justice, 166
Blairblock, Mr, 104
Blanchard, Mrs, 14
Blantyre, Lady, 109
Blewett, George, 157-8
Blyth, Mrs, 174
Boakes, James Edward, 142
Boden, PC, 166-7
Bodkin, Mr, 74
Bonaparte, Lucien, 117
Bond, Mr Thomas, 234
Bonwell, Reverend, 229
Bouillion, Madame, 224-5
Bow Street Runners, 13, 20-1, 40, 44-5,
    50-1, 119, 132, 247
Bradshaw, John William, 221
Bragg, Mr, 102

Bravo, Charles, 236
Brett, Sergeant, 213
Briggs, Mr Thomas, 173-6
Brigham, Mrs, 195-6, 234-5, 239
Bright, Dr, 61
Brill, John, 21
Brothers, Mary Ann, 85-6
Brown, Ann, 221
Brown, Hannah, 14-17
Brown, Mary, 221
Browns, the, 232
Burdett Coutts, Baroness Angela Georgina,
    73, 171
Burgess, James, 148-9
Burke, Ricard O'Sullivan, 213, 215-16
Burton, PC, 110
Bush, Mr, 70
Buswell, Harriet, 236
Butfoy, PC Abia, 94-7, 100-1, 103

Campion, William, 36
Carnell, Mr, 166
Carnell, Mrs, 166
Carr, 44
Carron, Nicholas William, 37-40
Carruthers, James, 73
Carter, Mr, 61
Cartwright, William, 39
Casey, 215
Cauty, William, 144-5
Cavendish, John Walter, 29-30
Chalk, George, 157-8
Chambers, Mr, 70
Chandler, Stephen, 66
Childe, James, 188
Childe, Thomas, 191
Chilman, PC Thomas, 31
Christie, Sergeant, 191
Church, John, 243-4
Churchill, Robert, 247
Clark, PC George, 90-106, 157-9
Clarke, Chief Inspector George, 171-2, 175,
    179-80, 195-6, 233-5, 239
Clinton, John Cornstock, 70-1
Clouson, Jane, 236
Coathupe, Sergeant Edwin, 171, 200
Cole, Sergeant, 170
Collier, PC, 44
Collins, Charles, 143-4
Collins, Mr Wilkie, 194, 236
Connor, Joseph, 86
Cooke, Mr, 23
Cooper, John William, 219-20, 222
Cooper, Sarah Ann, 219
Corydon, John, 213, 216
Cotton, Edward Youngman, 65-6

Courvoisier, Francois Benjamin, 42-6, 64
Coward, Superintendent, 164
Cox, Sarah, 138
Cox, Sergeant, 188, 191-2
Cully, PC, 21, 51
Cureton, Chief Constable Lt. Col. Edward
   Burgoyne, 187, 192-3

Dadd, Richard, 68-70
Dalmas, Augusta, 56-7
Dalmas, Augustus (*alias* Chaplin), 56-61
Dalmas, Caroline, 56-7
Dalmas, Charlotte, 56-60
Daly, PC Timothy, 50
Davis, Eliza, 18-19, 59, 85, 156
Davy, Inspector Daniel, 203-4
Deasy, 213
Death, Mr John, 174-5
De la Rue, Daniel, 79
De la Rue, James, 79-84
Desart, Earl of, 144
Devaney, 215
Dickens, Charles, 23, 50, 52, 80, 97,
   113-14, 118-24, 128, 135, 147, 175,
   208
Dixblanc, Marguerite, 222-6
Dixon, Mr, 167
Dobbs, Hannah, 244
Dodd, Mrs Elizabeth, 98, 103
Donovan, Mary, 242
Dorrell, William, 190
Douglas, Bill, 198-200
Douglas, Tom, 198-200
Dowdall, Inspector John, 243-4
Drake, Sarah, 228-9
Driscoll, Margaret, 100
Driver, Mr, 65-6
Druscovitch, Chief Inspector Nathaniel,
   171, 204, 207, 224-5, 235, 237-9
Dudley, Lord, 182
Duncannon, Lord, 41
Dunlap, Superintendent, 222
Dunning, PC George, 102
Dyer, George, 209-11

Edlin, Mr Peter, 139
Edwards, Edward, 187-94
Edwards, Mrs, 82
Edwin, Catherine, 28
Emberson, Harriet, 221
Emm, Walter, 160-3
Emsley, Mrs, 160-3
Euston, PC James, 83

Faraday, Dr Michael, 117-18
Farnes, PC John Burnside, 95, 100, 103

Feltham, Inspector George, 11-12, 14, 17
Field, Inspector Charles Frederick, 24-30,
   51, 110, 114, 119-24, 141, 146-7, 194
Fisher, Mary, 23-4
Fitzgerald & Vesci, Lord, 64
Fletcher, Timothy, 188
Flinn, Dennis, 99-100
Flores, General Juan Jose, 116-17
Flynn, Mr, 108-9
Foley, Superintendent, 138
Forrester, Daniel, 59, 67
Forrester, John, 59, 67
Forward, Emily, 185
Forward, Mary, 185
Francis, John, 72
Franz, Johann Carl, 164-6
Fuhrop, Theodore Christian, 178
Fuller, 65

Gale, Sarah, 14, 16
Gardner, Mr, 232
Gardner, PC, 48
Gatland, Inspector, 244
Gay, William, 14
Gee, 156-7
Gerard, Mr, 32
Gerrett, Sergeant, 52
Gill, Dr, 162-3
Gimlet, PC Timothy, 31
Girdwood, Mr, 14
Gleeson, 198
Glendinning, Ann, 131
Goddard, Henry, 20, 40
Goff, Sergeant Charles Burgess, 23-4, 26,
   28, 30, 52, 120
Gold, Frederick Isaac, 245
Gomez, Antonio, 153
Goncourt, Comtesse de, 238
Good, Daniel, 48-50, 58-9
Good, Jane, 49
Good, Molly, 49-50
Gough, Elizabeth, 138-9
Goulburn, Mr Commissioner, 125
Gould, Richard, 40, 47-8, 51
Graves, George, 166
Greenacre, James, 14-17
Greenham, Inspector George, 202, 204
Grimwood, Eliza, 23-30, 39, 52, 59, 80,
   85, 120
Groves, 214-15
Guerin, Mme, 224-5

Hacker, Miss Matilda, 244
Hagen, Inspector Karl Max, 244
Hale, Robert, 150-1
Hale, William, 150-1

253

Hall, Charles, 61-2
Hall, Charlotte, 61-2
Hall, Mrs, 230
Hall, Thomas, 55
Halliday, Mrs Martha, 164-6
Hardwick, John, 23
Harris, Elizabeth, 188-9
Harris, Samuel, 188
Hart, Sarah, 107
Harvey, Richard, 176
Harvey, Sergeant, 103
Harwood, Levi, 128-31
Harwood, Samuel, 130
Hatfield, Captain, 206
Haynes, Superintendent John, 51, 57-8,
   62, 65-6, 70, 73, 77, 81, 83, 110-12, 114,
   117-18, 124
Henderson, Commissioner Col. Sir
   Edmund, 218, 227, 233
Hennessy, John, 99-100
Herbert, Inspector, 153
Herschel, Sir John, 117
Hickton, PC Isaac, 90-1, 98, 100-6
Hill, Private, 120
Hill, William, 132-3
Hilton, Mr, 78
Hocker, James, 82
Hocker, Thomas Henry, 80-4
Holland, 156-7
Hollest, Caroline, 126, 130-1
Hollest, Reverend George Edward, 126-31
Hollington, Inspector, 128-9, 131
Holmes, Robert Fulton, 210-11
Howard, Mr, 200
Howie, Superintendent, 179-80
Howse, George, 64-5
Hoydonck, Constant Von, 206-7
Hubbard, Inspector, 209
Hubbard, William, 24-6, 28-30, 120
Hubner, Baron, 153

Jackson, Edward, 160
Jack the Ripper, 246-7
James, Edward, 155
James, Sergeant Robert Fulton, 210-11
Jenkins, Thomas, 65
Jervis, Inspector John, 32
Johnson, Mrs, 228-9
Joinville, Prince de, 151-2
Jones, Inspector Henry, 243
Jones, James, 128-30

Kelly, Colonel Thomas J., 212-13, 215-16
Kendall, Sergeant Edward, 100-1, 103-5,
   119, 127-31, 135
Kent, Constance, 138-9, 194-5

Kent, Elizabeth, 138
Kent, Eveline, 138
Kent, Francis Saville, 136-9, 187, 228
Kent, Mrs Mary, 137-8
Kent, Mary Amelia, 138
Kent, Mary Ann, 138
Kent, Samuel, 137-8
Kent, Mr William, 138-9
Kerley, Inspector, 243
Kerslake, Sarah, 138
Kimpton, PC, 93-4, 97, 99-106
King, PC, 164
Kohl, Edward Karl, 178-9
Kossuth, Lajos, 150-1
Kurr, William, 235, 239

Labalmondiér, Asst. Commissioner Lt. Col.
   Douglas, 220
Langley, Sergeant Edward, 101, 111-12,
   117-18, 142
Langton, PC Frederick, 55-6
Lankester, Dr Edwin, 229-30
Lansdowne, Inspector Andrew, 144
Latham, PC William, 86
Leeson, 198, 200
Lefroy, Percy, 245
Leon, Comte, 40
Letheby, Dr, 63, 180, 190
Lettis, 207
Littlechild, Chief Inspector John George,
   217, 239, 246
Lloyd, John, 38-9
Lockwood, Lady Julia, 46
Lockyer, PC, 112
Lucan, Lord, 222, 226
Lund, Inspector John, 124, 132, 142, 144-5
Lytton, Sir Edward Bulmer, 183

McLeod, Donald, 39
Maddle, Mr, 123
Manning, Frederick, 109-10, 114, 119,
   132, 135
Manning, Maria, 109-15, 119, 132
Manning, Mrs Rebecca, 111
Matthews, Mr, 174-6
Mawer, Mr, 167
May, Inspector, 69
Maybury, Superintendent, 197-8, 200
Mayne, Chief Constable Captain Dawson,
   187
Mayne, Commissioner Sir Richard, 17, 19,
   35, 40-2, 50, 88, 124, 133, 139, 146, 153,
   155, 164, 181-4, 187-93, 198, 210, 216-
   18, 222, 245
Mazzini, Giuseppe, 150, 152
M'Donnell, Eddie, 213-15

254

Meadows, 85
Meeus, Gendarme, 204
Meiklejohn, Inspector John, 235-9
Melbourne, Lord, 41
Meredith, John, 187, 189-93
Meredith, Mary, 188-9
Meshek, Aaron, 208-9
Meyer, Leopold, 75-6
M'Farlane, Mrs Sarah, 55-61
M'Farlane, William, 60
Milner, Alfred, 231
Milner, Amelia, 231-2
Milner, Thomas, 231
Monte, Raphael, 171
Moser, Inspector Maurice, 201-3
Moxey, Superintendent, 112, 114-15
Mullard, Sergeant, 231-2
Muller, Franz, 174-6
Mullins, James, 161-3
Murphy, James, 216

Napoleon III, 40, 152-3
Norman, Agnes, 231-3
Normanby, Marquis of, 133

O'Connor, Patrick, 108-13
Oldfield, Mr, 233
Orsini, Felice, 152-5
Ostrowski, Count, 73
Otway, Sergeant Charles, 21, 35-6, 40, 47, 152

Page, Mrs Elizabeth, 94, 97, 105
Page, Priscilla, 99
Page, Ralph, 94, 99, 104-5, 158
Page, William, 157-8
Paget, Lord & Lady, 144
Palmer, Chief Inspector William, 237, 239
Palmer, Joseph, 102
Palmer, Mrs, 84
Palmerston, Lord, 151, 183
Parfitt, Charles, 232-3
Parke, Baron, 46, 48
Parker, Mr, 70
Parkman, Dr, 135
Parsons, Julia, 99, 102
Parsons, Mrs, 99, 102
Parsons, Sergeant, 92-7, 99-106, 109, 158
Partridge, Inspector, 81
Partridge, Mr, 86
Pay, Inspector James, 222, 224, 231
Payne, Superintendent, 165
Pearce, Superintendent Nicholas, 35-40, 42-6, 48-52, 57, 61-2, 65, 67, 73-7, 85-6, 96, 104-5, 132-3, 152
Pearson, Peter, 219

Peck, PC, 164-5
Peel, Sir Robert, 73, 88, 159
Pegler, PC Samuel, 9-19
Pellizzioni Affair, 183
Perrau, Henri, 195-6
Perrau, Mrs Henrietta, 195-6
Perry, James, 101
Perry, Susan, 101
Peterson, 207
Petty, Mrs, 184-5
Phillips, Charles, 45-6
Philps, Sarah Jane, 83
Pierce, William, 149
Pieri, Giuseppe, 153-5
Piolaine, Charlotte, 46
Platt, Mr Baron, 71
Pollock, Chief Baron, 195
Popay, Sergeant, 21
Porter, Henry, 243
Price, Sergeant, 26, 28
Pritty, Maria, 33

Ranelagh, Lord, 74
Rankin, Eileen, 99-100
Rawlinson, Mr, 15, 83-4, 157
Raynaud, Edward, 151-2
Reading, William, 37
Redhead, Thomas, 133
Reid, Inspector Edmund John James, 246-7
Relf, Sergeant Richard, 230-1
Richmond, Duke of, 183-4
Riel, Julie, 222, 226
Riel, Madame Maria Caroline Besant, 222-6
Robinson, Elizabeth, 132
Robinson, George, 33-4
Roderick, PC, 18
Roe, Sir Frederick, 19, 20-1, 41
Rogers, Sergeant, 155
Rose, Mr, 160
Rose, PC, 42
Rothschild, N.M. & Co., 117
Rowan, Commissioner Col. Sir Charles, 18-19, 116, 133, 218
Rudio, Carlo di, 153-5
Rudio, Eliza, 154-5
Russell, Lord John, 40-41, 182-3
Russell, Lord William, 41-7, 64, 182

Saltzmann, Auguste, 165
Samuels, Mrs Rachel, 242
Sattler, Christian, 202-3
Saunders, Inspector John, 150-2, 154
Sayer, Inspector Edward Daniel, 241
Schmidt, Adolph, 234
Scotney, Sergeant, 80-2

Searle, Superintendent, 180-1
Serouche, Charles Louis, 32-3
Shackell, Inspector Joseph, 20-1, 40, 74-5,
    81, 83-4, 124-5
Sharpe, Henrietta, 65-6
Sharpe, John, 27
Shaw, Inspector Frederick, 44, 52, 69, 97,
    111, 119, 122, 132
Shaw, Richard, 198-200, 207
Shore, Superintendent John, 171-2
Smith, Hiram, 128-30
Smith, Mrs Mary, 157-9
Smith, Reverend Joseph, 131
Smith, Sergeant Henry, 119, 123, 135,
    143-4, 149, 154, 171
Smith, William J.R., 141
Snelling, Sarah, 123
Soames, Mrs, 167-8
Southey, Ernest, 181-5
Sparrow, 135
Spilsbury, Bernard, 247
Stevens, PC Jonas, 92, 98, 100, 103
Stevenson, Caroline, 32-3
Stevenson, William, 32-3
Still, Robert George, 221
Squires, Mrs, 236

Taff, Eliza, 218
Taff, George, 218
Taffir, Flowery Land Second Mate, 205
Tanner, Inspector Richard, 149, 160-2,
    170-2, 174-5, 180-1, 184, 187-94
Tawell, John, 107-8, 132
Taylor, Mr, 153
Taylor, Mrs, 232
Taylor, Professor Alfred Swaine, 134, 163,
    168, 190, 192-3
Tedman, Inspector John, 42, 44, 49, 51,
    85, 156-7
Templeman, John, 40, 51
Tester, George William, 148-9
Thain, Charles, 202-3
Thomas, Mrs, 243-4
Thomas, Sergeant William, 160, 199, 208
Thomson, Superintendent James Jacob,
    171, 181-2, 185, 190, 197-200, 207-9,
    214-18, 220-2
Thomson, Tally-ho, 121-2
Thornton, Inspector Stephen, 51-2, 111,
    116, 119, 123, 134, 141, 149, 161, 163,
    171, 208-9
Tietjens, Madam, 164-5
Titley, 245
Tornow, Inspector Charles Louis
    Christopher Constantine Von, 234
Tourville, Henri de, 233-5, 239

Tourville, Mrs de, 233
Turner, John, 223
Tyers, Constable, 230
Tyler, John, 144-5

Vestris, Madame, 75
Victoria, Queen, 41, 50, 69-72, 74, 170-1,
    183
Vidocq, Eugene Francois, 86-7
Vincent, Howard, 239-41, 245

Wadley, Mr, 18
Wakley, Thomas, 79-82, 86
Walker, Amos, 96-7
Walker, Superintendent Robert, 119, 166
Walker, William, 95
Ward, The Honourable Dudley, 182-3
Waters, Mrs, 230-1
Watson, William, 80-1
Webster, Katherine, 243-4
Wensley, Chief Constable Fredrick Porter,
    246
Westmoreland, Earl of, 184
Westwood, Mrs, 32, 34, 36
Westwood, Robert, 31-40, 42, 45, 59, 80
Whicher, Inspector Jonathan, 52, 57, 110,
    118-19, 121, 132, 136-7, 139, 144-5, 155,
    158, 164-6, 171, 189, 194-5, 228
Whidborne, Dr, 167-8
White, Annie Elizabeth, 184-5
White, Luke, 93
White, Mr Saltwood, 181
White, Mrs, 182, 184-5
Wiggins, Inspector William, 107
Wightman, Mr Justice, 145
Williamson, Chief Constable Frederick
    Adolphus, 139, 149, 154-5, 171-2, 180-1,
    194, 207, 217, 224-5, 227, 238-9, 241,
    246
Wills, W.H., 118
Wilson, Catherine (*alias* Constance,
    alias Turner, *alias* Taylor), 166-8
Wilson, Emma, 210
Wilson, George, 209-11
Wood, Alderman T., 70-1
Wood, Ned, 157-8
Worels, Superintendent, 219-21
Wright, PC, 109

Zutch, Heinrich, 178